AFFORDABLE
TO BUILD
HOME PLANS
4 t h e d i t i o n

Cover Plan No. 34029	pp. 178
Two-Story Homes in Full Color	pp. 2
More Popular Designs	pp. 33-245
Zip Quote — Home Cost Calculator	pp. 250
Copyright Information	pp. 251
Blueprint Order Form	pp. 252
Index	pp. 253
Versatile Garage Plans	pp. 254-256

We welcome your feedback! Email us at:
DCochran@Garlinghouse.com.

ALL WEBSITE CREDIT CARD TRANSACTIONS ARE SECURED WITH VERISIGN ENCRYPTION.
http://www.garlinghouse.com

Publisher:
James D. McNair III
Chief Operating Officer:
Bradford J. Kidney
Staff Writers:
Debra Cochran/Sue Barile
Cover Photography:
John Ehrenclou
Cover Design:
Laura Scott
4/C Layout:
Marla Gladstone

Library of Congress No.: 97-77625
ISBN: 0-938708-84-8

Submit all Canadian plan orders to:
The Garlinghouse Company
60 Baffin Place, Unit #5
Waterloo, Ontario N2V 1Z7

Canadian Orders Only: 1-800-561-4169
Fax No. 1-800-719-3291
Customer Service No.: 1-519-746-4169

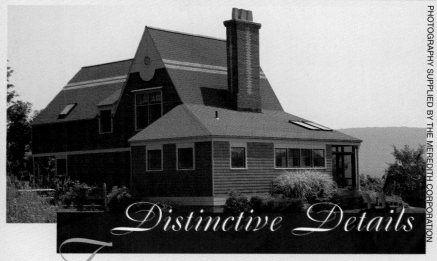

Distinctive Details

PHOTOGRAPHY SUPPLIED BY THE MEREDITH CORPORATION

The distinctive mix of architectural details of this home hint of Victorian roots. The small tiled foyer has a staircase to the second floor and the efficient kitchen to the left. A serving bar and open layout to the dining room highlight the kitchen. The expansive living room offers grand views of the outdoors. Enhanced by a vaulted ceiling and a fireplace this living room is the perfect living space for entertaining. Private access to the screen porch, a private bath and a vaulted ceiling pamper the master suite. Two secondary bedrooms share a bath on the upper level, where a loft overlooks the living room. No materials list is available for this plan. The photographed home may have been modified to suit individual tastes.

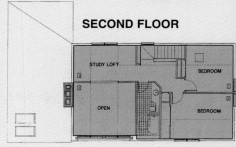

FIRST FLOOR
design 32084

M. SUITE · ENTRY · LIVING · DINING · KITCHEN · PORCH · DECK

WIDTH 55'-8"
DEPTH 37'-6"

SECOND FLOOR

STUDY LOFT · BEDROOM · OPEN · BEDROOM

first floor	1,291 sq. ft.
second floor	738 sq. ft.
basement	1,281 sq. ft.
bedrooms	three
bathrooms	2 full and 1 half
	basement
area — 2,029 sq. ft.

design 32084

10
6.95

Distinct Windows

The windows of this home give it character and distinction. The formal areas are located at the front of the home. The living room and the dining room enjoy the natural light from the bayed windows. The expansive family room is enhanced by a fireplace and the view of the rear yard. A U-shaped kitchen efficiently serves the dining room and the breakfast bay. Both the breakfast bay and the family room have access to the patio. The master suite is elegantly crowned by a decorative ceiling. The private master bath offers a garden tub and a step-in shower. Two large additional bedrooms share a full hall bath. There is a convenient second floor laundry center. This plan is available with a basement or slab foundation. Please specify when ordering. No materials list is available for this plan. The photographed home may have been modified to suit individual tastes.

first floor	1,126 sq. ft.
second floor	959 sq. ft.
basement	458 sq. ft.
garage	627 sq. ft.
bedrooms	three
bathrooms	2 full and 1 half
foundation	basement, slab

Total Living Area — 2,085 sq. ft.

← Abundant windows add light to the kitchen and breakfast area.

An
EXCLUSIVE DESIGN
By Jannis Vann & Associates, Inc.

SECOND FLOOR

BDRM.2 12'-0"X11'-0"

BATH

M.BATH

BALCONY 7'-0"X9'-0"

M.BDRM. 13'-0"X17'-0"

BDRM.3 13'-0"X12'-8

OPEN TO FOYER

design 93213

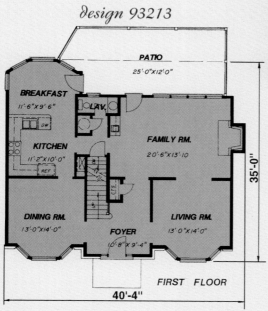

PATIO 25'-0"X12'-0"

BREAKFAST 11'-6"X9'-6"

LAV.

KITCHEN 11'-2"X10'-0" REF.

FAMILY RM. 20'-6"X13'-10

DINING RM. 13'-0"X14'-0"

LIVING RM. 13'-0"X14'-0"

FOYER 10'-8" X 9'-4"

FIRST FLOOR

35'-0"

40'-4"

↑ Put your feet up and relax. Enjoy a romantic fire in your family room.

design 93213

refer to price code C

Contemporary Ranch

*S*loping cathedral ceilings are found throughout the entirety of this home. A kitchen holds the central spot in the floor plan. It is partially open to a Great hall room with a firebox and deck access on one side, the daylight room lit by ceiling glass and full length windows on the other. The daylight room leads out onto a unique double deck. Bedrooms lie to the outside of the plan. Two smaller bedrooms at the rear share a full bath. The more secluded master bedroom at the front has its own full bath and access to a private deck. The photographed home may have been modified to suit individual tastes.

main floor	1,512 sq. ft.
garage	478 sq. ft.
bedrooms	three
bathrooms	2 full
foundation	bsmt, crawl

Total Living Area — 1,512 sq. ft.

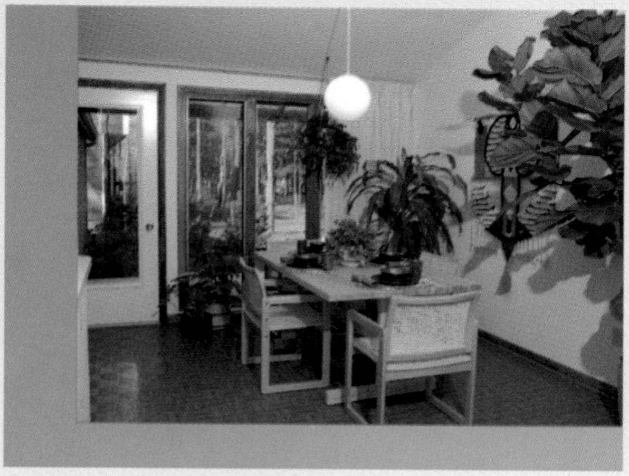

Spend quality time with the family as you enjoy the great outdoors from your daylight room.

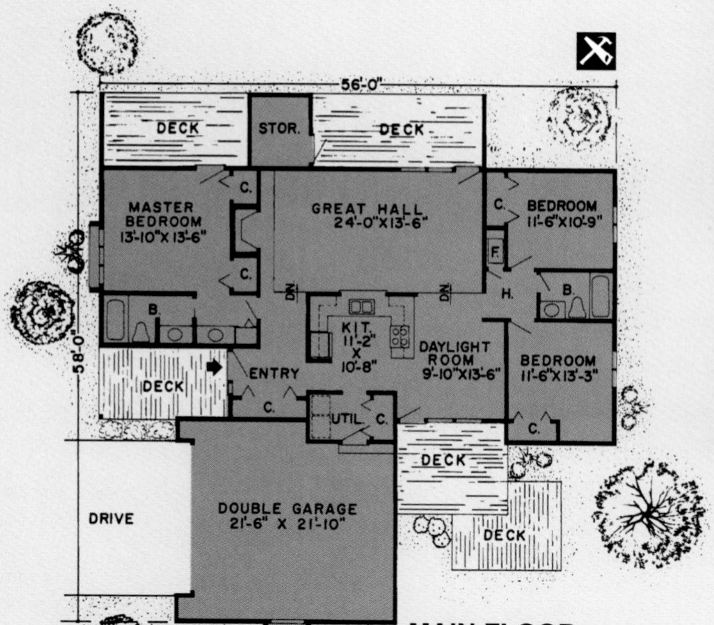
56'-0"
58'-0"
DECK
STOR.
DECK
MASTER BEDROOM 13'-10"X13'-6"
C.
GREAT HALL 24'-0"X13'-6"
C.
BEDROOM 11'-6"X10'-9"
F.
C.
B.
DN.
DN.
H.
B.
KIT. 11'-2" X 10'-8"
DAYLIGHT ROOM 9'-10"X13'-6"
BEDROOM 11'-6"X13'-3"
DECK
ENTRY
C.
UTIL.
C.
C.
DECK
DRIVE
DOUBLE GARAGE 21'-6" X 21'-10"
DECK

MAIN FLOOR
design 26740

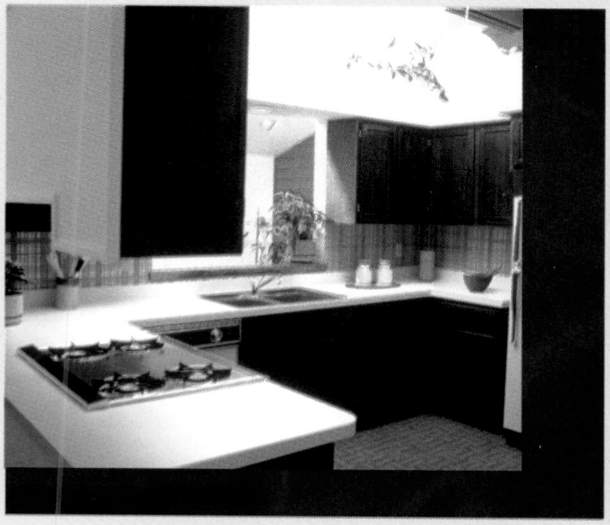

This efficient kitchen provides plenty of counter space for food preparation.

design 26740

refer to price code B

PHOTOGRAPHY BY JOHN EHRENCLOU

Spacious Stucco

*I*f open space suits your taste, here's a sturdy stucco classic that fits the bill with style. The vaulted foyer is flanked by the soaring living room with a huge palladium window, and the formal dining room. Step up the stairs to the loft for a great view of the fireplaced family room, separated from the huge kitchen/dinette arrangement by a two-way fireplace. And while you're upstairs, be sure to notice the two bedrooms with walk-in closets and adjoining bath. You'll find the master suite, with its garden spa, private deck access and walk-in closet on the first floor, just off the foyer. The photographed home may have been modified to suit individual tastes.

first floor	1,752 sq. ft.
second floor	620 sq. ft.
basement	1,726 sq. ft.
garage	714 sq. ft.
bedrooms	three
bathrooms	2 full and 1 half
foundation	bsmt, slab, crawl
Total Living Area —	**2,372 sq. ft.**

Enjoy the
outdoor
sunlight right
from your very
own family
room

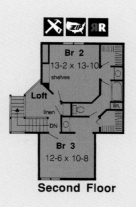

Br 2
13-2 x 13-10
shelves

Loft
linen
DN lin.

Br 3
12-6 x 10-8

Second Floor

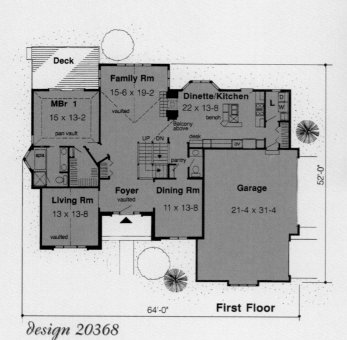

Deck

Family Rm
15-6 x 19-2
vaulted

Dinette/Kitchen
22 x 13-8
bench

D W

L

MBr 1
15 x 13-2
pan vault

Balcony
above

UP DN
desk
ov

spa

pantry

Foyer
vaulted

Dining Rm
11 x 13-8

Garage
21-4 x 31-4

52'-0"

Living Rm
13 x 13-8
vaulted

64'-0"

First Floor

design 20368

Dramatic
staircase leads
to loft overlook-
ing fireplaced
family room.

design 20368

refer to price code D

Streetside Appeal

This three bedroom beauty is loaded with convenience and charm. A traditional covered porch shelters entering guests. Lead them into the formal elegance of the living and dining room combination, divided by columns for a spacious feeling and a front-to-back view. When you want to kick off your shoes, show friends into the family room, where a two-way fireplace creates a warm, comfortable atmosphere. At the rear of the house, the kitchen and breakfast room adjoin in an open arrangement overlooking the rear deck. The master suite, tucked behind the garage in a quiet corner of the house, shares the backyard view. The open loft, that shares the second floor with two bedrooms and a full bath, would make a great rainy-day playroom for the kids. The photographed home may have been modified to suit individuals tastes.

first floor	1,590 sq. ft.
second floor	567 sq. ft.
basement	1,576 sq. ft.
garage	456 sq. ft.
bedrooms	three
bathrooms	2 full and 1 half
foundation	bsmt, slab, crawl

Total Living Area — 2,157 sq. ft.

◀ Cozy Living Room with plenty of space for entertaining the guests or catching up with the family.

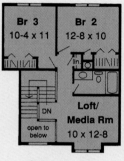

Second Floor

Br 3
10-4 x 11

Br 2
12-8 x 10

DN

open to below

Loft/ Media Rm
10 x 12-8

An
EXCLUSIVE DESIGN
By Karl Kreeger

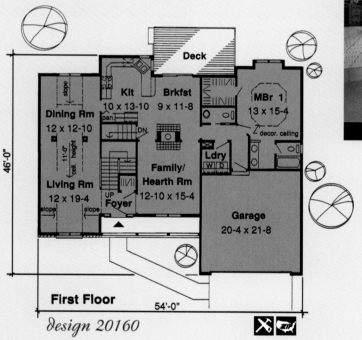

Deck

Kit
10 x 13-10

Brkfst
9 x 11-8

MBr 1
13 x 15-4

decor. ceiling

Dining Rm
12 x 12-10

pan.

DN

Ldry
W D

Living Rm
12 x 19-4

slope

Family/ Hearth Rm
12-10 x 15-4

UP **Foyer**

Garage
20-4 x 21-8

46'-0"

First Floor   54'-0"

design 20160

▲ Two-sided hearth for added pleasure in both the family room and breakfast nook.

design 20160

PHOTOGRAPHY BY BETH SINGER

Contemporary Design

Wood adds its warmth to the contemporary features of this solar design. Generous use of southern glass doors and windows, an air-lock entry, skylights and a living room fireplace reduce energy needs. R-26 insulation is used for floors and sloping ceilings. Decking rims the front of the home and gives access through sliding glass doors to a bedroom/den area and living room. The dining room lies up several steps from the living room and is separated from it by a half-wall. The dining room flows into the kitchen through an eating bar. A second floor landing balcony overlooks the living room. Two bedrooms, one with its own private deck, and a full bath finish the second level. The photographed home may have been modified to suit individual tastes.

first floor	911 sq. ft.
second floor	576 sq. ft.
basement	911 sq. ft.
bedrooms	three
bathrooms	1 full and 1 half
foundation	basement

Total Living Area — 1,487 sq. ft.

A stone fire-place and high beamed ceilings create a welcoming atmosphere for friends and family.

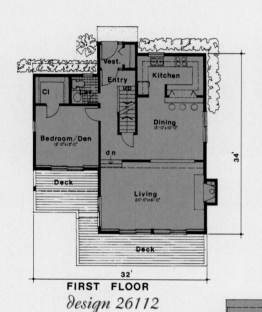

FIRST FLOOR
design 26112

Vest.

Entry
up

Kitchen

CI

Bedroom/Den
12'-0"x12'-0"

Dining
13'-0"x10'-0"

dn

Deck

Living
20'-0"x16'-0"

Deck

34'

32'

This rear deck adds many options for entertaining or relaxing on the weekend.

CI

Bath

CI   CI

Bedroom
12'-0"x12'-0"

Bedroom
13'-0"x14'-0"

dn

Balcony

Deck

Open to Living

Skylights

32'

SECOND FLOOR

design 26112

A Little Drama

*T*his home's dramatic exterior features a 12' high entry with transom and sidelights, multible gables and a box window. The foyer and sunken Great room feel very open with 12' high ceilings. The Great room and the breakfast room access a rear porch. A large closet is located in the laundry area hall. On the second floor is the master bedroom suite with a whirlpool tub and a walk-in closet. This is a classic home with large rooms in a compact package. No materials list is available for this plan. The photographed home may have been modified to suit individual tastes.

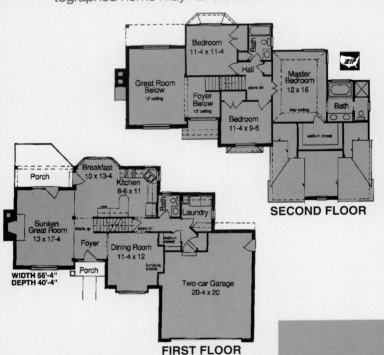

SECOND FLOOR

FIRST FLOOR
design 92609

first floor	960 sq. ft.
second floor	808 sq. ft.
basement	922 sq. ft.
garage	413 sq. ft.
bedrooms	three
bathrooms	2 full and 1 half
foundation	basement

Total Living Area — 1,768 sq. ft.

design 92609

refer to price code B

PHOTOGRAPHY BY RON & DONNA KOLB EXPOSURES UNLIMITED

Double Gables

Double gables and an exciting entry with an arched window, wood trim and sidelights create an impressive exterior on this family friendly home. The foyer introduces you to the formal areas; a living room or private library to one side and a formal dining room to the other. Split stairs decorated with rich wood rails lead to the second floor. A wrap-around balcony offers a view to the foyer and opens visually to the outside through the large window. Family members can relax in comfort in their spacious bedrooms with large closets. The master bedroom suite pampers the homeowner with its spaciousness, dual vanity, whirlpool tub and shower stall. Family activities will center around the roomy kitchen/breakfast bay and large family room with fireplace, multiple windows and convenient access to the rear yard. No materials list is available for this plan. No materials list is available for this plan. The photographed home may have been modified to suit individual tastes.

design 92692

SECOND FLOOR

first floor	1,207 sq. ft.
second floor	1,181 sq. ft.
basement	1,207 sq. ft.
garage	484 sq. ft.
bedrooms	four
bathrooms	2 full and 1 half
foundation	basement

Total Living Area — 2,388 sq. ft.

design 92692

refer to price code **D**

Country Farmhouse

Ready, set, grow with this lovely country farmhouse wreathed in windows and a covered wrap-around porch. A palladian window in the clerestory dormer bathes the two-story foyer in natural light. Nine foot ceilings throughout the first level, except kitchen, add drama. The private, first floor master suite has it all: whirlpool tub, shower, double vanity, and large walk-in closet. Upstairs, two bedrooms with dormers and attic storage access share a full bath. Keep growing with skylit bonus space over the garage and optional unfinished basement. This plan is available with a basement or crawl space foundation. Please specify when ordering.

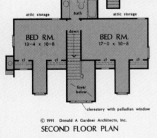

design 99852

© 1991 Donald A Gardner Architects, Inc.

SECOND FLOOR PLAN

FIRST FLOOR PLAN

first floor	1,356 sq. ft.
second floor	542 sq. ft.
bonus room	393 sq. ft.
garage	543 sq. ft.
bedrooms	three
bathrooms	2 full and 1 half
foundation	bsmt, crawl

Total Living Area — 1,898 sq. ft.

design 99852

refer to price code

Amazing Home

*U*pon entering the foyer, your view will go directly to the cozy fireplace and stylish French doors of the Great room. A grand entry into the formal dining room, coupled with the volume ceiling, pulls these two rooms together for a spacious feeling. From the roomy, well-equipped kitchen, there is a pass-through to the Great room. Natural light will flood the breakfast area through large windows. Located between the first floor master bedroom suite and the garage is the laundry, adding convenience and protecting the living areas from noise and disorder. Split stairs, graced with wood railings, lead to the versatile second floor with two additional bedrooms. No materials list is available for this plan. The photographed home may have been modified to suit individual tastes.

design 92642

first floor	1,524 sq. ft.
second floor	558 sq. ft.
basement	1,460 sq. ft.
bedrooms	three
bathrooms	2 full and 1 half
foundation	basement

Total Living Area — 2,082 sq. ft.

design 92642

refer to price code

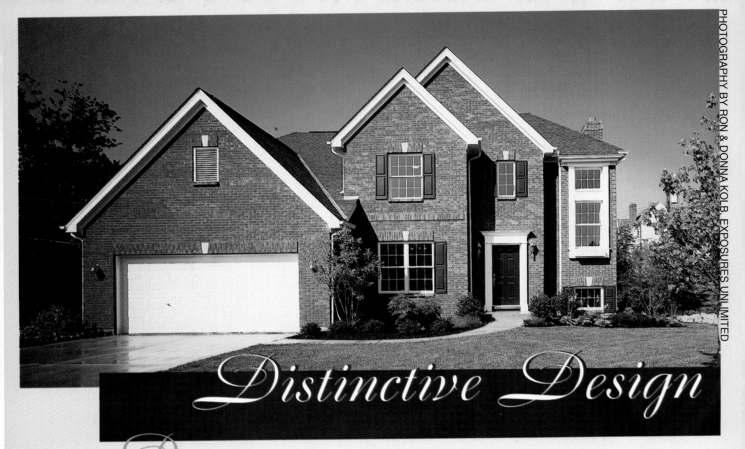

Distinctive Design

*D*esigned with your family in mind this home boasts many features. There is a furniture alcove in the formal dining room, a high ceiling and French doors topped with arched windows in the Great room, a wood rail at the split stairs, large pantry in the kitchen and a roomy laundry room. The spacious kitchen and breakfast area encourages relaxing gatherings. The master suite offers a whirlpool tub, his-n-her vanities, a shower stall and a walk-in closet. Two additional bedrooms share a full hall bath. No materials lsit is availalbe for this plan. The photographed home may have been modified to suit individual tastes.

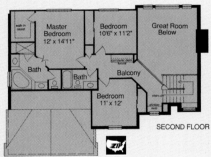

first floor	1,036 sq. ft.
second floor	861 sq. ft.
garage	420 sq. ft.
bedrooms	three
bathrooms	2 full and 1 half
foundation	basement

Total Living Area — 1,897 sq. ft.

design 92644

design 92644

refer to price code

Sixteen

Luxury Plan

An octagonal master bedroom with a vaulted ceiling, a sunken Great room with a balcony above, and an exterior with an exciting roof line; provide this home with all the luxurious ammenities in a moderate size. The first floor master bedroom targets this home to the empty-nester market. The elegant exterior has a rich solid look that is very important to the discriminating buyer. The kitchen features a center island and a breakfast nook. The sunken Great room has a cozy fireplace. Elegant and luxurious in a moderate size, this home has what your looking for. No materials list is available for this plan. The photographed home may have been modified to suit individual tastes.

SECOND FLOOR

FIRST FLOOR
design 92610

first floor ·········· 1,626 sq. ft.
second floor ·········· 475 sq. ft.
basement ·········· 1,512 sq. ft.
garage ·········· 438 sq. ft.
bedrooms ·········· three
bathrooms ·········· 2 full and 1 half
foundation ·········· basement
Total Living Area — 2,101 sq. ft.

design 92610

refer to price code

Perfect Ranch

This Ranch home features a large sunken Great room, centralized with a cozy fireplace. The master bedroom has an unforgettable bathroom with a super skylight. The huge three-car plus garage can include a work area for the family carpenter. In the center of this home, a kitchen includes an eating nook for family gatherings. The porch at the rear of the house has easy access from the dining room. One other bedroom and a den, which can easily be converted to a bedroom, are on the opposite side of the house from the master bedroom.

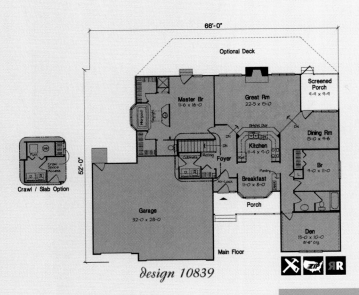

design 10839

main floor	1,738 sq. ft.
basement	1,083 sq. ft.
garage	796 sq. ft.
bedrooms	two
bathrooms	2 full
foundation	bsmt, slab, crawl

Total Living Area — 1,738 sq. ft.

design 10839

refer to price code B

Affordable Design

There's a lot of convenience packed into this affordable design. Flanking the kitchen to the right is the dining room which has a sliding glass door to the backyard, and to the left is the laundry room with an entrance to the garage. The master bedroom boasts its own full bathroom and the additional two bedrooms share the hall bath. An optional two-car garage plan is included.

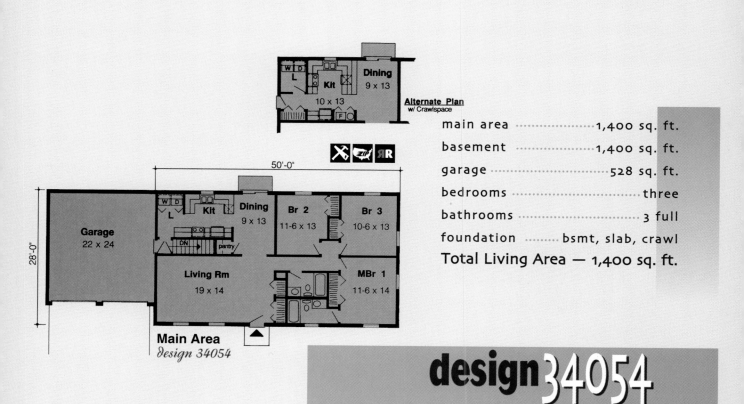

Alternate Plan
w/ Crawlspace

W D
L
Kit
10 x 13
Dining
9 x 13

main area	1,400 sq. ft.
basement	1,400 sq. ft.
garage	528 sq. ft.
bedrooms	three
bathrooms	3 full
foundation	bsmt, slab, crawl

Total Living Area — 1,400 sq. ft.

Garage
22 x 24

W D
L
Kit
Dining
9 x 13

Br 2
11-6 x 13

Br 3
10-6 x 13

DN
pantry

Living Rm
19 x 14

MBr 1
11-6 x 14

50'-0"

28'-0"

Main Area
design 34054

design**34054**

refer to price code **A**

Single Level

This home features a well designed floor plan, offering convenience and style. The roomy living room includes a two-sided fireplace shared with the dining room. An efficient U-shaped kitchen, equipped with a peninsula counter/breakfast bar, is open to the dining room. An entrance from the garage into the kitchen eliminates tracked in dirt and affords step-saving convenience when unloading groceries. The private master suite includes a whirlpool tub, a double vanity and a step-in shower. A large walk-in closet adds ample storage space to the suite. The secondary bedroom and the den/guest room share use of the full hall bath.

Alternate Foundation Plan

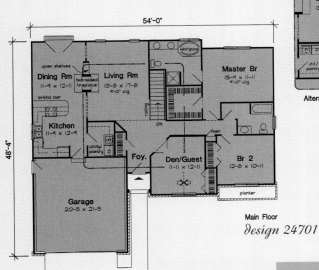

Main Floor
design 24701

main floor	1,625 sq. ft.
basement	1,625 sq. ft.
garage	455 sq. ft.
bedrooms	three
bathrooms	3 full and 2 half
foundation	bsmt, slab, crawl
Total Living Area —	**1,625 sq. ft.**

design 24701

Multiple Gables

An enchanting one level home with grand openings between rooms creates a spacious effect. The functional kitchen provides an abundance of counter space. Additional room for quick meals or serving an oversized crowd is provided at the breakfast bar. Double hung windows and angles add light and dimension to the dining area. The bright and cheery Great room with a sloped ceiling and a wood burning fireplace opens to the dining area and the foyer, making this three bedroom ranch look and feel much larger than its actual size. No materials list is available for this plan.

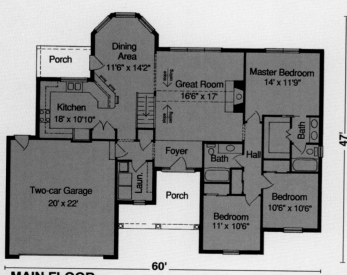

MAIN FLOOR
design 92649

main floor	1,590 sq. ft.
basement	1,576 sq. ft.
garage	456 sq. ft.
bedrooms	three
bathrooms	2 full
foundation	basement

Total Living Area — 1,508 sq. ft.

design 92649

refer to price code B

Casually Elegant

This country classic offers a casually elegant exterior with arched windows, dormers, and charming front and back porches with columns. Inside, the open, casual mood is continued in the central Great room which features a cathedral ceiling, a fireplace and a clerestory window that splashes the room with natural light. Other special touches include a breakfast bay and interior columns. The master suite with cathedral ceiling is privately located and features a skylit bath with whirlpool tub, shower and a double vanity. Two additional bedrooms share a full bath, and a garage with storage completes the plan.

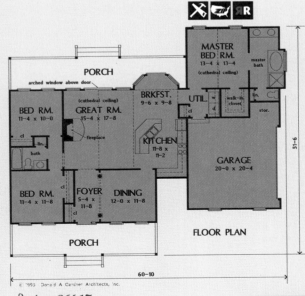

design 96417

main floor	1,561 sq. ft.
garage/storage	346 sq. ft.
bedrooms	three
bathrooms	2 full
foundation	crawlspace
Total Living Area —	**1,561 sq. ft.**

design 96417

refer to price code

Dramatic Ranch

The exterior of this ranch home is all wood with interesting lines. More than an ordinary ranch home, it has an expansive feeling to drive up to. The large living area has a stone fireplace and decorative beams. The kitchen and dining room lead to an outside deck. The laundry room has a large pantry, and is off the eating area. The master bedroom has a wonderful bathroom with a huge walk-in closet. In the front of the house, there are two additional bedrooms with a bathroom. This house offers one floor living and has nice big rooms.

An
EXCLUSIVE DESIGN
By Karl Kreeger

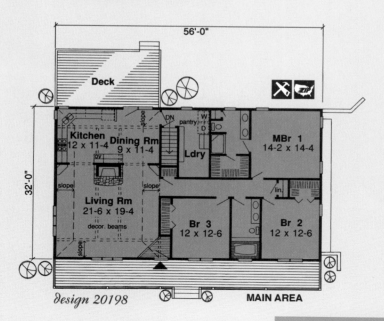

design 20198   **MAIN AREA**

main area	1,792 sq. ft.
basement	818 sq. ft.
garage	857 sq. ft.
bedrooms	three
bathrooms	2 full
foundation	basement

Total Living Area — 1,792 sq. ft.

design 20198

refer to price code **B**

Rustic Exterior

*A*lthough rustic in appearance, the interior of this cabin is quiet, modern and comfortable. Small in overall size, it still contains three bedrooms and two baths in addition to a large, two-story living room with exposed beams. As a hunting/fishing lodge or mountain retreat, this compares well.

Upper Floor

main floor	1,013 sq. ft.
upper floor	315 sq. ft.
basement	1,013 sq. ft.
bedrooms	three
bathrooms	2 full
foundation	bsmt, slab, crawl

Total Living Area — 1,328 sq. ft.

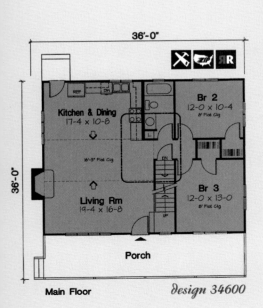

Main Floor

design 34600

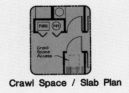

Crawl Space / Slab Plan

design 34600

refer to price code **A**

Country Cottage

We hardly wasted an inch creating a spacious interior for this dormered and gabled country cottage that lives much bigger than it looks. The front bedroom, master bedroom, and open Great room/kitchen gain vertical space from cathedral ceilings while the open foyer pulls the dining room and Great room together visually. The wrap-around front porch, breakfast bay window, and a skylit back porch add charm and expand living space. The master bath pampers the owner with a whirlpool tub, separate shower and dual vanity. A bonus room adds flexibilty to the plan.

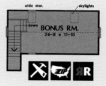

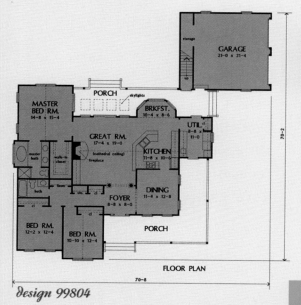

design 99804

main floor	1,815 sq. ft.
bonus room	336 sq. ft.
garage	522 sq. ft.
bedrooms	three
bathrooms	3 full and 2 half
foundation	crawlspace
Total Living Area — 1,815 sq. ft.	

design 99804

refer to price code

C

Country Influence

A cozy porch sets the tone for this comfortable home. Enter into the sun room that includes a coat closet and convenient access to a half bath. A simple half wall separates the living room and the dining room. The efficient kitchen is equipped with a laundry center and a sunny bayed area. The bedrooms are on the second floor. A walk-in closet, private bath with an oval tub and a decorative ceiling and bay window highlight the master suite. The two additional bedrooms share a full bath.

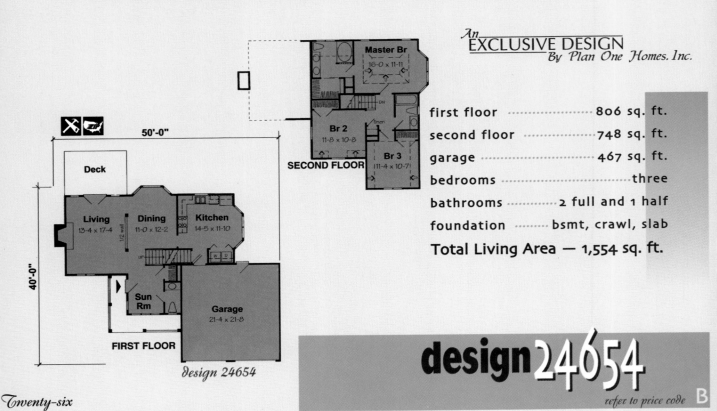

An
EXCLUSIVE DESIGN
By Plan One Homes, Inc.

first floor .... 806 sq. ft.

second floor .... 748 sq. ft.

garage .... 467 sq. ft.

bedrooms ....three

bathrooms .... 2 full and 1 half

foundation .... bsmt, crawl, slab

Total Living Area — 1,554 sq. ft.

design 24654

design**24654**

refer to price code **B**

© 1996 Donald A. Gardner Architects, Inc.

Dramatic Dormers

The foyer is open to the dramatic dormer and is defined by elegant columns, while the dining room is augmented by a tray ceiling. The front room does double duty as a bedroom or a study. A cathedral ceiling and a clerestory accentuating the rear porch opens the Great room. The Great room is further expanded into the open kitchen and breakfast room by a cased opening with accent columns. The master suite, privately removed to one side of the house, features a tray ceiling in the bedroom. A garden tub with a picture window is the focal point of the master bath. Buyers will love the roomy walk-in closet. Two bedrooms on the other side of the home share a full bath and linen closet.

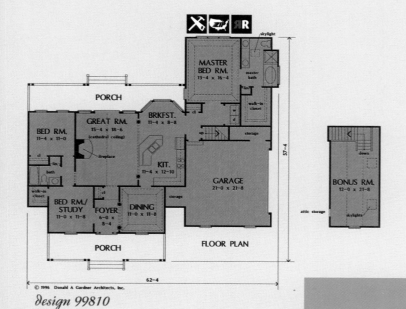

© 1996 Donald A Gardner Architects, Inc.

design 99810

main floor	1,685 sq. ft.
bonus room	331 sq. ft.
garage	536 sq. ft.
bedrooms	three
bathrooms	2 full
foundation	crawlspace

Total Living Area — 1,685 sq. ft.

design 99810

refer to price code C

B. NATHAN

Great Beginnings

Privacy as well as an open Great room for gathering make this exciting three bedroom country home perfect for the active young family. The Great room features a fireplace, cathedral ceiling, and built-in bookshelves. The kitchen is designed for efficient use with its food preparation island and pantry. The master suite with cathedral ceiling, walk-in closet, and a luxurious bath provides a welcome retreat. Two additional bedrooms, one with a cathedral ceiling and walk-in closet, share a skylit bath. A second floor bonus room makes a perfect study or play area. This plan is available with a basement or crawl space foundation. Please specify when ordering.

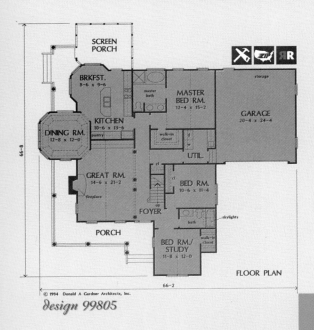

FLOOR PLAN

© 1994 Donald A Gardner Architects, Inc.
design 99805

BONUS RM.
14-2 x 17-10

main floor	1,787 sq. ft.
bonus room	326 sq. ft.
garage	521 sq. ft.
bedrooms	three
bathrooms	2 full
foundation	bsmt, crawl

Total Living Area — 1,787 sq. ft.

design 99805

refer to price code

Extra Style

You don't have to sacrifice style when buying a smaller home. Notice the palladian window with a fan light above at the front of the home. The entrance porch includes a turned post entry. Once inside, the living room is topped by an impressive vaulted ceiling. A fireplace accents the room. A decorative ceiling enhances both the master bedroom and the dining room. Efficiently designed, the kitchen includes a peninsula counter and serves the dining room with ease. A private bath and double closet highlight the master suite. Two additional bedrooms are served by a full hall bath.

MAIN FLOOR
design 24700

main floor	1,312 sq. ft.
basement	1,293 sq. ft.
garage	459 sq. ft.
bedrooms	three
bathrooms	2 full
foundation	bsmt, slab, crawl
Total Living Area	**1,312 sq. ft.**

design 24700

refer to price code A

Great Starter

© 1993 Donald A. Gardner Architects, Inc.

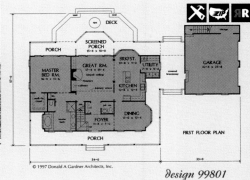

design 99801

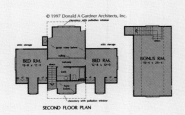

© 1997 Donald A Gardner Architects, Inc.

SECOND FLOOR PLAN

Two-story Great room

A two-story Great room and two-story foyer, both with dormer windows, welcome natural light into this graceful country classic with wrap-around porch. The large kitchen, featuring a center cooking island with counter and large breakfast area, opens to the Great room for easy entertaining. Columns punctuate the interior spaces and a separate dining room provides a formal touch to the plan. The master suite, privately situated on the first floor, has a double vanity, garden tub, and separate shower. The semi-detached garage features a large bonus room.

first floor	1,618 sq. ft.
second floor	570 sq. ft.
bonus room	495 sq. ft.
garage	649 sq. ft.
bedrooms	three
bathrooms	2 full and 1 half
foundation	crawlspace
Total Living Area — 2,188 sq. ft.	

design 99801

refer to price code D

This functional, all on one level, home plan features a lovely country porch entry into a spacious living room that is accented by a fireplace. The efficient U-shaped kitchen has direct access to both the dining and the living room. A screened porch is accessed directly from the kitchen. The master bedroom includes a private double vanity bath with a whirlpool tub and separate shower. The two additional bedrooms share a full double vanity bath which has the added convenience of a laundry center. No materials list is available for this plan.

Alternate Crawl/Slab Plan

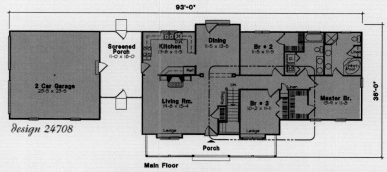

design 24708

Main Floor

93'-0"

38'-0"

main floor .... 1,576 sq. ft.
basement .... 1,454 sq. ft.
garage .... 576 sq. ft.
bedrooms .... three
bathrooms .... 2 full
foundation .... bsmt, slab, crawl
Total Living Area — 1,576 sq. ft.

design 24708

refer to price code B

Whimsical Appeal

Double gables with clerestory palladian window and a colonnaded wrap-around porch give this four bedroom, two-story farmhouse whimsical appeal. Palladian windows flood the two-level foyer and Great room with natural light. A balcony connects the two spaces on the second level, the first floor enjoys nine-foot ceilings throughout. Both master bedroom and Great room with fireplace access the covered rear porch. The master bath features a walk-in closet, double vanity, separate shower, and whirlpool tub.

One of three upstairs bedrooms enjoys a private bath and walk-in closet.

design 96442

refer to price code D

© Donald A. Gardner Architects, Inc.
design 96442

FIRST FLOOR PLAN

49-5

45-4

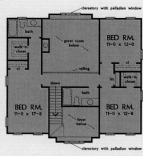

first floor .... 1,346 sq. ft.
second floor .... 836 sq. ft.
bedrooms .... four
bathrooms .... 3 full and 1 half
foundation .... crawlspace
Total Living Area — 2,182 sq. ft.

Classic Country

ual porches, gables, and circle-top windows give this home its special country charm. The foyer, expanded by a vaulted ceiling, introduces a formal colonnaded dining room. The open kitchen features columns and an island for easy entertaining. The vaulted Great room is always bright with light from the circle-top clerestory. Extra room for growth is waiting in the skylit bonus room. The front bedroom doubles as a study for versatility. A tray ceiling adds volume to the private master suite that has a bath with skylight, garden tub, double bowl vanity, and both linen and walk-in closets.

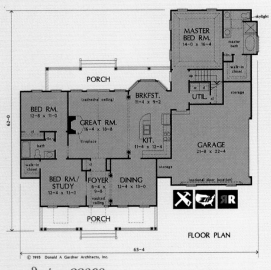

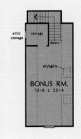

design 99808

main floor	1,832 sq. ft.
bonus	425 sq. ft.
garage	562 sq. ft.
bedrooms	three
bathrooms	2 full
foundation	crawlspace

Total Living Area — 1,832 sq. ft.

design 99808

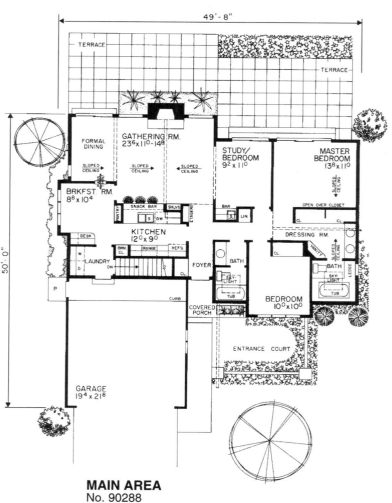

MAIN AREA
No. 90288

Soaring Ceilings Add Space and Drama

◼ This plan features:

— Two bedrooms (with optional third bedroom)

— Two full baths

◼ A sunny Master Suite with a sloping ceiling, private terrace entry, and luxurious garden bath with an adjoining Dressing Room

◼ A Gathering Room with a fireplace, study and formal Dining Room, flowing together for a more spacious feeling

◼ A convenient pass-through that adds to the efficiency of the galley Kitchen and adjoining Breakfast Room

MAIN AREA — 1,387 SQ. FT.
GARAGE — 440 SQ. FT.

TOTAL LIVING AREA:
1,387 SQ. FT.

Wonderful Open Spaces

■ This plan features:

— Three bedrooms

— Two full baths

■ A Family Room, Kitchen and Breakfast Area that all connects to form a great space

■ A central, double fireplace adding warmth and atmosphere to the Family Room, Kitchen and the Breakfast area

■ An efficient Kitchen that is highlighted by a peninsula counter and doubles as a snack bar

■ A Master Suite that includes a walk-in closet, a double vanity, separate shower and tub bath

■ Two additional bedrooms sharing a full hall bath

■ A wooden deck that can be accessed from the Breakfast Area

■ An optional crawl space or slab foundation — please specify when ordering

MAIN FLOOR — 1,388 SQ. FT.
GARAGE — 400 SQ. FT.

An EXCLUSIVE DESIGN
By Jannis Vann & Associates, Inc.

TOTAL LIVING AREA: 1,388 SQ. FT.

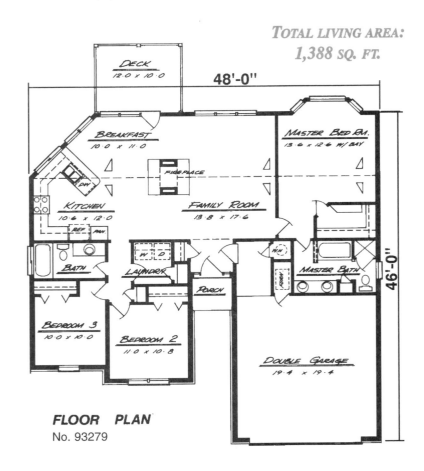

FLOOR PLAN
No. 93279

To order your Blueprints, call 1-800-235-5700

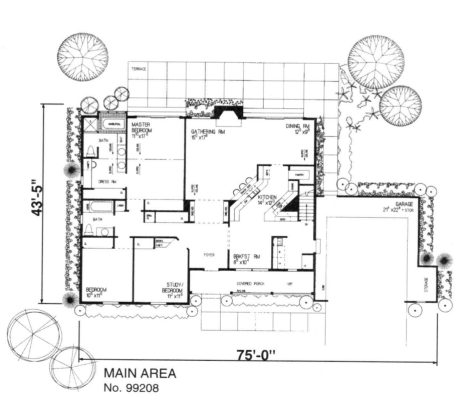

MAIN AREA
No. 99208

43'-5"

75'-0"

Cozy Traditional with Style

■ This plan features:

— Three bedrooms

— Two full baths

■ A convenient one-level design

■ A galley-style Kitchen that shares a snack bar with the spacious Gathering Room

■ A focal point fireplace making the Gathering Room warm and inviting

■ An ample Master Suite with a luxury Bath which contains a whirlpool tub and separate Dressing Room

■ Two additional bedrooms, one that could double as a Study, located at the front of the house

MAIN AREA — 1,830 SQ. FT.
BASEMENT — 1,830 SQ. FT.

TOTAL LIVING AREA:
1,830 SQ. FT.

Refer to **Pricing Schedule A** on the order form for pricing information

Family Favorite

■ This plan features:

— Three bedrooms

— Two full baths

■ An open arrangement with the Dining Room that combines with ten foot ceilings to make the Living Room seem more spacious

■ Glass on three sides of the Dining Room which overlooks the deck

■ An efficient, compact Kitchen with a built-in pantry and peninsula counter

■ A Master Suite with a window seat, a compartmentalized private bath and a walk-in closet

■ Two additional bedrooms that share a full hall closet

MAIN AREA — 1,359 SQ. FT.
BASEMENT — 1,359 SQ. FT.
GARAGE — 501 SQ. FT.

An
EXCLUSIVE DESIGN
By Karl Kreeger

TOTAL LIVING AREA:
1,359 SQ. FT.

58'-0"

Crawl Space/Slab Option

Deck

Dining
11-0 × 11-2

Decor. Ceiling

Br #2
10-10 × 11-10

Den/Br #3
10-0 × 11-10

Optional Door Location

Kit
10-0 × 11-2

Sink
Range
DW
Ret.
Pan.

Ldry

Railing

Solid Wall w/ Opt. Door Location

DN

Plant Ledge

34'-4"

Decor. Ceiling

lin.

MBr #1
11-7 × 13-0

Living Rm
14-10 × 17-0

10' clg

Garage
20-4 × 21-8

Seat

MAIN AREA
No. 20156

To order your Blueprints, call 1-800-235-5700

38'-0"

Br 1
14-8 x 9-6

Nook **Kit.**
8x 11-6

pantry

line of loft above

linen

Living
14 x 17

ladder

26'-0"

grill

Br 2
14-8 x 9-6

Deck

Main Floor
No. 24309

Loft
9 x 12

railing

An
EXCLUSIVE DESIGN
By Marshall Associates

Rustic Retreat

■ This plan features:

— Two bedrooms

— One full bath

■ A wrap-around deck equipped with a built-in bar-b-que for easy outdoor living

■ An entry, in a wall of glass, opens the Living area to the outdoors

■ A large fireplace in the Living area opens into an efficient Kitchen, with a built-in pantry, that serves the Nook area

■ Two bedrooms share a centrally located full bath with a window tub

■ A loft area ready for multiple uses

MAIN FLOOR — 789 SQ. FT.
LOFT — 108 SQ. FT.

TOTAL LIVING AREA:
897 SQ. FT.

Refer to **Pricing Schedule D** on the order form for pricing information

Rich Classic Lines

■ This plan features:

— Four bedrooms

— Three full and one half baths

■ A vaulted ceiling in the Great Room and the Master Suite

■ A corner fireplace in the Great Room with French doors to the Breakfast/Kitchen area

■ A center island in the Kitchen with an angled sink and a built-in desk and pantry

■ A tray ceiling and recessed hutch area in the formal Dining Room

■ A Master Suite with a walk-in closet, a whirlpool tub, and a double vanity

■ No materials list is available for this plan

FIRST FLOOR — 1,496 SQ. FT.
SECOND FLOOR — 716 SQ. FT.
BASEMENT — 1,420 SQ. FT.
GARAGE — 460 SQ. FT.

TOTAL LIVING AREA:
2,212 SQ. FT.

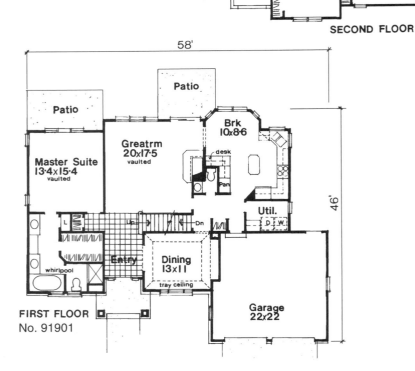

SECOND FLOOR

FIRST FLOOR
No. 91901

Spectacular Traditional

- This plan features:
— Three bedrooms
— Two full baths
- The use of gable roofs and the blend of stucco and brick to form a spectacular exterior
- A high vaulted ceiling and a cozy fireplace, with built-in cabinets in the Den
- An efficient, U-shaped Kitchen with an adjacent Dining Area
- A Master Bedroom, with a raised ceiling, that includes a private bath and a walk-in closet
- Two family bedrooms that share a full hall bath
- An optional crawl space or slab foundation — please specify when ordering

MAIN AREA — 1,237 SQ. FT.
GARAGE — 436 SQ. FT.

TOTAL LIVING AREA:
1,237 SQ. FT.

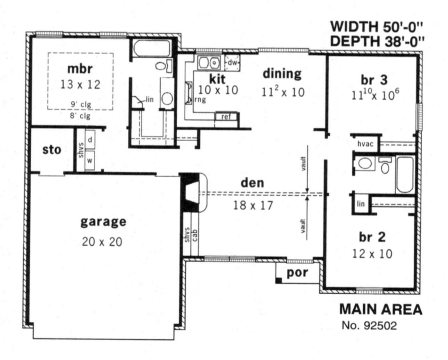

WIDTH 50'-0"
DEPTH 38'-0"

mbr 13 x 12
9' clg
8' clg

sto

kit 10 x 10

dining 11^2 x 10

br 3 11^{10} x 10^6

den 18 x 17

br 2 12 x 10

garage 20 x 20

por

MAIN AREA
No. 92502

Inviting Porch Has Dual Function

■ This plan features:

— Three bedrooms

— One full and one three quarter bath

■ An inviting, wrap-around porch Entry with sliding glass doors leading right into a bayed Dining Room

■ A Living Room with a cozy feeling, enhanced by the fireplace

■ An efficient Kitchen opening to both Dining and Living Rooms

■ A Master Suite with a walk-in closet and private Master Bath

■ An optional basement, slab or crawl space foundation — please specify when ordering

MAIN FLOOR — 1,295 SQ. FT.
GARAGE — 400 SQ. FT.

TOTAL LIVING AREA:
1,295 SQ. FT.

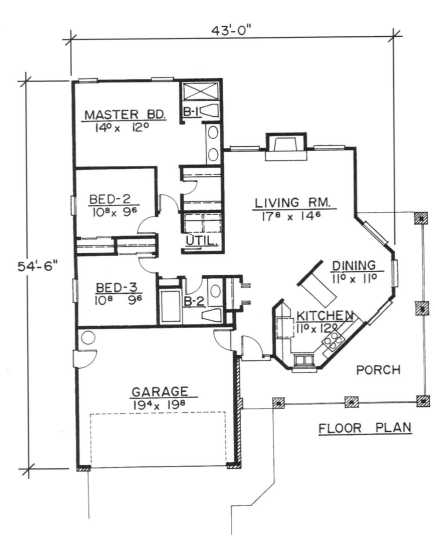

43'-0"

54'-6"

MASTER BD.
14⁰ x 12⁰

B-1

BED-2
10⁸ x 9⁶

UTIL.

LIVING RM.
17⁸ x 14⁶

BED-3
10⁸ 9⁶

B-2

DINING
11⁰ x 11⁰

KITCHEN
11⁰ x 12⁹

PORCH

GARAGE
19⁴ x 19⁸

FLOOR PLAN

To order your Blueprints, call 1-800-235-5700

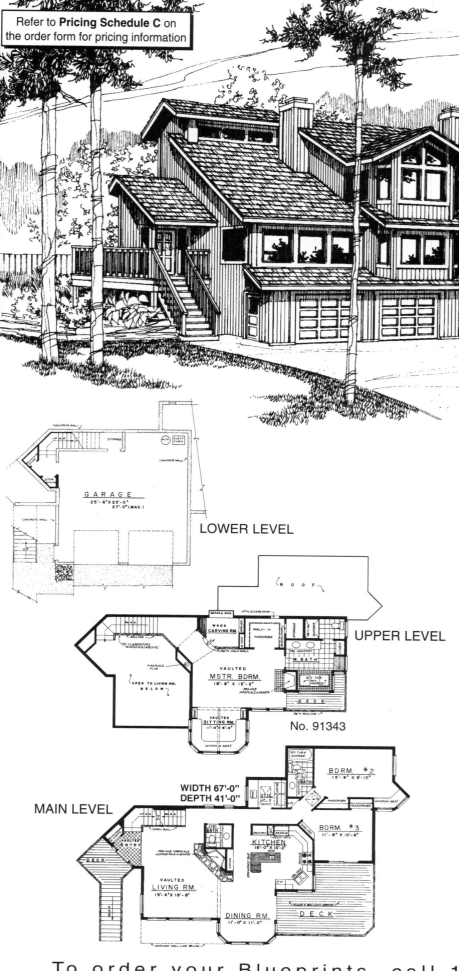

LOWER LEVEL

UPPER LEVEL

No. 91343

MAIN LEVEL

WIDTH 67'-0"
DEPTH 41'-0"

Customized for Sloping View Site

■ This plan features:

— Three bedrooms

— Two full and one half baths

■ A stone-faced fireplace and vaulted ceiling in the Living Room

■ An island food preparation center with a sink and a Breakfast bar in the Kitchen

■ Sliding glass doors leading from the Dining Room to the adjacent deck

■ A Master Suite with a vaulted ceiling, a sitting room, and a lavish Master Bath with a whirlpool tub, skylights, double vanity and a walk-in closet

MAIN LEVEL — 1,338 SQ. FT.
UPPER LEVEL — 763 SQ. FT.
LOWER LEVEL — 61 SQ. FT.

TOTAL LIVING AREA:
2,162 SQ. FT.

Refer to **Pricing Schedule A** on the order form for pricing information

Split Bedroom Plan

■ This plan features:

— Three bedrooms

— Two full baths

■ A tray ceiling giving a decorative touch to the Master Bedroom and a vaulted ceiling topping the five-piece Master Bath

■ A full bath located between the secondary bedrooms

■ A corner fireplace and a vaulted ceiling highlighting the heart of the home, the Family Room

■ A wetbar/serving bar to the Family Room and a built-in pantry add to the convenience of the Kitchen

■ A formal Dining Room crowned in an elegant high ceiling

■ An optional basement, crawl space or slab foundation — please specify when ordering

MAIN FLOOR — 1,429 SQ. FT.
BASEMENT — 1,472 SQ. FT.
GARAGE — 438 SQ. FT.

© Frank Betz Associates

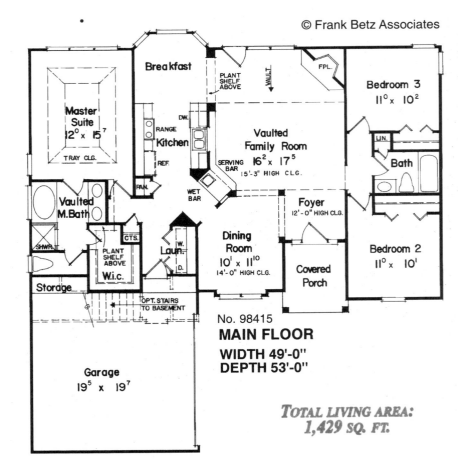

No. 98415

MAIN FLOOR

WIDTH 49'-0"
DEPTH 53'-0"

TOTAL LIVING AREA:
1,429 SQ. FT.

To order your Blueprints, call 1-800-235-5700

Refer to **Pricing Schedule C** on the order form for pricing information

An
EXCLUSIVE DESIGN
By Karl Kreeger

SECOND FLOOR

BEDROOM
13'-2" x 11'-4"
SLOPED CEILING
B.
OPEN TO LIVING ROOM
HALL
RAILING
C.
ATTIC
BEDROOM
11'-4" x 11'-2"
OPEN TO FOYER
SLOPED CEILING
DN

Tower Stimulates Interest

■ This plan features:

— Four bedrooms

— Three full baths

■ Sloping ceilings and lofty open spaces

■ A rustic, fireplaced Living Room with sloped ceilings to enhance the atmosphere

■ A Master Suite with vaulted ceilings, walk-in closet, dressing area and Master Bath

■ Two upstairs bedrooms sharing a full bath

FIRST FLOOR — 1,496 SQ. FT.
SECOND FLOOR — 520 SQ. FT.
GARAGE — 424 SQ. FT.
BASEMENT — 1,487 SQ. FT.

TOTAL LIVING AREA:
2,016 SQ. FT.

FIRST FLOOR
NO. 34049

61'-0"
40'-4"

OPTIONAL PATIO
DECK
CEILING BEAMS
LIVING ROOM LEVEL
SLOPED CLG
SLOPED CLG
15'-0" x 19'-4"
BRKFST
7'-10" x 12'-6"
KITCHEN
ISLAND
LAUND.
10'-8" x 11'-2"
PANTRY
DESK
STEP
M. BEDROOM
VAULTED CEILING
13'-4" x 14'-4"
B.
HALL
C.
LIN
DRESSING
GARAGE
20'-4" x 19'-6"
DINING ROOM
11'-2" x 11'-4"
FOYER
OPEN
STEP
DN
UP
BEDROOM
11'-0" x 12'-4"
B.
PORCH
RAILING
APRON
DRIVEWAY
STEP
WALK
C.

Refer to **Pricing Schedule B** on the order form for pricing information

Cozy Front Porch

■ This plan features:

— Three bedrooms

— Two full and one half bath

■ Living Room enhanced by a large fireplace

■ Formal Dining Room that is open to the Living Room, giving a more spacious feel to the rooms

■ Efficient Kitchen with ample counter and cabinet space, double sinks and pass thru window to living area

■ Sunny Breakfast Area with vaulted ceiling and a door to the sun deck

■ First floor Master Suite with separate tub and shower stall, and walk-in closet

■ First floor powder room with a hide-away laundry center

■ Two additional bedrooms that share a full hall bath

An
EXCLUSIVE DESIGN
By Jannis Vann & Associates, Inc.

FIRST FLOOR — 1,045 SQ. FT.
SECOND FLOOR — 690 SQ. FT.
BASEMENT — 465 SQ. FT.
GARAGE — 580 SQ. FT.

TOTAL LIVING AREA:
1,735 SQ. FT.

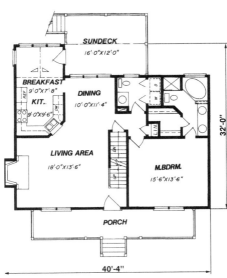

FIRST FLOOR
No. 93269

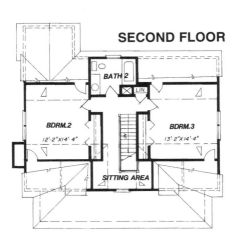

SECOND FLOOR

To order your Blueprints, call 1-800-235-5700

© 1996 Donald A Gardner Architects, Inc.

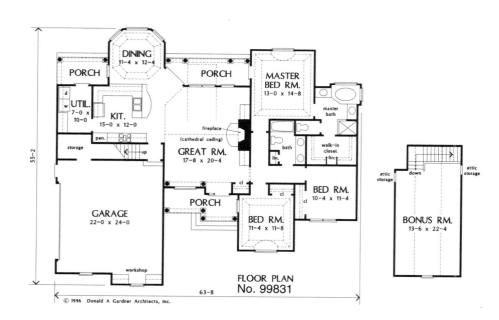

FLOOR PLAN
No. 99831

© 1996 Donald A Gardner Architects, Inc.

TOTAL LIVING AREA:
1,699 SQ. FT.

European Sophistication

■ This plan features:

— Three bedrooms

— Two full baths

■ Keystone arches, gables, and stucco give the exterior European sophistication

■ Large Great Room with fireplace, and U-shaped Kitchen and a large utility room nearby

■ Octagonal tray ceiling dresses up the Dining Room

■ Special ceiling treatments include a cathedral ceiling in the Great Room and tray ceilings in both the Master and front bedrooms

■ Indulgent Master Bath with a separate toilet area, a garden tub, shower, and twin vanities

■ Bonus room over the garage adds flexibility

MAIN FLOOR — 1,699 SQ. FT.

GARAGE — 637 SQ. FT.

Refer to **Pricing Schedule B** on the order form for pricing information

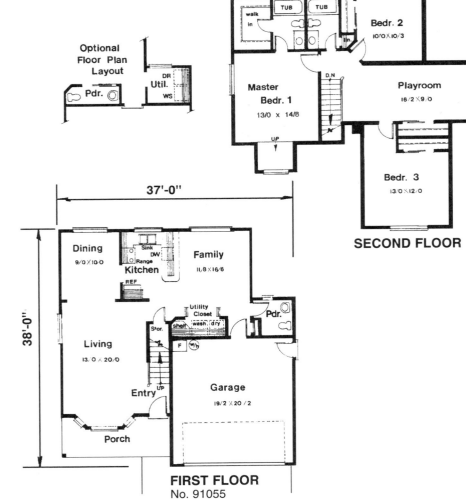

Excellent Choice for First Time Buyer

■ This plan features:

— Three bedrooms

— Two full and one half baths

■ A formal Living Room with a floor-to-ceiling triple window

■ Family Room with a sliding glass door to the backyard, a Utility Closet for washer and dryer and access to the Kitchen

■ Kitchen with a peninsula counter/snackbar

■ Master Bedroom with a recessed dormer window, an oversized, walk-in closet and a private Bath

■ Two bedrooms on the second floor, sharing a full bath and a Playroom

FIRST FLOOR — 805 SQ. FT.
SECOND FLOOR — 961 SQ. FT.
GARAGE — 540 SQ. FT.

TOTAL LIVING AREA:
1,766 SQ. FT.

Optional Floor Plan Layout

DR
Util.
Pdr.
WS

SECOND FLOOR

walk in
TUB
TUB
Bedr. 2
10/0 X 10/3

Master Bedr. 1
13/0 x 14/8

D.N

Playroom
16/2 X 9/0

UP

Bedr. 3
13/0 X 12/0

37'-0"

38'-0"

Dining
9/0 X 10-0

Sink
DW
Range
Kitchen

Family
11/8 X 16/6

REF

Utility Closet
wash. dry

Pdr.

Stor.
shelf

Living
13/0 X 20/0

F
W/H

UP

Entry

Garage
19/2 X 20/2

Porch

FIRST FLOOR
No. 91055

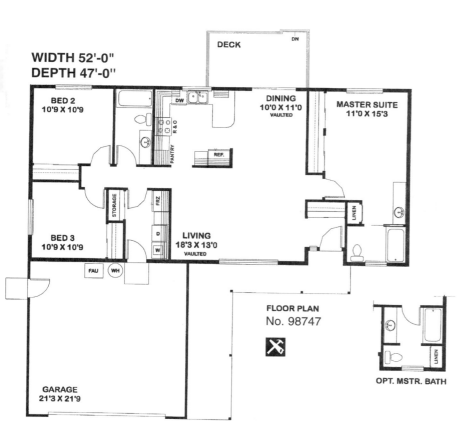

WIDTH 52'-0"
DEPTH 47'-0"

DECK   DN

BED 2
10'9 X 10'9

DINING
10'0 X 11'0
VAULTED

MASTER SUITE
11'0 X 15'3

DW

R & O

PANTRY

REF.

STORAGE

FRZ

LINEN

BED 3
10'9 X 10'9

LIVING
18'3 X 13'0
VAULTED

D

W

FAU   WH

FLOOR PLAN
No. 98747

GARAGE
21'3 X 21'9

OPT. MSTR. BATH

LINEN

L-Shaped Front Porch

■ This plan features:

— Three bedrooms

— Two full baths

■ Attractive wood siding and a large L-shaped covered porch

■ Generous Living Room with a vaulted ceiling

■ Large two car garage with access through Utility Room

■ Roomy secondary bedrooms share the full bath in the hall

■ Kitchen highlighted by a built-in pantry and a garden window

■ Vaulted ceiling adds volume to the Dining Room

■ Master Suite in isolated location enhanced by abundant closet space, separate vanity, and linen storage

MAIN FLOOR — 1,280 SQ. FT.

TOTAL LIVING AREA:
1,280 SQ. FT.

Refer to **Pricing Schedule B** on the order form for pricing information

Ten Foot Entry

- This plan features:
- —Three bedrooms
- —Two full baths
- Large volume Great Room highlighted by a fireplace flanked by windows
- See-through wetbar enhancing the Breakfast area and the Dining Room
- Decorative ceiling treatment giving elegance to the Dining Room
- Fully equipped Kitchen with a planning desk and a pantry
- Roomy Master Bedroom suite has a volume ceiling and special amenities; a skylighted dressing bath area, plant shelf, a large walk-in closet, a double vanity and a whirlpool tub
- Secondary bedrooms with ample closets sharing a convenient hall bath

MAIN FLOOR — 1,604 SQ. FT.
GARAGE — 466 SQ. FT.

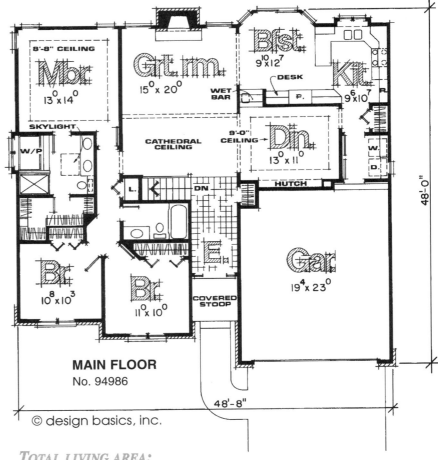

MAIN FLOOR
No. 94986

© design basics, inc.

TOTAL LIVING AREA:
1,604 SQ. FT.

To order your Blueprints, call 1-800-235-5700

FIRST FLOOR
No. 91053

FIRST FLOOR — 1,150 SQ. FT.
SECOND FLOOR — 949 SQ. FT.
GARAGE — 484 SQ. FT.

TOTAL LIVING AREA:
2,099 SQ. FT.

SECOND FLOOR

Updated Victorian

■ This plan features:

— Three bedrooms

— Two full and one half baths

■ Classic Victorian exterior design accented by a wonderful turret room and second floor covered porch

■ Spacious formal Living Room leading into a formal Dining Room for ease in entertaining

■ Efficient, U-shaped Kitchen with loads of counter space and a peninsula snackbar, opens to an eating Nook and Family Room for informal gatherings and activities

■ Elegant Master Suite with a unique, octagon Sitting area, a private Porch, an oversized, walk-in closet and private bath with a double vanity and a window tub

■ Two additional bedrooms with ample closets share a full bath

Refer to **Pricing Schedule A** on the order form for pricing information

An EXCLUSIVE DESIGN
By Karl Kreeger

Simple Lines Enhanced by Elegant Window Treatment

■ This plan features:

— Two bedrooms (optional third)

— Two full baths

■ A huge, arched window that floods the front room with natural light

■ A homey, well-lit Office or Den

■ Compact, efficient use of space

■ An efficient Kitchen with easy access to the Dining Room

■ A fireplaced Living Room with a sloping ceiling and a window wall

■ A Master Bedroom sporting a private Master Bath with a roomy walk-in closet

MAIN AREA — 1,492 SQ. FT.
BASEMENT — 1,486 SQ. FT.
GARAGE — 462 SQ. FT.

TOTAL LIVING AREA: 1,492 SQ. FT.

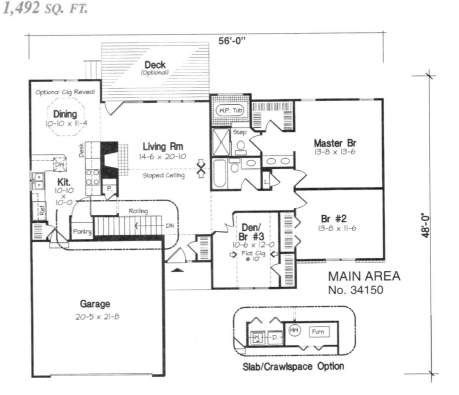

56'-0"

Deck (Optional)

Optional Clg Reveal

Dining 10-10 x 11-4

W.P. Tub

Step

Master Br 13-8 x 13-6

Living Rm 14-6 x 20-10

Sloped Ceiling

Kit. 10-10 x 10-0

Desk

DW

Ref

Pantry

Railing

DN

Den/ Br #3 10-6 x 12-0
Flat Clg @ 10'

Br #2 13-8 x 11-6

48'-0"

Garage 20-5 x 21-8

MAIN AREA
No. 34150

W D HW Furn

Slab/Crawlspace Option

© design basics, inc.

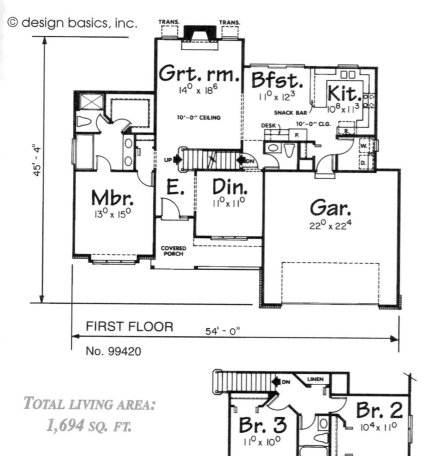

FIRST FLOOR 54' - 0"

No. 99420

TOTAL LIVING AREA:
1,694 SQ. FT.

Br. 3 11⁰ x 10⁰
Br. 2 10⁴ x 11⁰

SECOND FLOOR

Simplicity at it's Finest

■ This plan features:

— Three bedrooms

— Two full and one half baths

■ Covered porch providing a
nostalgic feel for the elevation

■ Volume Great Room offering a
fireplace with transom windows
to either side

■ Built-in planning desk and pantry
in the Breakfast Area

■ Snack bar for informal meals
highlighting the Kitchen

■ Formal dining room overlooking
the porch with easy access to the
Kitchen

■ Isolated Master Suite with private
five-piece bath and walk-in closet

FIRST FLOOR — 1,298 SQ. FT.
SECOND FLOOR — 396 SQ. FT.
BASEMENT — 1,298 SQ. FT.
GARAGE — 513 SQ. FT.

Refer to **Pricing Schedule C** on the order form for pricing information

Country Styled Home

■ This plan features:

— Three bedrooms

— Two full and one half baths

■ A country styled front Porch provides a warm welcome

■ The Family Room is highlighted by a fireplace and front windows

■ The Dining Room is separated from the U-shaped Kitchen by only an extended counter

■ The first floor Master Suite pampers the owners with a walk-in closet and a five-piece bath

■ There are two additional bedrooms with a convenient bath in the hall

FIRST FLOOR — 1,288 SQ. FT.
SECOND FLOOR — 545 SQ. FT.
GARAGE — 540 SQ. FT.

TOTAL LIVING AREA:
1,833 SQ. FT.

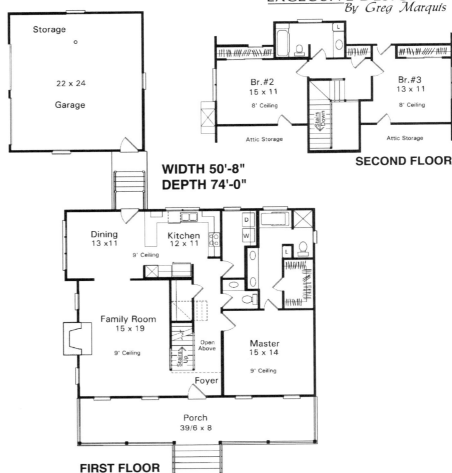

An EXCLUSIVE DESIGN
By Greg Marquis

WIDTH 50'-8"
DEPTH 74'-0"

Storage

22 x 24

Garage

Br. #2
15 x 11
8' Ceiling

Attic Storage

Stairs Down

Br. #3
13 x 11
8' Ceiling

Attic Storage

SECOND FLOOR

Dining
13 x11
9' Ceiling

Kitchen
12 x 11

D
W

Family Room
15 x 19
9' Ceiling

Open Above

Stairs Up

Master
15 x 14
9' Ceiling

Foyer

Porch
39/6 x 8

FIRST FLOOR
No. 93432

To order your Blueprints, call 1-800-235-5700

An
EXCLUSIVE DESIGN
By Independent Designs

MAIN FLOOR
No. 93909

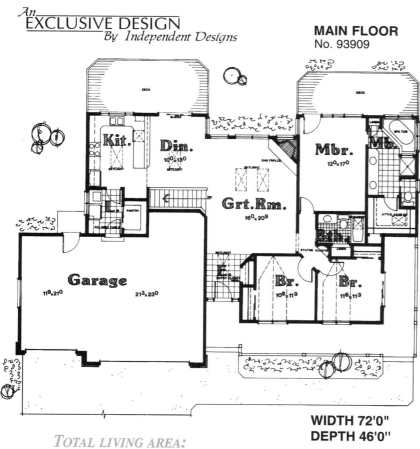

WIDTH 72'0"
DEPTH 46'0"

TOTAL LIVING AREA:
1,716 SQ. FT.

Inviting Wrap-Around Porch

■ This plan features:

— Three bedrooms

— Two full baths

■ A warm and inviting welcome, achieved by a wrap-around porch

■ A corner gas fireplace and two skylights in the Great Room

■ The Dining Room naturally lighted by the sliding glass doors to a rear deck and a skylight above

■ U-shaped Kitchen separated from the Dining Room by a breakfast bar and including another skylight

■ Luxurious Master Bedroom equipped with a plush Bath and access to a private deck

■ Two additional bedrooms sharing the full bath in the hall

■ No materials list is available for this plan

MAIN FLOOR — 1,716 SQ. FT.

Refer to **Pricing Schedule B** on the order form for pricing information

Compact Victorian
Ideal for Narrow Lot

■ This plan features:

— Three bedrooms

— Three full baths

■ A large, front Parlor with a raised hearth fireplace

■ A Dining Room with a sunny bay window

■ An efficient galley Kitchen serving the formal Dining Room and informal Breakfast Room

■ A beautiful Master Suite with two closets, an oversized tub and double vanity, plus a private sitting room with a bayed window and vaulted ceiling

■ An optional basement, crawl space or slab foundation — please specify when ordering

FIRST FLOOR — 954 SQ. FT.
SECOND FLOOR — 783 SQ. FT.

TOTAL LIVING AREA:
1,737 SQ. FT.

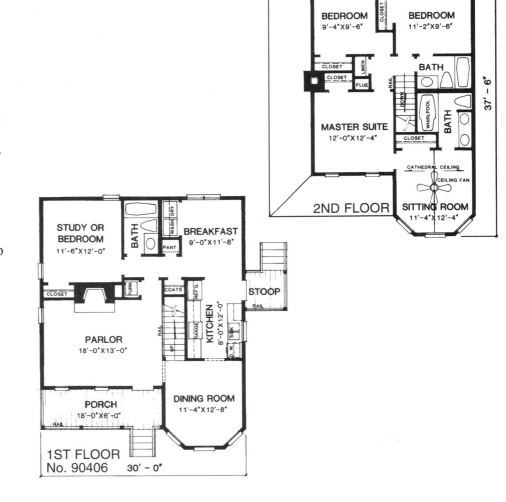

© 1995 Donald A. Gardner Architects, Inc.

attic storage

BED RM.
10-4 x 10-0

bath

MASTER BED RM.
13-6 x 15-8

cl

BONUS RM.
20-0 x 14-2

down

walk-in closet

attic storage

BED RM.
11-4 x 11-10

master bath

walk-in closet

SECOND FLOOR PLAN

TOTAL LIVING AREA:
1,792 SQ. FT.

Appealing Farmhouse Design

■ This plan features:

— Three bedrooms

— Two full and one half baths

■ Comfortable farmhouse features easy to build floor plan with many extras

■ Great Room which is open to the Kitchen and Breakfast bay, and expanded living space provided by the full back porch

■ For narrower lot restrictions, the Garage can be modified to open in front

■ Second floor Master Bedroom Suite contains a walk-in closet and a private bath with a garden tub and separate shower

■ Two more bedrooms on the second floor, one with a walk-in closet, share a full bath

FIRST FLOOR — 959 SQ. F.T
SECOND FLOOR — 833 SQ. FT.
BONUS ROOM — 344 SQ. FT.
GARAGE & STORAGE — 500 SQ. FT.

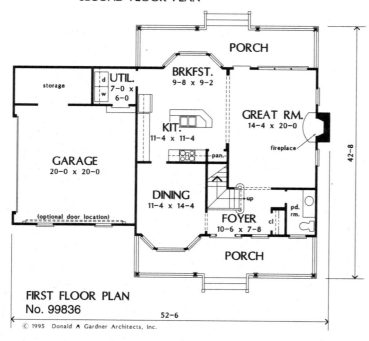

storage

d
w

UTIL.
7-0 x 6-0

BRKFST.
9-8 x 9-2

PORCH

KIT.
11-4 x 11-4

GREAT RM.
14-4 x 20-0

fireplace

pan.

GARAGE
20-0 x 20-0

DINING
11-4 x 14-4

up

(optional door location)

FOYER
10-6 x 7-8

pd. rm.

cl

PORCH

42-8

52-6

FIRST FLOOR PLAN
No. 99836

© 1995 Donald A Gardner Architects, Inc.

Refer to **Pricing Schedule B** on the order form for pricing information

A Home for Today and Tomorrow

■ This plan features:

— Three bedrooms

— Two full baths

■ An intriguing Breakfast nook off the Kitchen

■ A wide open, fireplaced Living Room with glass sliders to an optional deck

■ A step-saving arrangement of the Kitchen between the Breakfast area and formal Dining Room

■ A handsome Master Bedroom with sky-lit compartmentalized bath

MAIN AREA — 1,583 SQ. FT.
BASEMENT — 1,573 SQ. FT.
GARAGE — 484 SQ. FT.

TOTAL LIVING AREA:
1,583 SQ. FT.

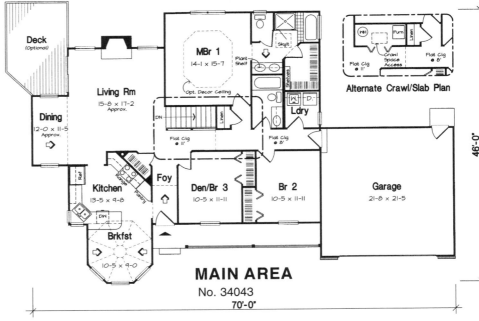

MAIN AREA
No. 34043
70'-0"

An EXCLUSIVE DESIGN
By Karl Kreeger

To order your Blueprints, call 1-800-235-5700

Refer to **Pricing Schedule C** on the order form for pricing information

PLAN NO. 93212

An EXCLUSIVE DESIGN
By Jannis Vann & Associates, Inc.

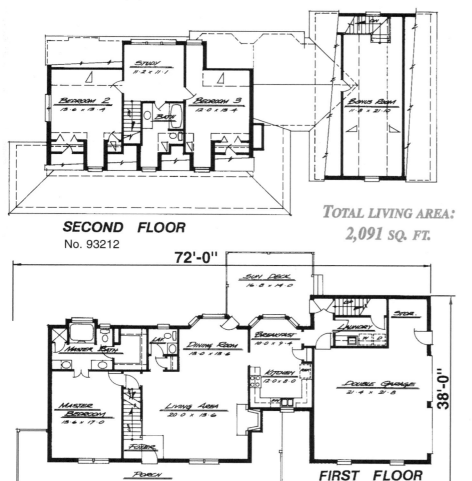

SECOND FLOOR
No. 93212

STUDY
11·2 x 11·1

BEDROOM 2
13·6 x 13·4

BEDROOM 3
12·0 x 13·4

BATH

BONUS ROOM
11·8 x 21·10

TOTAL LIVING AREA:
2,091 SQ. FT.

72'-0"

SUN DECK
16·8 x 14·0

MASTER BATH

LAV.

DINING ROOM
15·0 x 13·6

BREAKFAST
10·0 x 9·4

LAUNDRY

STOR.

W/D

KITCHEN
12·0 x 8·0

DOUBLE GARAGE
21·4 x 21·8

MASTER BEDROOM
13·6 x 17·0

LIVING AREA
20·0 x 13·6

FOYER

PORCH

38'-0"

FIRST FLOOR

Modern Conveniences

■ This plan features:
— Three bedrooms
— Two full and one half baths

■ Living Room with a cozy fireplace

■ Formal Dining Room with a bay window

■ A sunny Breakfast Nook with a bay window overlooking the deck

■ Master Suite with jacuzzi and a step-in shower, double vanity, and a walk-in closet

■ A second floor study or hobby room overlooking the deck

■ A future Bonus Room

■ No materials list is available for this plan

■ An optional basement, slab or crawl space foundation — please specify when ordering

FIRST FLOOR — 1,362 SQ. FT.
SECOND FLOOR — 729 SQ. FT.
BONUS ROOM — 384 SQ. FT.
BASEMENT — 988 SQ. FT.
GARAGE — 559 SQ. FT.

© 1995 Donald A Gardner Architects, Inc.

Tremendous Curb Appeal

■ This plan features:

— Three bedrooms

— Two full baths

■ Wrap-around porch sheltering entry

■ Great Room topped by a cathedral ceiling and enhanced by a fireplace

■ Great Room, Dining Room and Kitchen open to each other for a feeling of spaciousness

■ Pantry, skylight and peninsula counter add to the comfort and efficiency of the Kitchen

■ Cathedral ceiling crowns the Master Suite and has many amenities; walk-in and linen closets, luxurious private bath

■ Bedroom/Study, topped by a cathedral ceiling

■ Skylight over full hall bath naturally illuminates the room

MAIN FLOOR — 1,246 SQ. FT.
GARAGE — 420 SQ. FT.

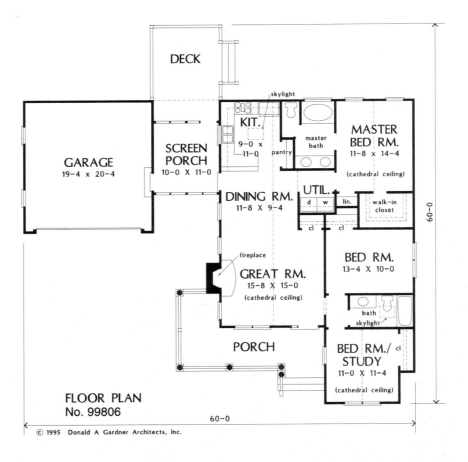

FLOOR PLAN
No. 99806

© 1995   Donald A Gardner Architects, Inc.

DECK

GARAGE
19-4 x 20-4

SCREEN PORCH
10-0 X 11-0

skylight

KIT.
9-0 x 11-0

pantry

master bath

MASTER BED RM.
11-8 x 14-4
(cathedral ceiling)

DINING RM.
11-8 X 9-4

UTIL.
d   w   lin.

walk-in closet

cl   cl

fireplace

GREAT RM.
15-8 X 15-0
(cathedral ceiling)

BED RM.
13-4 x 10-0

bath
skylight

PORCH

BED RM./ STUDY
11-0 X 11-4
(cathedral ceiling)

cl

60-0

60-0

TOTAL LIVING AREA:
1,246 SQ. FT.

To order your Blueprints, call 1-800-235-5700

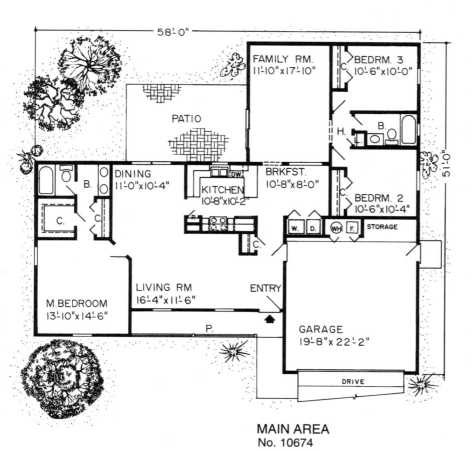

58'-0"

51'-0"

FAMILY RM.
11'-10"x17'-10"

BEDRM. 3
10'-6"x10'-0"

PATIO

H.

B.

DINING
11'-0"x10'-4"

BRKFST.
10'-8"x8'-0"

KITCHEN
10'-8"x10'-2"

DW.

B.

C.

C.

BEDRM. 2
10'-6"x10'-4"

W. D.

WH. F.

STORAGE

M.BEDROOM
13'-10"x14'-6"

LIVING RM
16'-4"x11'-6"

ENTRY

P.

GARAGE
19'-8"x22'-2"

DRIVE

MAIN AREA
No. 10674

Carefree Convenience

■ This plan features:

— Three bedrooms

— Two full baths

■ A galley Kitchen, centrally located between the Dining, Breakfast and Living Room areas

■ A huge Family Room which exits onto the Patio

■ A Master Suite with double closets and vanity with two additional bedrooms share a full-half bath

MAIN AREA — 1,600 SQ. FT.
GARAGE — 465 SQ. FT.

TOTAL LIVING AREA:
1,600 SQ. FT.

A Stylish, Open Concept Home

■ This plan features:

— Three bedrooms

— Two full baths

■ An angled Entry creating the illusion of space

■ Two square columns that flank the bar and separate the Kitchen from the Living Room

■ A Dining Room that may service both formal and informal occasions

■ A Master Bedroom with a large walk-in closet

■ A large Master Bath with a dual vanity, linen closet and whirlpool tub/shower combination

■ Two additional bedrooms that share a full bath

■ No materials list available for this plan

MAIN FLOOR — 1,282 SQ. FT.
GARAGE — 501 SQ. FT.

TOTAL LIVING AREA:
1,282 SQ. FT.

WIDTH 48-10

MAIN FLOOR
No. 93021

© Larry E. Belk

To order your Blueprints, call 1-800-235-5700

Refer to **Pricing Schedule D** on the order form for pricing information

Laun.
9'10" x 8'5"

Kitchen

Breakfast
19'7" x 12' 3"

French Doors

French Doors w/ arched window

Great Room
15'8" x 16'5"
high ceiling

slope ceiling

Master Bedroom
13'8" x 14'8"

slope ceiling

Bath

Hall

hanging space

butler's pantry

pantry

Foyer

Hall

Dressing

Two-car Garage
19'10" x 21'4"

Dining Room
11' x 15'9"

furniture alcove

Porch

stairs up

stairs

Court Yard

walk-in closet

FIRST FLOOR

41'8"

61'0"

No. 92646

TOTAL LIVING AREA: 2,320 SQ. FT.

Bedroom
10'8" x 13'5"

Bedroom
10'9" x 10'

slope ceiling

Great Room Below

linen linen

Hall

Bath

Balcony

stairs dn

Bedroom
11' x 11'2"

desk

bookshelves

Porch

slope ceiling   slope ceiling

SECOND FLOOR

A Touch of Old World Charm

■ This plan features:

— Four bedrooms

— Two full and one half baths

■ Authentic balustrade railings and front courtyard greet one and all

■ High ceiling in Great Room tops corner fireplace and French doors with arched window

■ Formal Dining Room enhanced by a decorative window and furniture alcove

■ Country Kitchen with work island, two pantrys, Breakfast area with French door to rear yard, Laundry and Garage entry

■ Master Bedroom wing offers a sloped ceiling, plush bath and a huge walk-in closet

■ No materials list is available for this plan

FIRST FLOOR — 1,595 SQ. FT.
SECOND FLOOR — 725 SQ. FT.
GARAGE — 409 SQ. FT.

Refer to **Pricing Schedule B** on the order form for pricing information

Open Space Living

■ This plan features:

— Three bedrooms

— Two full and one half baths

■ A wrap-around Deck providing outdoor living space, ideal for a sloping lot

■ Two and a half-story glass wall and two separate atrium doors providing natural light for the Living/Dining Room area

■ An efficient galley Kitchen with easy access to the Dining area

■ A Master Bedroom suite with a half bath and ample closet space

■ Another bedroom on the first floor adjoins a full hall bath

■ A second floor Bedroom/Studio, with a private Deck, adjacent to a full hall bath and a Loft area

FIRST FLOOR — 1,086 SQ. FT.
SECOND FLOOR — 466 SQ. FT.
BASEMENT — 1,080 SQ. FT.

An
EXCLUSIVE DESIGN
By Westhome Planners. Ltd.

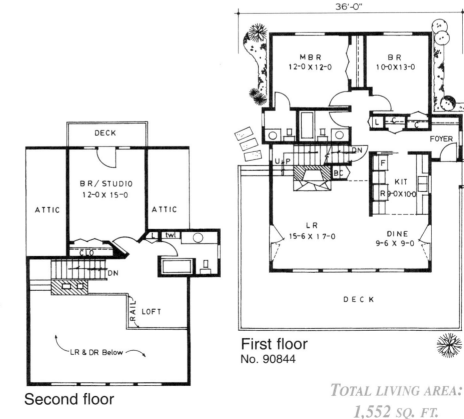

Second floor

First floor
No. 90844

TOTAL LIVING AREA:
1,552 SQ. FT.

To order your Blueprints, call 1-800-235-5700

© design basics, inc.

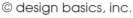

FIRST FLOOR
No. 99450

TOTAL LIVING AREA:
2,695 SQ. FT.

SECOND FLOOR

Fashionable Country Style

- This plan features:

— Four bedrooms

— Two full, one three quarter and one half baths

- The large covered front Porch adds old fashioned appeal to this modern floor plan

- Dining Room with a decorative ceiling and a built-in hutch

- Kitchen has a center island and access to gazebo shaped Nook

- Great Room is accented by transom windows and a fireplace with bookcases on each side

- The Master Bedroom has a cathedral ceiling, a door to the front porch, and a large bath with a whirlpool tub

- An optional basement or slab foundation — please specify when ordering

FIRST FLOOR — 1,881 SQ. FT.
SECOND FLOOR — 814 SQ. FT.
BASEMENT — 1,020 SQ. FT.
GARAGE — 534 SQ. FT.

Refer to **Pricing Schedule B** on the order form for pricing information

Carefree Comfort

■ This plan features:

— Three bedrooms

— Two full baths

■ A dramatic vaulted Foyer

■ A range top island Kitchen with a sunny eating Nook surrounded by a built-in planter

■ A vaulted ceiling in the Great Room with a built-in bar and corner fireplace

■ A bayed Dining Room that combines with the Great Room for a spacious feeling

■ A Master Bedroom with a private reading nook, vaulted ceiling, walk-in closet, and a well appointed private Bath

■ Two additional bedrooms sharing a full hall bath

■ An optional basement, slab or crawl space foundation— please specify when ordering

MAIN AREA — 1,665 SQ. FT.
GARAGE — 2-CAR

TOTAL LIVING AREA:
1,665 SQ. FT.

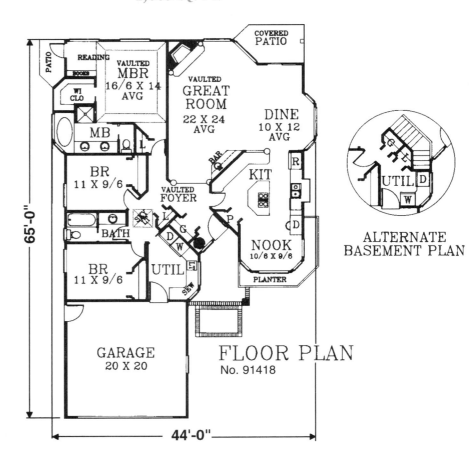

FLOOR PLAN
No. 91418

ALTERNATE
BASEMENT PLAN

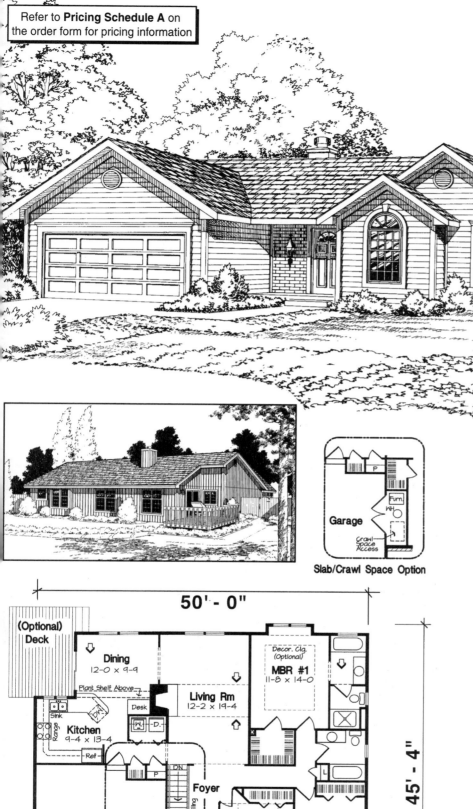

Slab/Crawl Space Option

Garage

Crawl Space Access

Furn.
WH
P

MAIN FLOOR
No. 20164

50' - 0"

45' - 4"

(Optional) Deck

Dining
12-0 x 9-9

Plant Shelf Above

Kitchen
9-4 x 13-4

Sink
Range
Ref
DW

Desk
W - D

Living Rm
12-2 x 19-4

Decor. Clg. (Optional)

MBR #1
11-8 x 14-0

DN
P

Foyer

DN
Railing

Garage
19-4 x 23-6

Den/BR #3
10-5 x 11-6

BR #2
10-5 x 10-5

An
EXCLUSIVE DESIGN
By Karl Kreeger

Easy Living

■ This plan features:

— Three bedrooms

— Two full baths

■ A dramatic sloped ceiling and a massive fireplace in the Living Room

■ A Dining Room crowned by a sloping ceiling and a plant shelf also having sliding doors to the deck

■ A U-shaped Kitchen with abundant cabinets, a window over the sink and a walk-in pantry

■ A Master Suite with a private full bath, decorative ceiling and walk-in closet

■ Two additional bedrooms that share a full bath

MAIN FLOOR — 1,456 SQ. FT.
BASEMENT — 1,448 SQ. FT.
GARAGE — 452 SQ. FT.

TOTAL LIVING AREA:
1,456 SQ. FT.

Refer to **Pricing Schedule B** on the order form for pricing information

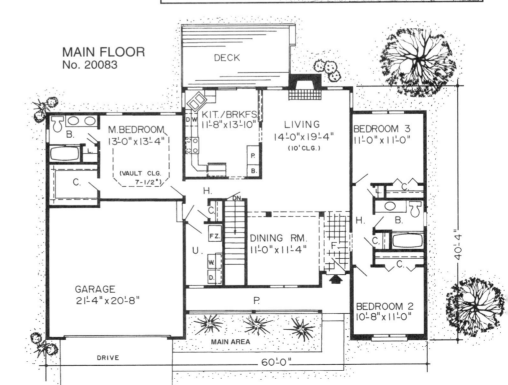

One-Level with a Twist

■ This plan features:

— Three bedrooms

— Two full baths

■ Wide-open active areas that are centrally-located

■ A spacious Dining, Living, and Kitchen area

■ A Master Suite at the rear of the house with a full bath

■ Two additional bedrooms that share a full hall bath and the quiet atmosphere that results from an intelligent design

MAIN AREA — 1,575 SQ. FT.
BASEMENT — 1,575 SQ. FT.
GARAGE — 475 SQ. FT.

TOTAL LIVING AREA:
1,575 SQ. FT.

An
EXCLUSIVE DESIGN
By Karl Kreeger

MAIN FLOOR
No. 20083

DECK

KIT./BRKFS.
11'-8"x13'-10"

LIVING
14'-0"x19'-4"
(10'CLG.)

BEDROOM 3
11'-0"x11'-0"

B.

M.BEDROOM
13'-0"x13'-4"

(VAULT CLG.
7-1/2")

C.

H.

DN

C.

DINING RM.
11'-0"x11'-4"

F.Z.

U.

W.
D.

H.

B.

C.

GARAGE
21'-4"x20'-8"

P.

BEDROOM 2
10'-8"x11'-0"

40'-4"

MAIN AREA

DRIVE

60'-0"

To order your Blueprints, call 1-800-235-5700

Refer to **Pricing Schedule D** on the order form for pricing information

© 1997 Donald A. Gardner Architects, Inc.

B. NATHAN

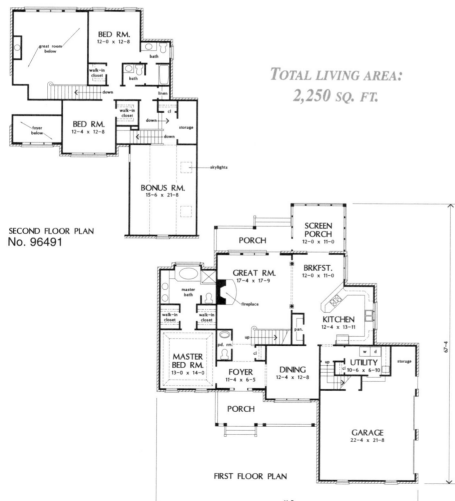

SECOND FLOOR PLAN
No. 96491

TOTAL LIVING AREA:
2,250 SQ. FT.

FIRST FLOOR PLAN

© 1997 Donald A. Gardner Architects, Inc.

Traditional Two-Story Home

■ This plan features:

— Three bedrooms

— Two full and two half baths

■ Facade handsomely accented by multiple gables, keystone arches and transom windows

■ Arched clerestory window lights two-story Foyer for dramatic entrance

■ Two-story Great Room exciting with inviting fireplace, wall of windows and back Porch access

■ Open Kitchen with easy access to Screen Porch and Dining Room

■ Private Master Bedroom suite offers two walk-in closets and deluxe bath

FIRST FLOOR — 1,644 SQ. FT.
SECOND FLOOR — 606 SQ. FT.
BONUS ROOM — 548 SQ. FT.
GARAGE & STORAGE — 657 SQ. FT.

Refer to **Pricing Schedule D** on the order form for pricing information

Traditional Ranch has Many Modern Features

■ This plan features:

— Three bedrooms

— Three full baths

■ A vaulted-ceiling Great Room with skylights and a fireplace

■ A double L-shaped Kitchen with an eating bar opening to a bayed Breakfast Room

■ A Master Suite with a walk-in closet, corner garden tub, separate vanities and a linen closet

■ Two additional bedrooms each with a walk-in closet and built-in desk, sharing a full hall bath

■ A loft that overlooks the Great Room which includes a vaulted ceiling and open rail balcony

■ An optional basement or crawlspace foundation — please specify when ordering

FIRST FLOOR — 1,996 SQ. FT.
LOFT — 305 SQ. FT.

  TOTAL LIVING AREA: 2,301 SQ. FT.

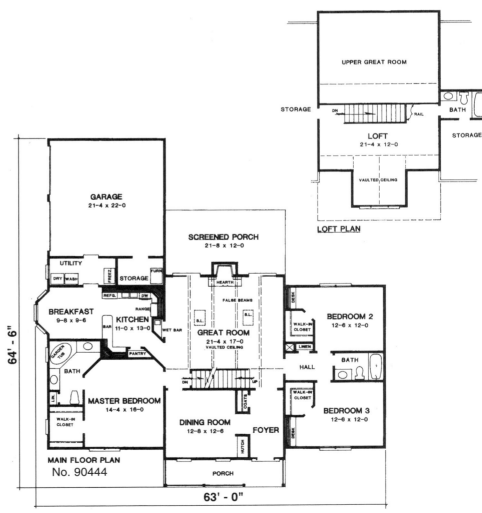

UPPER GREAT ROOM

STORAGE DN RAIL BATH

LOFT
21-4 x 12-0

STORAGE

VAULTED CEILING

LOFT PLAN

GARAGE
21-4 x 22-0

UTILITY

DRY WASH FREEZ STORAGE FURN.

SCREENED PORCH
21-8 x 12-0

HEARTH

REFG. DW

RANGE

BREAKFAST
9-8 x 9-6

KITCHEN
11-0 x 13-0

BAR

WET BAR

FALSE BEAMS

B.L. B.L.

GREAT ROOM
21-4 x 17-0
VAULTED CEILING

DESK

WALK-IN
CLOSET

BEDROOM 2
12-6 x 12-0

GARDEN
TUB

PANTRY

LINEN

BATH

DN

HALL

BATH

MASTER BEDROOM
14-4 x 16-0

WALK-IN
CLOSET

COATS

WALK-IN
CLOSET

BEDROOM 3
12-6 x 12-0

DINING ROOM
12-8 x 12-6

FOYER

DESK

MAIN FLOOR PLAN
No. 90444

HUTCH

64' - 6"

PORCH

63' - 0"

To order your Blueprints, call 1-800-235-5700

Refer to **Pricing Schedule B** on the order form for pricing information

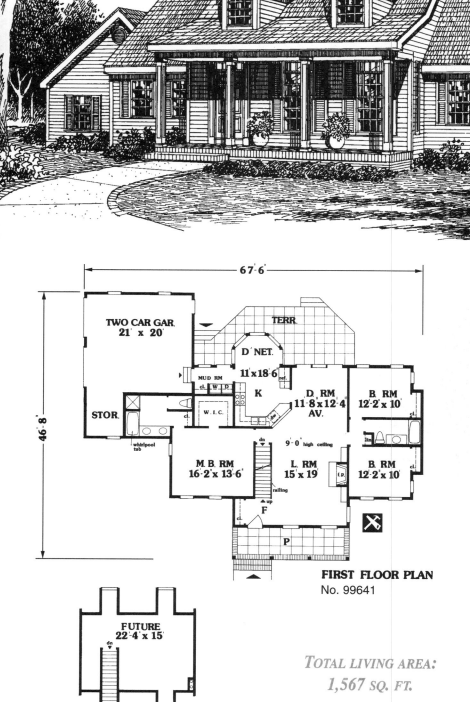

FIRST FLOOR PLAN
No. 99641

67'-6"

46'-8"

TWO CAR GAR.
21' x 20'

TERR.

D´NET.
11' x 18'-6"

STOR.

MUD RM
cl. W D
cl.
W. I. C.

whirlpool tub

K

ref.

D. RM.
11'-8 x 12'-4"
AV.

B. RM.
12'-2" x 10'

cl.

9'-0" high ceiling

dn

M. B. RM.
16'-2' x 13'-6'

L. RM.
15' x 19'

f.p.

B. RM.
12'-2" x 10'

cl.

railing

F

up

cl.

P

FUTURE
22'-4" x 15'

dn

SECOND FLOOR PLAN

TOTAL LIVING AREA:
1,567 SQ. FT.

Southern Traditional Flavor

◼ This plan features:

— Three bedrooms

— Two full baths

◼ A varied roof line with dormers and a charming colonnaded front porch sheltering the entrance

◼ Living Room enhanced by nine foot ceilings and a bookcase flanked fireplace

◼ Two mullioned French doors leading from the Dining Room to the rear terrace

◼ Laundry area/Mudroom between the Garage and Kitchen

◼ Master Suite with walk-in closet and a compartmented bath with a separate stall shower, whirlpool tub and double vanity

◼ Two additional bedrooms that share a full hall bath

FIRST FLOOR — 1,567 SQ. FT.
SECOND FLOOR(BONUS) — 462 SQ. FT.
BASEMENT — 1,567 SQ. FT.
GARAGE — 504 SQ. FT.

Two-Way Fireplace

■ This plan features:

— Three bedrooms

— Two full and one half baths

■ A large Kitchen with cook-top island and a breakfast area opening to the deck

■ Built-in cedar closets and spacious bedrooms

■ A Master Suite loaded with a walk-in closet, skylight, double vanities and a sunken tub

■ A vaulted formal Dining Room and ceiling fans in the Kitchen and Living Room

FIRST FLOOR — 1,789 SQ. FT.
SECOND FLOOR — 568 SQ. FT.
BASEMENT — 1,789 SQ. FT.
GARAGE — 529 SQ. FT.

TOTAL LIVING AREA:
2,357 SQ. FT.

An
EXCLUSIVE DESIGN
By Karl Kreeger

SECOND FLOOR

BEDROOM 3
11'-4"x12'-6"

BEDROOM 2
11'-4"x11'-10"

CEDAR CLOSET

ATTIC STOR.

SECOND FLOOR

DECK

KIT./BRKFST.
14'-4"x22'-4"

LIVING ROOM
17'-0"x23'-4"
(11'-0" CLG.)

M. BEDROOM
14'-10"x15'-4"

ISLAND

DESK   BOOKS

FOYER

DINING
12'-2"x12'-4"

LAUNDRY

SKYLIGHT

GARAGE
22'-4"x22'-8"

FIRST FLOOR

55' - 0"

61' - 0"

FIRST FLOOR
No. 10652

Refer to **Pricing Schedule B** on
the order form for pricing information

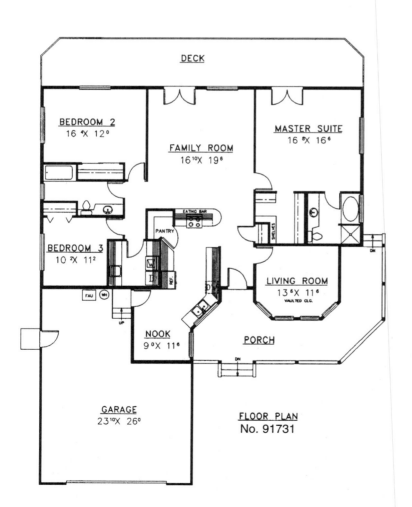

DECK

BEDROOM 2
16⁴ X 12⁰

FAMILY ROOM
16¹⁰ X 19⁶

MASTER SUITE
16⁸ X 16⁶

EATING BAR

PANTRY

SHELVES

BEDROOM 3
10² X 11²

LIVING ROOM
13⁶ X 11⁶
VAULTED CLG.

FAU

UP

NOOK
9⁰ X 11⁶

PORCH

DN

GARAGE
23¹⁰ X 26⁰

FLOOR PLAN
No. 91731

Country Style & Charm

◼ This plan features:

— Three bedrooms

— Two full baths

◼ Brick accents, front facing gable, and railed wrap-around covered porch

◼ A built-in range and oven in a L- shaped Kitchen

◼ A Nook with garage access for convenient unloading of groceries and other supplies

◼ A bay window wrapping around the front of the formal Living Room

◼ A Master Suite with French doors opening to the deck

MAIN AREA — 1,857 SQ. FT.
GARAGE — 681 SQ. FT.
WIDTH — 51'-6"
DEPTH — 65'-0"

TOTAL LIVING AREA:
1,857 SQ. FT.

Refer to **Pricing Schedule D** on the order form for pricing information

Two-Story Farmhouse

■ This plan features:

— Three bedrooms

— Two full and one half baths

■ The wrap-around Porch gives a nostalgic appeal to this home

■ The Great Room with fireplace is accessed directly from the Foyer

■ The formal Dining Room has direct access to the efficient Kitchen

■ An island, double sink, plenty of counter/cabinet space and a built-in pantry complete the Kitchen

■ The second floor Master Suite has a five-piece, private bath and a walk-in closet

■ Two other bedrooms have walk-in closets and a share a separate bath

■ An optional basement or crawl-space foundation — please specify when ordering

FIRST FLOOR — 1,125 SQ. FT.
SECOND FLOOR — 1,138 SQ. FT.
BASEMENT — 1,125 SQ. FT.

TOTAL LIVING AREA:
2,263 SQ. FT.

SECOND FLOOR PLAN

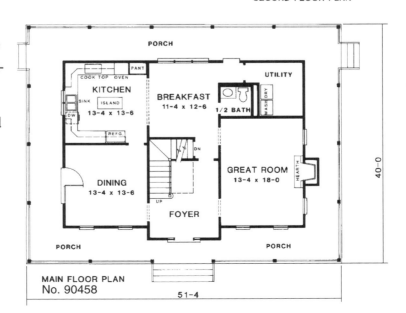

MAIN FLOOR PLAN
No. 90458

To order your Blueprints, call 1-800-235-5700

Refer to **Pricing Schedule D** on the order form for pricing information

FIRST FLOOR — 1,670 SQ. FT.
SECOND FLOOR — 580 SQ. FT.
BONUS ROOM — 222 SQ. FT.

Bedroom
13'4" x 10'8"

Bath

Bonus Room
10'0" x 13'11"

Balcony

Great Room
Below

slope ceiling

stairs dn

Bedroom
13'4" x 10'0"

window seat

SECOND FLOOR

WIDTH 70'-8"
DEPTH 42'-3"

TOTAL LIVING AREA:
2,250 SQ. FT.

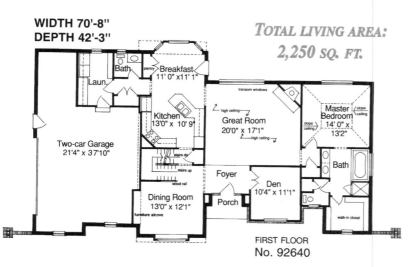

Bath
Laun.
pantry
Breakfast
11'0" x 11'1"

transom windows

Kitchen
13'0" x 10'9"

Great Room
20'0" x 17'1"

high ceiling

Master
Bedroom
14'0" x
13'2"

slope ceiling

Two-car Garage
21'4" x 37'10"

stairs dn
stairs up
wood rail

Foyer

Den
10'4" x 11'1"

Bath

Dining Room
13'0" x 12'1"

furniture alcove

Porch

walk-in closet

FIRST FLOOR
No. 92640

Impressive Styling

◼ This plan features:

— Three bedrooms

— Two full and one half baths

◼ Gracious entrance framed by windows, lanterns and a keystone arch

◼ Open Foyer with a lovely landing staircase and formal Dining Room with a furniture alcove and a decorative window

◼ Spacious Great Room enhanced by a corner fireplace, high ceiling and a transom windows

◼ Convenient Kitchen with peninsula counter sink, Pantry, Breakfast alcove with access to back yard, and nearby Laundry/Garage entry

◼ Master Bedroom wing offers a slope ceiling, a large, walk-in closet and a double vanity bath

◼ Two second floor bedrooms with ample closets share a double vanity bath and Bonus Room

◼ No materials list is available for this plan

Refer to **Pricing Schedule A** on the order form for pricing information

Spanish Style Affordable Home

■ This plan features:

— Two bedrooms

— Two full baths

■ A large Master Suite with vaulted ceilings and a handicap accessible private bath

■ Vaulted ceilings in the Great Room

■ An open Kitchen area with an eating bar

MAIN AREA — 1,111 SQ. FT.

TOTAL LIVING AREA:
1,111 SQ. FT.

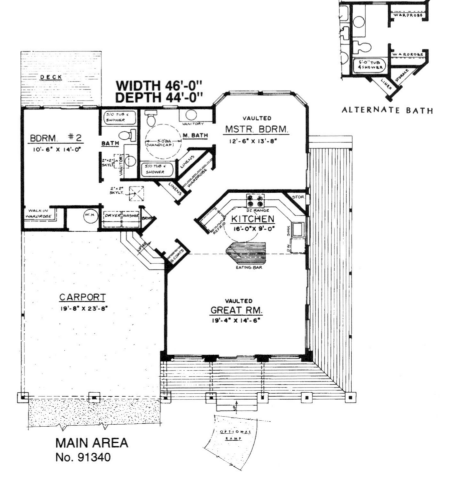

WIDTH 46'-0"
DEPTH 44'-0"

DECK

BDRM. #2
10'-6" X 14'-0"

BATH

M. BATH

VAULTED
MSTR. BDRM.
12'-6" X 13'-8"

WALK-IN WARDROBE

W.H.

DRYER WASHER

KITCHEN
16'-0" X 9'-0"

STOR.

EATING BAR

CARPORT
19'-8" X 23'-8"

VAULTED
GREAT RM.
19'-4" X 14'-6"

OPTIONAL RAMP

ALTERNATE BATH

MAIN AREA
No. 91340

To order your Blueprints, call 1-800-235-5700

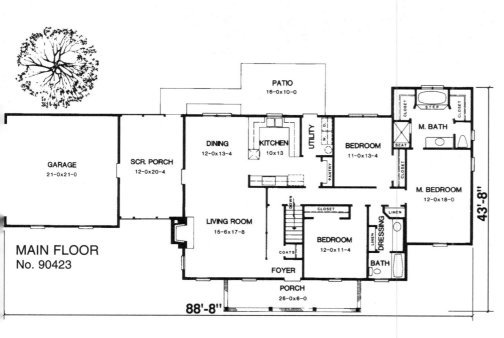

PATIO
16-0x10-0

GARAGE
21-0x21-0

SCR. PORCH
12-0x20-4

DINING
12-0x13-4

KITCHEN
10x13

UTILITY

PANTRY

BEDROOM
11-0x13-4

CLOSET

M. BATH

STEP

CLOSET

SEAT

CLOSET

M. BEDROOM
12-0x18-0

LIVING ROOM
15-6x17-8

DOWN

CLOSET

COATS

BEDROOM
12-0x11-4

LINEN

DRESSING

LINEN

LINEN

BATH

FOYER

PORCH
26-0x6-0

MAIN FLOOR
No. 90423

88'-8"

43'-8"

Expansive, Not Expensive

■ This plan features:

— Three bedrooms

— Two full baths

■ A Master Suite with his-n-her closets and a private Master Bath

■ Two additional bedrooms that share a full hall closet

■ A pleasant Dining Room that overlooks a rear garden

■ A well-equipped Kitchen with a built-in planning corner and eat-in space

■ An optional basement, slab or crawl space foundation — please specify when ordering

MAIN FLOOR — 1,773 SQ. FT.

TOTAL LIVING AREA:
1,773 SQ. FT.

Refer to **Pricing Schedule C** on the order form for pricing information

Open Plan Accented By Loft, Windows and Decks

■ This plan features:

— Three bedrooms

— Two and one half baths

■ A fireplaced Family Room and Dining Room

■ A large Kitchen sharing a preparation/eating bar with Dining Room

■ A first floor Master Bedroom featuring two closets and a five-piece bath

■ An ample Utility Room designed with a pantry and room for a freezer, a washer and dryer, plus a furnace and a hot water heater

FIRST FLOOR — 1,280 SQ. FT.
SECOND FLOOR — 735 SQ. FT.
GREENHOUSE — 80 SQ. FT.

TOTAL LIVING AREA:
2,015 SQ. FT.

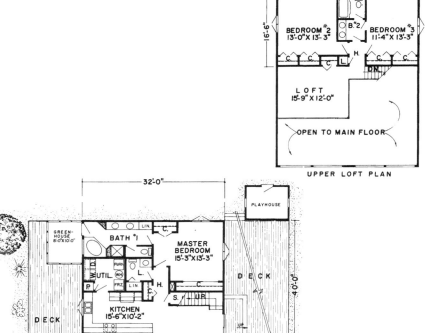

UPPER LOFT PLAN

MAIN FLOOR PLAN
No. 10515

To order your Blueprints, call 1-800-235-5700

©1994 Donald A. Gardner Architects. Inc.

B. NATHAN

TOTAL LIVING AREA:
1,475 SQ. FT.

DECK

spa

GARAGE
20-4 x 22-5

storage

fireplace

KIT.
10-4 x 13-6

UTIL.

w
d

walk-in
closet

BED RM.
11-4 x 10-0

cl   lin.

bath

(cathedral ceiling)

GREAT RM.
15-4 x 16-0

cl

MASTER
BED RM.
13-4 x 14-4

master
bath

54-7

cl   cl

FOYER
15-4 x 3-8

DINING
10-4 x 12-0

BED RM./
STUDY
11-4 x 10-4

PORCH

FLOOR PLAN
No. 96452

59-6

©Donald A. Gardner Architects, Inc.

Exciting Ceilings Add Appeal

◼ This plan features:

— Three bedrooms

— Two full baths

◼ Open design enhanced by cathedral and tray ceilings above arched windows

◼ Foyer with columns defining Great Room with central fireplace and Deck access

◼ Cooktop island in Kitchen provides great cooks with convenience and company

◼ Ultimate Master Suite offers walk-in closet, tray ceiling, and whirlpool bath

◼ Front Bedroom/Study offers multiple uses with tray ceiling and arched window

MAIN FLOOR — 1,475 SQ. FT.
GARAGE & STORAGE — 478 SQ. FT.

Refer to **Pricing Schedule A** on the order form for pricing information

Lots of Space in this Small Package

■ This plan features:

— Two bedrooms with possible third bedroom/loft

— Two full baths

■ A Living Room with dynamic, soaring angles and a fireplace

■ A first floor Master Suite with full bath and walk in-closet

■ Walk-in closets in all bedrooms

MAIN FLOOR — 878 SQ. FT.
UPPER FLOOR — 405 SQ. FT.

TOTAL LIVING AREA:
1,283 SQ. FT.

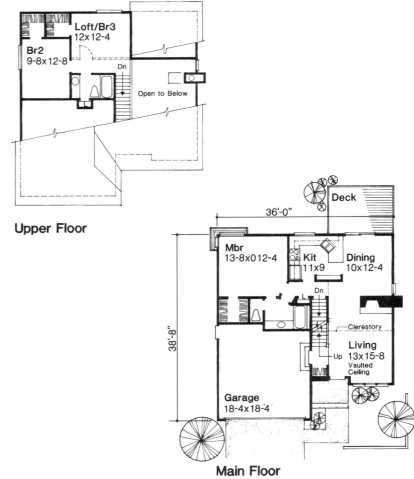

Upper Floor

Loft/Br3
12x12-4

Br2
9-8x12-8

Dn

Open to Below

Main Floor
No. 90378

36'-0"

Deck

Mbr
13-8x012-4

Kit
11x9

Dining
10x12-4

Dn

38'-8"

Clerestory

Living
13x15-8
Up
Vaulted Ceiling

Garage
18-4x18-4

To order your Blueprints, call 1-800-235-5700

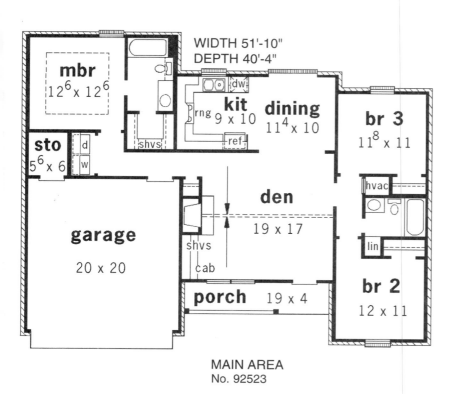

WIDTH 51'-10"
DEPTH 40'-4"

mbr
12^6 x 12^6

sto
5^6 x 6

d
w

kit
9 x 10
rng

dining
11^4 x 10

br 3
11^8 x 11

dw

shvs

ref

hvac

lin

den
19 x 17

garage
20 x 20

shvs

cab

br 2
12 x 11

porch   19 x 4

MAIN AREA
No. 92523

Private Master Suite

■ This plan features:

— Three bedrooms

— Two full baths

■ A spacious Great Room enhanced
by a vaulted ceiling and fireplace

■ A well-equipped Kitchen with
windowed double sink

■ A secluded Master Suite with
decorative ceiling, private Master
Bath, and walk-in closet

■ Two additional bedrooms sharing
hall bath

■ An optional crawl space or slab
foundation — please specify
when ordering

MAIN FLOOR — 1,293 SQ. FT.
GARAGE — 433 SQ. FT.

TOTAL LIVING AREA:
1,293 SQ. FT.

Refer to **Pricing Schedule C** on the order form for pricing information

© Frank Betz Associates

Small, Yet Lavishly Appointed

■ This plan features:

— Three bedrooms

— Two full and one half baths

■ The Dining Room, Living Room, Foyer and Master Bath all topped by high ceilings

■ Master Bedroom includes a decorative tray ceiling and a walk-in closet

■ Kitchen open to the Breakfast Room enhanced by a serving bar and a pantry

■ Living Room with a large fireplace and a French door to the rear yard

■ Master Suite located on opposite side from secondary bedrooms, allowing for privacy

■ Please specify basement or crawl space foundation when ordering

MAIN FLOOR — 1,845 SQ. FT.
BONUS — 409 SQ. FT.
GARAGE — 529 SQ. FT.

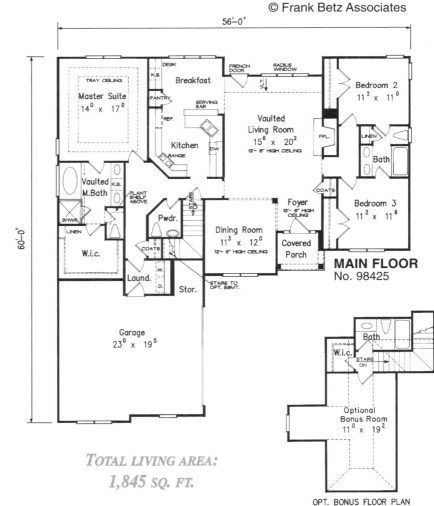

56'-0"

60'-0"

TRAY CEILING

Master Suite
14⁰ x 17⁰

DESK

Breakfast

FRENCH DOOR

RADIUS WINDOW

Bedroom 2
11² x 11⁰

PANTRY

SERVING BAR

REF.

Kitchen

RANGE

DW

Vaulted Living Room
15⁶ x 20²
13'- 6" HIGH CEILING

FPL.

LINEN

Bath

Vaulted M.Bath

K.S.

PLANT SHELF ABOVE

SHWR.

LINEN

W.i.c.

Pwdr.

STAIRS UP

COATS

Foyer
13'- 6" HIGH CEILING

Bedroom 3
11² x 11⁶

Laund.

COATS

W. D.

Dining Room
11³ x 12⁰
13'- 6" HIGH CEILING

Covered Porch

Stor.

STAIRS TO OPT. BSMT.

MAIN FLOOR
No. 98425

Garage
23⁰ x 19⁵

TOTAL LIVING AREA:
1,845 SQ. FT.

Bath

W.i.c.

STAIRS DN

Optional Bonus Room
11⁰ x 19²

OPT. BONUS FLOOR PLAN

To order your Blueprints, call 1-800-235-5700

© 1995 Donald A. Gardner Architects, Inc.

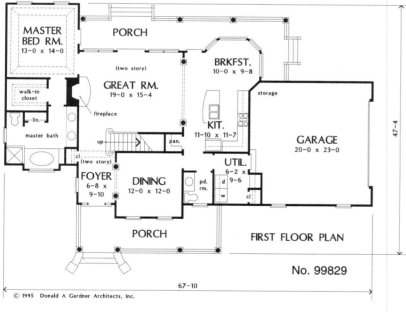

MASTER BED RM.
13-0 x 14-0

PORCH

walk-in closet

lin.

master bath

BRKFST.
10-0 x 9-8

(two story)

GREAT RM.
19-0 x 15-4

storage

fireplace

KIT.
11-10 x 11-7

GARAGE
20-0 x 23-0

up

pan.

47-4

cl

(two story)

FOYER
6-8 x 9-10

DINING
12-0 x 12-0

pd. rm.

UTIL.
6-2 x 9-6

d

w

cl

PORCH

FIRST FLOOR PLAN

No. 99829

© 1995 Donald A Gardner Architects, Inc.

67-10

Distinctive Detailing

■ This plan features:

— Three bedrooms

— Two full and one half baths

■ Interior columns distinguish the inviting two-story Foyer from the Dining Room

■ Spacious Great Room set off by two-story windows and opening to the Kitchen and Breakfast Bay

■ Nine foot ceilings add volume and drama to the first floor

■ Secluded Master Suite topped by a space amplifying tray ceiling and enhanced by a plush bath

■ Two generous additional bedrooms with ample closet and storage space

■ Skylit bonus room enjoying second floor access

FIRST FLOOR — 1,436 SQ. FT.
SECOND FLOOR — 536 SQ. FT.
GARAGE & STORAGE — 520 SQ. FT.
BONUS ROOM — 296 SQ. FT.

TOTAL LIVING AREA:
1,972 SQ. FT.

great room below

BED RM.
11-10 x 13-0

skylights

cl

sto.

down

BONUS RM.
20-0 x 13-0

foyer below

sto.

bath

lin.

BED RM.
12-0 x 12-0

walk-in closet

attic storage

SECOND FLOOR PLAN

To order your Blueprints, call 1-800-235-5700

81

Refer to **Pricing Schedule C** on the order form for pricing information

Farmhouse Flavor

■ This plan features:

— Three bedrooms

— Two full and one half baths

■ A inviting wrap-around porch with old-fashioned charm

■ Two-story foyer

■ A wood stove in the Living Room that warms the entire house

■ A modern Kitchen flowing easily into the bayed Dining Room

■ A first floor Master Bedroom with private Master Bath

■ Two additional bedrooms with walk-in closets and cozy gable sitting nooks

FIRST FLOOR — 1,269 SQ. FT.
SECOND FLOOR — 638 SQ. FT.
BASEMENT — 1,269 SQ. FT.

TOTAL LIVING AREA:
1,907 SQ. FT.

An
EXCLUSIVE DESIGN
By Karl Kreeger

SECOND FLOOR

Br 2
10-4 x 14

skylight
open to below

Balcony

Br 3
11 x 14

plant ledge

DN

slope

FIRST FLOOR
No. 10785

Optional Deck

Living Rm
13 x 19-6

Ldry

W D

pan.

Kitchen
11 x 12

wood stove

MBr 1
13-6 x 14

DN

Dining Rm
12-10 x 13-6

Foyer

47'-0"

39'-0"

Slab/Crawl Space Option

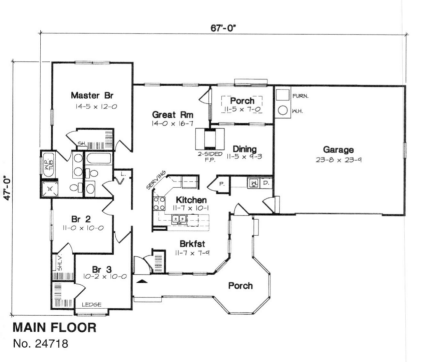

MAIN FLOOR
No. 24718

67'-0"

47'-0"

Master Br
14-5 x 12-0

Great Rm
14-0 x 16-7

Porch
11-5 x 7-0

FURN.

W.H.

Garage
23-8 x 23-9

2-SIDED F.P.

Dining
11-5 x 9-3

SERVING

Kitchen
11-7 x 10-1

P.

W D.

Br 2
11-0 x 10-0

Br 3
10-2 x 10-0

Brkfst
11-7 x 7-9

Porch

SHLV

LEDGE

W/P TUB

SH.

Gazebo Porch Creates Old-Fashioned Feel

■ This plan features:

— Three bedrooms

— Two full baths

■ An old-fashioned welcome is created by the covered Porch

■ The Breakfast area overlooks the Porch and is separated from the Kitchen by an extended counter

■ The Dining room and the Great room are highlighted by a two sided fireplace, enhancing the temperature as well as the atmosphere

■ The roomy Master suite is enhanced by a whirlpool bath with double vanity and a walk-in closet

■ No materials list is available for this plan

MAIN FLOOR — 1,452 SQ. FT.
GARAGE — 584 SQ. FT.

TOTAL LIVING AREA:
1,452 SQ. FT.

Great Room
Heart of Home

■ This plan features:

— Three bedrooms

— Two full baths

■ Sheltered porch leads into the Entry with arches and a Great Room

■ Spacious Great Room with a ten foot ceiling above a wall of windows and rear yard access

■ Efficient Kitchen with a built-in pantry, a laundry closet and a Breakfast area accented by a decorative window

■ Bay of windows enhances the Master Bedroom suite with a double vanity bath and a walk-in closet

■ Two additional bedrooms with ample closets, share a full bath

■ No materials list is available for this plan.

MAIN AREA — 1,087 SQ. FT.

TOTAL LIVING AREA:
1,087 SQ. FT.

© Larry E. Belk

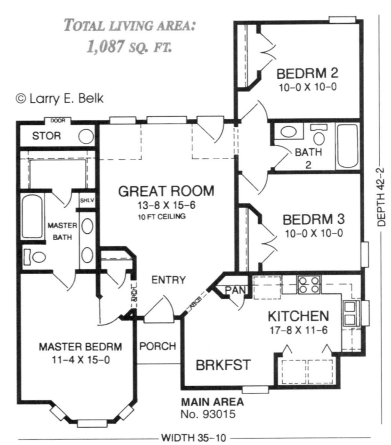

STOR

GREAT ROOM
13-8 X 15-6
10 FT CEILING

MASTER BATH

SHLV

BEDRM 2
10-0 X 10-0

BATH 2

BEDRM 3
10-0 X 10-0

ENTRY

PAN

KITCHEN
17-8 X 11-6

MASTER BEDRM
11-4 X 15-0

PORCH

BRKFST

DEPTH 42-2

MAIN AREA
No. 93015

WIDTH 35-10

An
EXCLUSIVE DESIGN
By Karl Kreeger

DECK

M. BEDROOM
15'-4"
X
13'-4"

LIVING RM.
14'-0"
X
20'-0"

DINING
10'-6"
X
10'-0"

SLOPE CLG.

DOWN

KIT.
12'-0"
X
12'-0"

DW

BRKFST

C. B. L. B. C.

L. W. D.

BEDROOM 2
10'-0"
X
11'-0"

BEDROOM 3
10'-0"
X
11'-0"

H.

FOYER

C.

P.

GARAGE
19'-4" X 20'-4"

44'-4"

P.

MAIN AREA
No. 20062

49'-8"

Inexpensive Ranch Design

■ This plan features:

— Three bedrooms

— Two full baths

■ A large picture window brightening the Breakfast area

■ A well planned Kitchen

■ A Living Room which is accented by an open beam across the sloping ceiling and wood burning fireplace

■ A Master Bedroom with an extremely large bath area

MAIN AREA — 1,500 SQ. FT.
BASEMENT — 1,500 SQ. FT.
GARAGE — 482 SQ. FT.

TOTAL LIVING AREA:
1,500 SQ. FT.

Refer to **Pricing Schedule D** on the order form for pricing information

Exciting Arched Accents Give Impact

■ This plan features:

— Three bedrooms

— Two full and one half baths

■ Keystone arch accents entrance into open Foyer with angled staircase and sloped ceiling

■ Great Room enhanced by an entertainment center, hearth fireplace and a wall of windows

■ Efficient, angled Kitchen offers work island/snackbar, Breakfast area with access to back yard

■ Master Bedroom wing with a lavish Bath with two vanities, and corner window tub

■ Two bedrooms with walk-in closets share a skylit Study, double vanity bath and a Bonus Room

■ No materials list is available for this plan

FIRST FLOOR — 1,542 SQ. FT.
SECOND FLOOR — 667 SQ. FT.
BONUS ROOM — 236 SQ. FT.
BASEMENT — 1,470 SQ. FT.

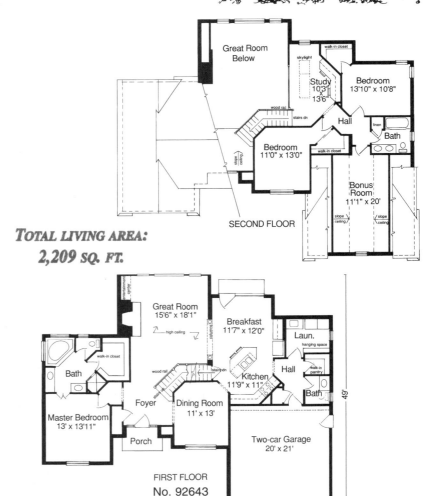

TOTAL LIVING AREA: 2,209 SQ. FT.

To order your Blueprints, call 1-800-235-5700

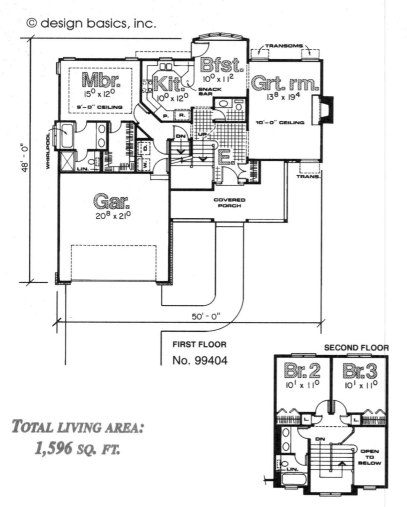

© design basics, inc.

48' - 0"

Mbr.
15⁰ x 12⁰
9'-0" CEILING

Kit.
10⁰ x 12⁰

Bfst.
10⁰ x 11²
SNACK BAR

Grt. rm.
13⁸ x 19⁴
10'-0" CEILING

TRANSOMS

P. R.

DN UP

LIN.

Gar.
20⁸ x 21⁰

COVERED
PORCH

TRANS.

50' - 0"

FIRST FLOOR
No. 99404

SECOND FLOOR

Br. 2
10¹ x 11⁰

Br. 3
10¹ x 11⁰

DN

OPEN
TO
BELOW

LIN.

TOTAL LIVING AREA:
1,596 SQ. FT.

Charming Country Style

■ This plan features:

— Three bedrooms

— Two full and one half baths

■ Specious Great Room enhanced by a fireplace and transom windows

■ Breakfast Room with a bay window and direct access to the Kitchen

■ Snack bar extending work space in the Kitchen

■ Master Suite enhanced by a crowning in a boxed nine foot ceiling, a compartmental whirlpool bath and a large walk-in closet

■ Second floor balcony overlooking the U-shaped stairs and Entry

■ Two second floor bedrooms share a full hall bath

FIRST FLOOR — 1,191 SQ. FT.
SECOND FLOOR — 405 SQ. FT.
BASEMENT — 1,191 SQ. FT.
GARAGE — 454 SQ. FT.

Refer to **Pricing Schedule A** on the order form for pricing information

Easy Living Design

■ This plan features:

— Three bedrooms

— Two full baths

■ A handicaped Master Bath plan is available

■ Vaulted Great Room, Dining Room and Kitchen areas

■ A Kitchen accented with angles and an abundance of cabinets for storage

■ A Master Bedroom with an ample sized wardrobe, large covered private deck, and private bath

MAIN AREA — 1,345 SQ. FT.
WIDTH — 47'-8"
DEPTH — 56'-0"

TOTAL LIVING AREA:
1,345 SQ. FT.

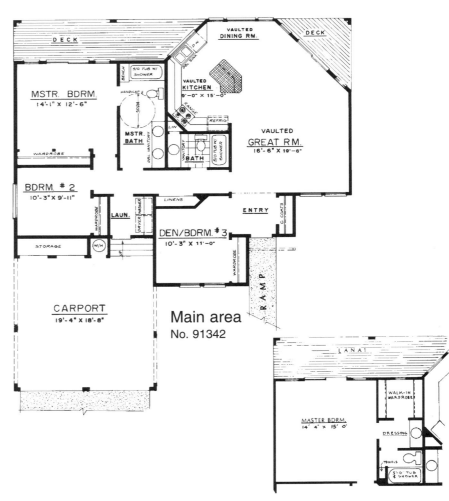

Main area
No. 91342

ALTERNATE BATH

To order your Blueprints, call 1-800-235-5700

Refer to **Pricing Schedule B** on
the order form for pricing information

A Comfortable Informal Design

- This plan features:
- — Three bedrooms
- — Two full baths
- Warm, country front Porch with wood details
- Spacious Activity Room enhanced by a pre-fab fireplace
- Open and efficient Kitchen/Dining area highlighted by bay window, adjacent to Laundry and Garage entry
- Corner Master Bedroom offers a pampering bath with a garden tub and double vanity topped by a vaulted ceiling
- Two additional bedrooms with ample closets, share a full bath
- An optional slab or crawl space foundation — please specify when ordering

MAIN FLOOR — 1,300 SQ. FT.
GARAGE — 576 SQ. FT.

MAIN FLOOR
No. 94801

GARAGE 22'-6"x 21'-0"

STORAGE

LAUNDRY

DINING & KITCHEN 18'-0"x 11'-6"

GARDEN TUB

VAULTED BATH CEILING

BED ROOM 14'-0"x 11'-6"

ACTIVITY ROOM 18'-0"x 13'-6"

PRE-FAB FIREPLACE

BED ROOM 11'-0"x 10'-0"

WALK-IN CLOSET

BED ROOM 11'-6"x 11'-6"

PORCH

68'-0"

28'-0"

TOTAL LIVING AREA:
1,300 SQ. FT.

To order your Blueprints, call 1-800-235-5700

89

Refer to **Pricing Schedule C** on the order form for pricing information

Split Bedroom Ranch

■ This plan features:

— Three bedrooms

— Two full baths

■ The formal Foyer opens into the Great room which features a vaulted ceiling and a hearth fireplace

■ The U-shaped Kitchen is located between the Dining room and the Breakfast nook

■ The secluded Master bedroom is spacious and includes amenities such as walk-in closets and a full bath

■ Two secondary Bedrooms have ample closet space and share a full bath

■ The covered front Porch and rear Deck provide additional space for entertaining

■ An optional basement, slab or a crawl space foundation — please specify when ordering

MAIN FLOOR — 1,804 SQ. FT.
BASEMENT — 1,804 SQ. FT.
GARAGE — 506 SQ. FT.

TOTAL LIVING AREA:
1,804 SQ. FT.

MAIN FLOOR
No. 90476

Refer to **Pricing Schedule D** on the order form for pricing information

SECOND FLOOR PLAN

BEDROOM
13-6 x 13-0

GREAT ROOM
(BELOW)

BOOKS

CLOSET

BATH

OPTIONAL BATH
AND CLOSET

OFFICE OR
BONUS ROOM
11-4 x 25-4

OPEN RAIL

BOOKS

CLOSET

BEDROOM
13-6 x 12-0

BALCONY

OPEN RAIL

BEDROOM
13-6 x 12-0

FOYER
(BELOW)

FIRST FLOOR — 1,637 SQ. FT.
SECOND FLOOR — 761 SQ. FT.
BONUS AREA — 453 SQ. FT.

TOTAL LIVING AREA:
2,398 SQ. FT.

MAIN FLOOR PLAN
No. 90450

70'-10"

54'-6"

STORAGE

BREAKFAST
12-0 x 10-4

WOOD DECK
22-0 x 12-0

M. BATH

M. BEDROOM
13-6 x 18-0

GREAT ROOM
21-6 x 13-6
(TWO STORY)

HEARTH

OPEN RAIL

KITCHEN
12-0 x 13-0

GARAGE
22-0 x 22-0

CLOSET CLOSET

LAUNDRY
10-2 x 8-2

1/2 BA.

DINING
13-6 x 12-0

FOYER

STUDY
13-6 x 10-0

PORCH

Elegant Brick Two-Story

◼ This plan features:

— Four bedrooms

— Two full and one half baths

◼ A large two-story Great Room with a fireplace and access to a wood deck

◼ A secluded Master Suite with two walk-in closets and a private, lavish, Master Bath

◼ A large island Kitchen serving the formal Dining Room and the sunny Breakfast Nook with ease

◼ Three additional bedrooms, two with walk-in closets, sharing a full hall bath

◼ An optional Bonus Room with a private entrance from below

◼ An optional basement or crawl space foundation — please specify when ordering

Refer to **Pricing Schedule A** on the order form for pricing information

Quoin Accents Distinguish this Plan

■ This plan features:

— Three bedrooms

— Two full baths

■ A traditional brick elevation with quoin accents

■ A large Family Room with a corner fireplace and direct access to the outside

■ An arched opening leading to the Breakfast Area

■ A bay window illuminating the Breakfast Area with natural light

■ An efficiently designed, U-shaped Kitchen with ample cabinet and counter space

■ A Master Suite with a private master bath

■ Two additional bedrooms that share a full hall bath

■ No materials list is available for this plan

MAIN FLOOR — 1,142 SQ. FT.
GARAGE — 428 SQ. FT.

TOTAL LIVING AREA:
1,142 SQ. FT.

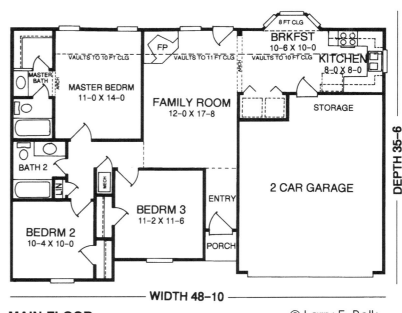

MAIN FLOOR
No. 93017

© Larry E. Belk

To order your Blueprints, call 1-800-235-5700

Refer to **Pricing Schedule A** on the order form for pricing information

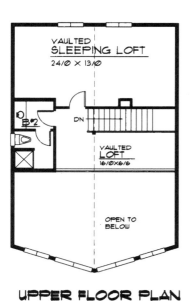

UPPER FLOOR PLAN

VAULTED
SLEEPING LOFT
24/0 × 13/0

B #2
DN

VAULTED
LOFT
16/0×6/6

OPEN TO
BELOW

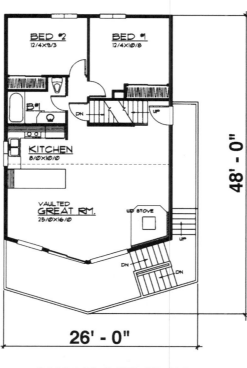

BED #2
12/4×9/3

BED #1
12/4×10/8

B #1

KITCHEN
8/0×10/0

VAULTED
GREAT RM.
25/0×16/0

WD STOVE

48' - 0"

26' - 0"

MAIN FLOOR PLAN
No. 91026

Home on a Hill

■ This plan features:

— Two bedrooms

— One full and one three-quarter baths

■ Sweeping panels of glass and a wood stove, creating atmosphere for the Great Room

■ An open plan that draws the Kitchen into the warmth of the Great Room's wood stove

■ A sleeping loft that has a full bath all to itself

FIRST FLOOR — 988 SQ. FT.
SECOND FLOOR — 366 SQ. FT.
BASEMENT — 742 SQ. FT.
GARAGE — 283 SQ. FT.

TOTAL LIVING AREA:
1,354 SQ. FT.

PLAN NO. 90966

Refer to **Pricing Schedule D** on the order form for pricing information

Stately Manor

■ This plan features:

— Three bedrooms

— Two full and one half baths

■ A porch serving as a grand entrance

■ A very spacious Foyer with an open staircase and lots of angles

■ A beautiful Kitchen equipped with a cook top island and a full bay window wall that includes a roomy Breakfast Nook

■ A Living Room with a vaulted ceiling that flows into the formal Dining Room for ease in entertaining

■ A grand Master Suite equipped with a walk-in closet and five-piece private bath

FIRST FLOOR — 1,383 SQ. FT.
SECOND FLOOR — 997 SQ. FT.
BASEMENT — 1,374 SQ. FT.
GARAGE — 420 SQ. FT.

TOTAL LIVING AREA:
2,380 SQ. FT.

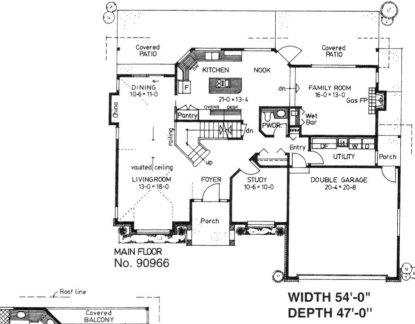

MAIN FLOOR
No. 90966

WIDTH 54'-0"
DEPTH 47'-0"

SECOND FLOOR

An EXCLUSIVE DESIGN
By Westhome Planners, Ltd.

Rocking Chair Living

■ This plan features:

— Three bedrooms

— Two full baths

■ A massive fireplace separating Living and Dining Rooms

■ An isolated Master Suite with a walk-in closet and a helpful compartmentalized bath

■ A galley-type Kitchen between the Breakfast Room and Dining Room

■ An optional basement, slab or crawl space foundation — please specify when ordering

MAIN AREA — 1,670 SQ. FT.

TOTAL LIVING AREA:
1,670 SQ. FT.

MAIN AREA
No. 90409

Floor plan labels:

STORAGE 8'-4"x7'-6"
UTILITY 8'-2"x7'-6"
BREAKFAST 10'-0"x9'-6"
KITCHEN 9'-8"x8'-8"
DINING RM. 19'-8"x11'-2"
BEDROOM 12'-10"x12'-0"
W. D.
PAN.
DRESS.
CL.
BATH
LIN.
BATH
GARAGE 21'-2"x20'-2"
M. BEDROOM 15'-8"x13'-10"
CATHEDRAL CLG.
GREAT RM. 19'-8"x18'-2"
BEDROOM 13'-0"x11'-0"
CL.
CL.
PATIO 14'-0"x10'-0"
PORCH 21'-0"x6'-0"
30'-0"
73'-8"

Refer to **Pricing Schedule C** on the order form for pricing information

Small, But Not Lacking

- This plan features:
  — Three bedrooms
  — One full and one three quarter baths

- Great Room adjoining the Dining Room for ease in entertaining

- Kitchen highlighted by a peninsula counter/snackbar extending work space and offering convenience in serving informal meals or snacks

- Split bedroom plan allowing for privacy for the Master Bedroom suite with a private bath and a walk-in closet

- Two additional bedrooms sharing the full family bath in the hall

- Garage entry convenient to the kitchen

FIRST FLOOR — 1,546 SQ. FT.
GARAGE — 440 SQ. FT.
BASEMENT — 1,530 SQ. FT.

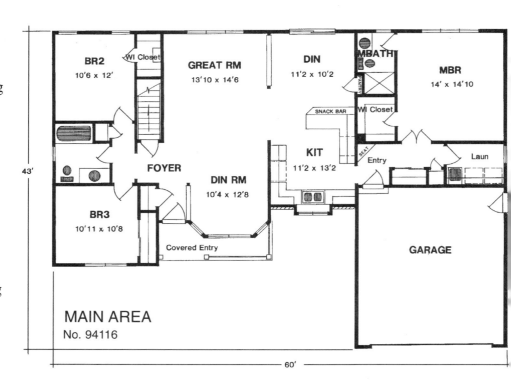

BR2
10'6 x 12'

WI Closet

GREAT RM
13'10 x 14'6

DIN
11'2 x 10'2

MBATH

MBR
14' x 14'10

FOYER

WI Closet

SNACK BAR

KIT
11'2 x 13'2

Entry

Laun

BR3
10'11 x 10'8

DIN RM
10'4 x 12'8

Covered Entry

43'

GARAGE

MAIN AREA
No. 94116

60'

TOTAL LIVING AREA:
1,546 SQ. FT.

To order your Blueprints, call 1-800-235-5700

Refer to **Pricing Schedule B** on the order form for pricing information

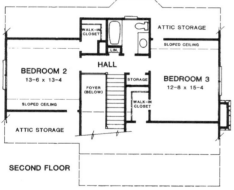

BEDROOM 2
13-6 x 13-4

WALK-IN CLOSET

ATTIC STORAGE

SLOPED CEILING

LIN.

HALL

FOYER (BELOW)

STORAGE

BEDROOM 3
12-8 x 15-4

WALK-IN CLOSET

SLOPED CEILING

ATTIC STORAGE

SECOND FLOOR

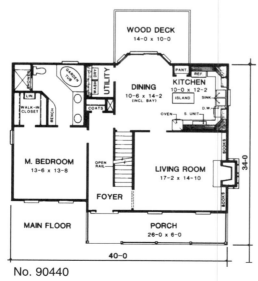

WOOD DECK
14-0 x 10-0

GARDEN TUB

WASH DRY

UTILITY

DINING
10-6 x 14-2
(INCL BAY)

PANT.

REF

KITCHEN
10-0 x 12-2

ISLAND

SINK

LIN.

WALK-IN CLOSET

BENCH

COATS

OVEN

S UNIT

D.W.

M. BEDROOM
13-6 x 13-8

OPEN RAIL

LIVING ROOM
17-2 x 14-10

BOOKS

BOOKS

34-0

FOYER

MAIN FLOOR

PORCH
26-0 x 6-0

40-0

No. 90440

Rustic Warmth

■ This plan features:

— Three bedrooms

— Two full baths

■ A fireplaced Living Room with built-in bookshelves

■ A fully-equipped Kitchen with an island

■ A sunny Dining Room with glass sliders to a wood deck

■ A first floor Master Suite with walk-in closet and lavish master bath

■ An optional basement or crawl space foundation — please specify when ordering

MAIN FLOOR — 1,100 SQ. FT.
SECOND FLOOR — 664 SQ. FT.
BASEMENT — 1,100 SQ. FT.

TOTAL LIVING AREA:
1,764 SQ. FT.

Refer to **Pricing Schedule B** on the order form for pricing information

© 1995 Donald A Gardner Architects, Inc.

Cathedral Ceiling

■ This plan features:

— Three bedrooms

— Two full baths

■ Cathedral ceiling expanding the Great room, Dining Room and Kitchen

■ A versatile bedroom or study topped by a cathedral ceiling accented by double circle-top windows

■ Master Suite complete with a cathedral ceiling, including a bath with a garden tub, linen closet and a walk-in closet

MAIN FLOOR — 1,417 SQ. FT.
GARAGE — 441 SQ. FT.

TOTAL LIVING AREA:
1,417 SQ. FT.

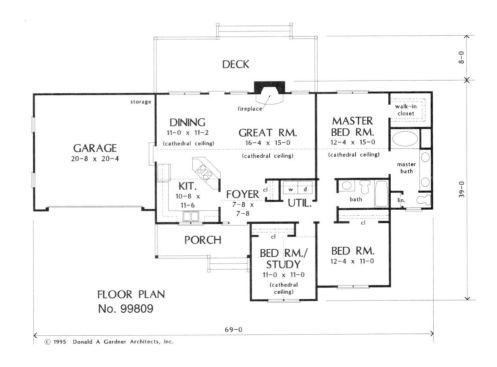

FLOOR PLAN
No. 99809

© 1995 Donald A Gardner Architects, Inc.

To order your Blueprints, call 1-800-235-5700

© 1991 Donald A. Gardner Architects, Inc.

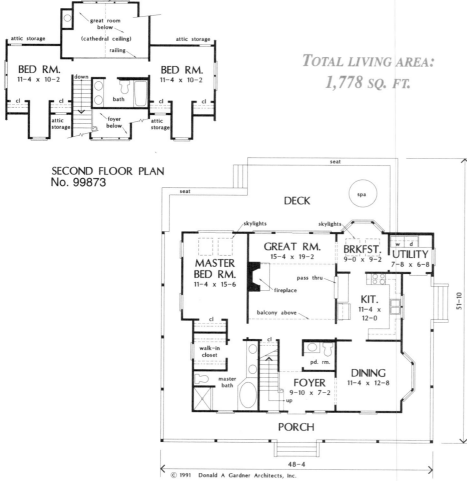

clerestory with palladian window

great room
below
(cathedral ceiling)
railing

attic storage

attic storage

BED RM.
11-4 x 10-2

BED RM.
11-4 x 10-2

cl

cl

down

bath

cl

cl

attic
storage

foyer
below

attic
storage

SECOND FLOOR PLAN
No. 99873

TOTAL LIVING AREA:
1,778 SQ. FT.

seat

DECK

spa

seat

skylights

skylights

MASTER
BED RM.
11-4 x 15-6

GREAT RM.
15-4 x 19-2

BRKFST.
9-0 x 9-2

w d
UTILITY
7-8 x 6-8

pass thru

fireplace

KIT.
11-4 x
12-0

balcony above

cl

walk-in
closet

cl

pd. rm.

51-10

master
bath

FOYER
9-10 x 7-2

up

DINING
11-4 x 12-8

PORCH

48-4

© 1991 Donald A Gardner Architects, Inc.

FIRST FLOOR PLAN

Deck Includes Spa

■ This plan features:

— Three bedrooms

— Two full and one half baths

■ An exterior porch giving the
home a traditional flavor

■ Great Room highlighted by a
fireplace and a balcony above as
well as a pass-through into the
kitchen

■ Kitchen eating area with sky
lights and bow windows overlooking the deck with a spa

■ Two additional bedrooms with a
full bath on the second floor

■ Master Suite on the first floor and
naturally illuminated by two skylights

■ An optional basement or crawl
space foundation — please
specify when ordering

FIRST FLOOR — 1,325 SQ. FT.
SECOND FLOOR — 453 SQ. FT.

Refer to **Pricing Schedule B** on the order form for pricing information

Home For the Discriminating Buyer

■ This plan features:

— Three bedrooms

— Two full baths

■ A sloped ceiling and a corner fireplace enhancing the Great Room

■ A Kitchen with a garden window above the double sink

■ A peninsula counter joins the Kitchen and the Breakfast Room in an open layout

■ A Master Suite with a large walk-in closet, a private bath with an oval corner tub, and a separate shower and double vanity

■ Two additional bedrooms that share a full hall bath

■ No materials list available for this plan

MAIN AREA — 1,710 SQ. FT.
BASEMENT — 1,560 SQ. FT.
GARAGE — 455 SQ. FT.

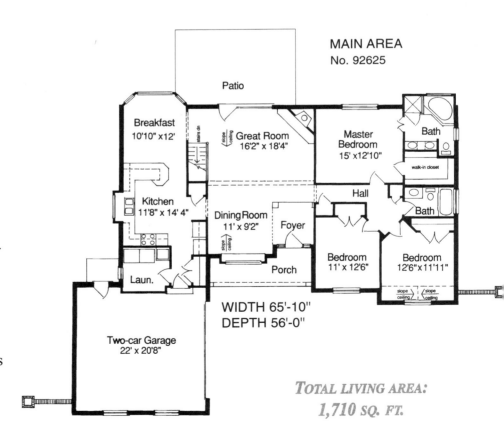

MAIN AREA
No. 92625

Patio

Breakfast
10'10" x12'

Great Room
16'2" x 18'4"

Master
Bedroom
15' x12'10"

Bath

walk-in closet

Kitchen
11'8" x 14' 4"

Hall

Bath

Dining Room
11' x 9'2"

Foyer

Laun.

Porch

Bedroom
11' x 12'6"

Bedroom
12'6" x11'11"

Two-car Garage
22' x 20'8"

WIDTH 65'-10"
DEPTH 56'-0"

TOTAL LIVING AREA:
1,710 SQ. FT.

To order your Blueprints, call 1-800-235-5700

Refer to **Pricing Schedule A** on the order form for pricing information

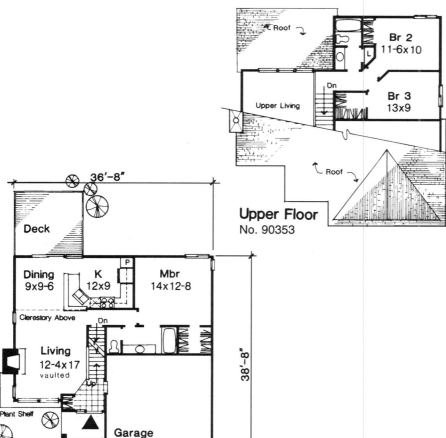

Upper Floor
No. 90353

Br 2
11-6 x 10

Br 3
13 x 9

Upper Living

Roof

Main Floor

36'-8"

Deck

Dining
9 x 9-6

K
12 x 9

Mbr
14 x 12-8

Clerestory Above

Living
12-4 x 17
vaulted

Plant Shelf

Garage
20 x 20

38'-8"

Living Room Features Vaulted Ceiling

■ This plan features:

— Three bedrooms

— Two full baths

■ A vaulted ceiling in the Living Room and the Dining Room, with a clerestory above

■ A Master Bedroom with a walk-in closet and private full bath

■ An efficient Kitchen, with a corner double sink and peninsula counter

■ A Dining Room with sliding doors to the Deck

■ A Living Room with a fireplace that adds warmth to open areas

■ Two additional bedrooms that share a full hall bath

FIRST FLOOR — 846 SQ. FT.
SECOND FLOOR — 400 SQ. FT.

TOTAL LIVING AREA:
1,246 SQ. FT.

Refer to **Pricing Schedule C** on the order form for pricing information

Quality and Diversity

■ This plan features:

— Four bedrooms

— Two full and one half bath

■ Elegant arched entrance from Porch into Foyer and Great Room

■ Corner fireplace and atrium door highlight Great Room

■ Hub Kitchen with walk-in pantry and peninsula counter easily accesses glass Breakfast bay

■ Master Bedroom wing crowned by tray ceiling offers plush bath and walk-in closet

■ Three additional bedrooms with decorative windows and large closets share a full bath

■ No materials list is available for this plan

FIRST FLOOR — 1,401 SQ. FT.
SECOND FLOOR — 621 SQ. FT.
BASEMENT — 1,269 SQ. FT.
GARAGE — 478 SQ. FT.

TOTAL LIVING AREA:
2,022 SQ. FT.

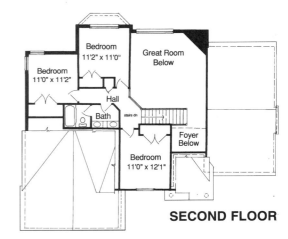

SECOND FLOOR

FIRST FLOOR
No. 92629

To order your Blueprints, call 1-800-235-5700

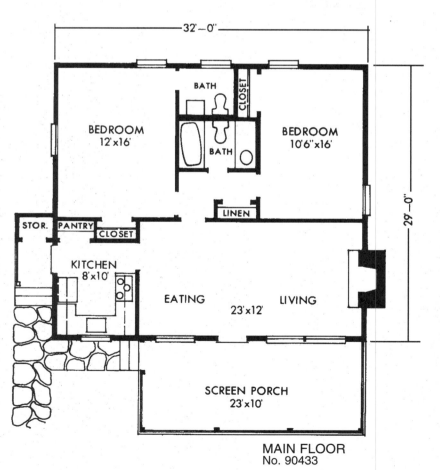

32'—0"

29'—0"

BEDROOM
12'x16'

BATH

CLOSET

BATH

BEDROOM
10'6"x16'

LINEN

STOR. | PANTRY
CLOSET

KITCHEN
8'x10'

EATING   LIVING
23'x12'

SCREEN PORCH
23'x10'

MAIN FLOOR
No. 90433

Cabin in the Country

◼ This plan features:

— Two bedrooms

— One full and one half baths

◼ A Screened Porch for enjoyment of your outdoor surroundings

◼ A combination Living and Dining area with cozy fireplace for added warmth

◼ An efficiently laid out Kitchen with a built-in pantry

◼ Two large bedrooms located at the rear of the home

◼ An optional slab or crawl space foundation — please specify when ordering

MAIN FLOOR — 928 SQ. FT.
SCREENED PORCH — 230 SQ. FT.
STORAGE — 14 SQ. FT.

TOTAL LIVING AREA:
928 SQ. FT.

Refer to **Pricing Schedule B** on the order form for pricing information

Large Front Window Provides Streaming Natural Light

■ This plan features:

— Three bedrooms

— Two full and one half baths

■ An outstanding, two-story Great Room with an unusual floor-to-ceiling, corner front window and cozy, hearth fireplace

■ Kitchen with a work island, pantry, a corner, double sink opening to the Great Room, and a bright, bay window eating Nook

■ Master Suite with a vaulted ceiling and a double vanity, spa tub and walk-in closet

■ Two additional bedrooms share a full hall bath and a Bonus area for multiple uses

FIRST FLOOR — 1,230 SQ. FT.
SECOND FLOOR — 477 SQ. FT.
BONUS ROOM — 195 SQ. FT.

TOTAL LIVING AREA:
1,707 SQ. FT.

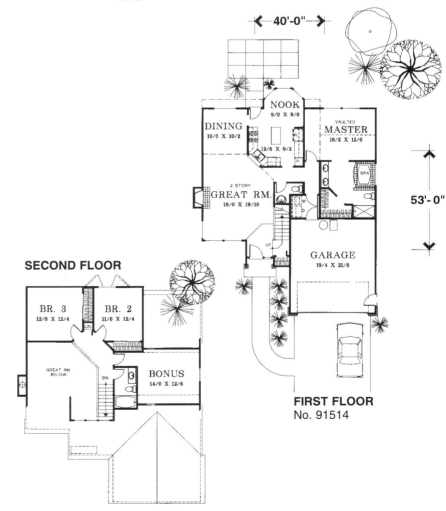

SECOND FLOOR

BR. 3
12/8 X 12/4

BR. 2
11/0 X 12/4

GREAT RM BELOW

DN

BONUS
14/0 X 12/6

FIRST FLOOR
No. 91514

40'-0"

53'-0"

NOOK
9/0 X 9/0

DINING
10/0 X 10/2

VAULTED
MASTER
16/2 X 12/0

12/6 X 9/2

2 STORY
GREAT RM.
16/0 X 19/10

SPA

UP

GARAGE
19/4 X 21/8

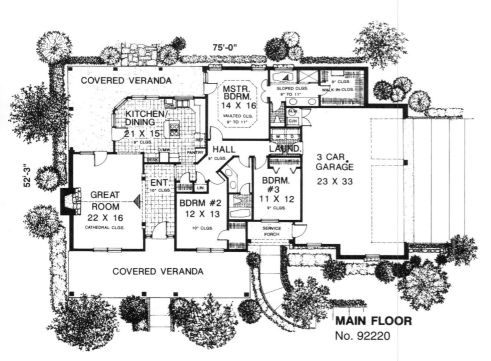

MAIN FLOOR
No. 92220

TOTAL LIVING AREA:
1,830 SQ. FT.

Southern Hospitality

■ This plan features:

— Three bedrooms

— Two full baths

■ Welcoming Covered Veranda

■ Easy-care, tiled Entry leads into Great Room with fieldstone fireplace and atrium door to another Covered Veranda topped by a cathedral ceiling

■ A bright Kitchen/Dining Room includes a stovetop island/ snackbar, built-in pantry and desk, and access to Covered Veranda

■ Vaulted ceiling crowns Master Bedroom that offers a plush bath and huge walk-in closet

■ Two additional bedrooms with ample closets share a double vanity bath

■ No materials list is available for this plan

MAIN FLOOR — 1,830 SQ. FT.

GARAGE — 759 SQ. FT.

Refer to **Pricing Schedule B** on the order form for pricing information

Easy One Floor Living

■ This plan features:

— Three bedrooms

— Two full baths

■ A spacious Family Room topped by a vaulted ceiling and high-lighted by a large fireplace and a French door to the rear yard

■ A serving bar open to the Family Room and the Dining Room, a pantry and a peninsula counter adding more efficiency to the Kitchen

■ A crowning tray ceiling over the Master Bedroom and a vaulted ceiling over the Master Bath

■ A vaulted ceiling over the cozy Sitting Room in the Master Suite

■ Two additional bedrooms, roomy in size sharing the full bath in the hall

■ An optional basement, crawl space or slab foundaiton — please specify when ordering

WIDTH 50'-0"
DEPTH 51'-0"

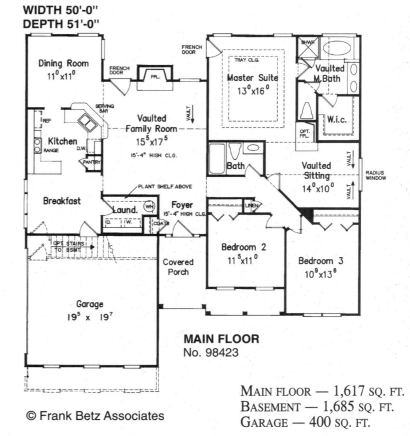

MAIN FLOOR
No. 98423

© Frank Betz Associates

MAIN FLOOR — 1,617 SQ. FT.
BASEMENT — 1,685 SQ. FT.
GARAGE — 400 SQ. FT.

TOTAL LIVING AREA:
1,671 SQ. FT.

To order your Blueprints, call 1-800-235-5700

47'-0"

54'-0"

PATIO

BDRM-2
11/0 x 10/10

BDRM-3
11/0 x 10/10

KIT.
10/4 x 10/10

PANT.

VAULTED
DINING RM.
10/8 x 11/2

LINEN

TUB

VAULTED
LIVING RM.
15/10 x 20/8

HEARTH

MASTER
12/10 x 15/2

COVERED PORCH

GARAGE
21/4 x 21/8

MAIN AREA
No. 91807

An Affordable, Stylish Floor Plan

■ This plan features:

— Three bedrooms

— One full and one three quarter baths

■ A covered porch entry

■ An old-fashioned hearth fireplace in the vaulted ceiling Living Room

■ A handy Kitchen with U-shaped counter that is accessible from the Dining Room

■ A Master Bedroom with a large walk-in closet and private bath

■ An optional crawl space or slab foundation — please specify when ordering

MAIN FLOOR — 1,410 SQ. FT.
GARAGE — 484 SQ. FT.

TOTAL LIVING AREA:
1,410 SQ. FT.

Extraordinary Split Level

■ This plan features:

— Three bedrooms

— Two full baths and opt. half bath

■ 10-foot high ceilings in the Living Room, Family Room and Dinette area

■ A heat-circulating fireplace

■ A master bath with separate stall shower and whirlpool tub

■ A two-car Garage with access through the Mudroom

MAIN AREA — 1,203 SQ. FT.
BASEMENT — 676 SQ. FT.
GARAGE — 509 SQ. FT.

TOTAL LIVING AREA:
1,203 SQ. FT.

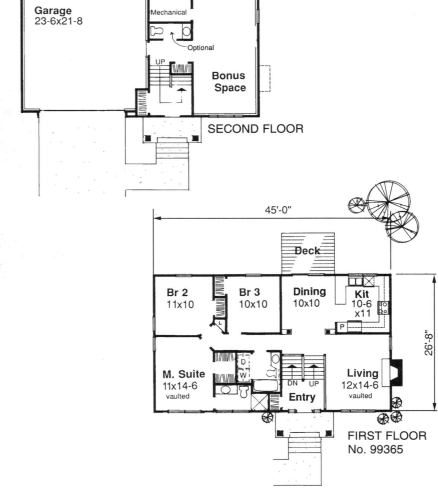

Garage
23-6x21-8

Mechanical

Optional

UP

Bonus Space

SECOND FLOOR

45'-0"

Deck

Br 2
11x10

Br 3
10x10

Dining
10x10

Kit
10-6
x11

26'-8"

M. Suite
11x14-6
vaulted

DN   UP

Entry

Living
12x14-6
vaulted

FIRST FLOOR
No. 99365

Refer to **Pricing Schedule A** on
the order form for pricing information

OPTIONAL
BASEMENT PLAN

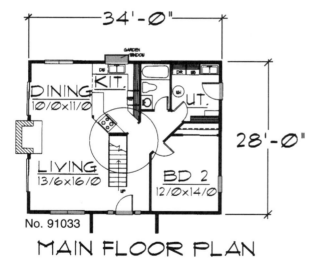

No. 91033

MAIN FLOOR PLAN

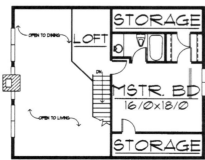

UPPER FLOOR PLAN

Neat and Tidy

■ This plan features:

— Two bedrooms

— Two full baths

■ A two story Living Room and Dining Room with a handsome stone fireplace

■ A well-appointed Kitchen with a peninsula counter

■ A Master Suite with a walk-in closet and private Master Bath

■ A large utility room with laundry facilities

■ An optional basement or crawl space foundation — please specify when ordering

FIRST FLOOR — 952 SQ. FT.
SECOND FLOOR — 297 SQ. FT.

TOTAL LIVING AREA:
1,249 SQ. FT.

Refer to **Pricing Schedule D** on the order form for pricing information

© 1993 Donald A. Gardner Architects, Inc.

Covered Porches Front and Back

■ This plan features:

— Three bedrooms

— Two full and one half baths

■ Open floor plan plus a Bonus Room great for today's family needs

■ Two-story Foyer with palladian, clerestory window and balcony overlooking Great Room

■ Great Room with cozy fireplace provides perfect gathering place

■ Columns visually separate Great Room from Breakfast area and smart, U-shaped Kitchen

■ Privately located Master Bedroom accesses Porch and luxurious Master Bath with separate shower and double vanity

FIRST FLOOR — 1,632 SQ. FT.
SECOND FLOOR — 669 SQ. FT.
BONUS ROOM — 528 SQ. FT.
GARAGE & STORAGE — 707 SQ. FT.

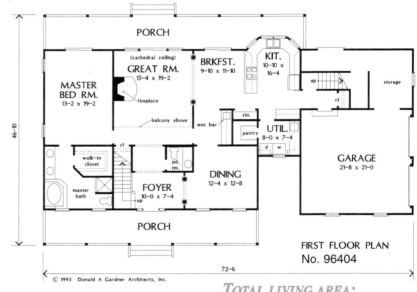

FIRST FLOOR PLAN
No. 96404

© 1993 Donald A Gardner Architects, Inc.

TOTAL LIVING AREA:
2,301 SQ. FT.

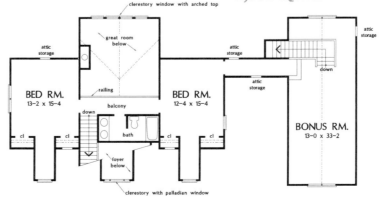

SECOND FLOOR PLAN

To order your Blueprints, call 1-800-235-5700

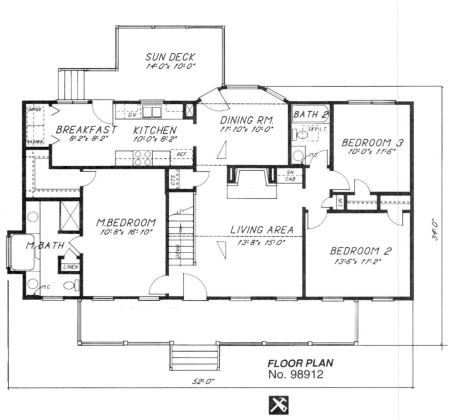

An
EXCLUSIVE DESIGN
By Jannis Vann & Associates, Inc.

SUN DECK
14'-0" x 10'-0"

BREAKFAST
8'-2" x 8'-2"

KITCHEN
10'-0" x 8'-2"

DINING RM.
11'-10" x 10'-0"

BATH 2

BEDROOM 3
10'-0" x 11'-6"

M. BEDROOM
10'-8" x 16'-10"

LIVING AREA
13'-8" x 15'-0"

BEDROOM 2
13'-6" x 11'-2"

M. BATH

LINEN

DRYER

WASHER

D.W.

REF.

SH. CAB.

LIN

34'-0"

52'-0"

FLOOR PLAN
No. 98912

Simply Cozy

■ This plan features:
— Three bedrooms
— Two full baths

■ Quaint front porch shelters Entry into the Living Area which is showcased by a massive fireplace and built-ins

■ Formal Dining Room with Deck access accented by a bay of glass

■ Efficient, galley Kitchen with Breakfast area, laundry facilities and outdoor access

■ Secluded Master Bedroom offers a roomy walk-in closet and plush bath with two vanities and a garden window tub

■ Two additional bedrooms with ample closets, share a full bath with a skylight

MAIN FLOOR — 1,325 SQ. FT.

TOTAL LIVING AREA:
1,325 SQ. FT.

Refer to **Pricing Schedule C** on the order form for pricing information

Secluded Master Suite

■ This plan features:

— Three bedrooms

— Two full baths

■ A convenient one-level design with an open floor plan between the Kitchen, Breakfast area and Great Room

■ A vaulted ceiling and a large cozy fireplace in the Great Room

■ A well-equipped Kitchen using a peninsula counter as an eating bar

■ A Master Suite with a luxurious Master Bath

■ Two additional bedrooms having use of a full hall bath

■ An optional crawl space or slab foundation — please specify when ordering

MAIN AREA — 1,680 SQ. FT.
GARAGE — 538 SQ. FT.

TOTAL LIVING AREA:
1,680 SQ. FT.

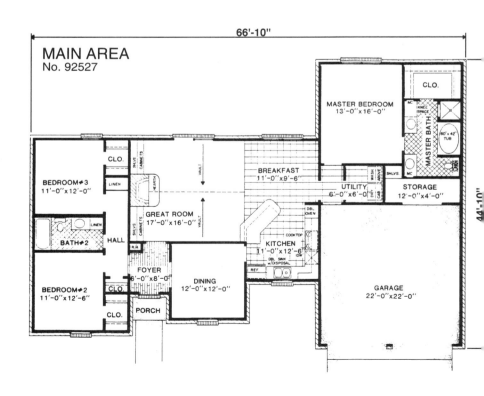

MAIN AREA
No. 92527

66'-10"

44'-10"

MASTER BEDROOM
13'-0"x16'-0"

CLO.

MASTER BATH

60"x42" TUB

BEDROOM #3
11'-0"x12'-0"

CLO.

LINEN

SHLVS
CABINETS

HEARTH

BREAKFAST
11'-0"x9'-6"

UTILITY
6'-0"x6'-0"

STORAGE
12'-0"x4'-0"

WASH

SHLVS.

VAULT

SHLVS
CABINETS

GREAT ROOM
17'-0"x16'-0"

VAULT

DBL
OVEN

BATH #2

LINEN

HALL

COOKTOP

KITCHEN
11'-0"x12'-6"

DBL SINK
w/DISPOSAL

FOYER
6'-0"x8'-0"

DINING
12'-0"x12'-0"

REF

GARAGE
22'-0"x22'-0"

BEDROOM #2
11'-0"x12'-6"

CLO.

CLO.

PORCH

To order your Blueprints, call 1-800-235-5700

© Frank Betz Associates

WIDTH 54'-0"
DEPTH 47'-6"

FIRST FLOOR

Bath

Bedroom 2
10⁰ x 11⁰

Breakfast

FRENCH DOOR

FPL.

VAULT

Master Suite
13⁰ x 15⁰
TRAY CLG.

D.W.
SERVING BAR

RANGE

Kitchen

STAIRS UP

REF.

Vaulted Family Room
15⁰ x 18⁸
13'-0" HIGH CLG.

Bedroom 3
10⁰ x 11⁰

Laund.

W. D.

PANTRY

DECORATIVE COLUMN

Foyer
13'-0" HIGH CLG.

COATS

Vaulted Master Bath

LINEN

SHWR.

Dining Room
11² x 11⁹
13'-0" HIGH CLG.

Covered Porch

PLANT SHELF ABOVE

W.i.c.

Garage
21⁵ x 19⁸

TOTAL LIVING AREA: 1,544 SQ. FT.

REF.

Laund.

W. D.

PANTRY

STAIRS DN.

OPT. BASEMENT STAIR LOCATION
No. 98460

STAIRS DN.

Opt. Bonus Room
13⁵ x 19⁸

OPTIONAL BONUS ROOM

European Flair

■ This plan features:
— Three bedrooms
— Two full baths

■ Large fireplace serving as an attractive focal point for the vaulted Family Room

■ Decorative columns defining the elegant Dining Room

■ Kitchen including a serving bar for the Family Room and a Breakfast area

■ Master Suite topped by a tray ceiling over the bedroom and a vaulted ceiling over the five-piece Master Bath

■ Optional bonus room for future expansion

■ An optional basement or crawl space foundation — please specify when ordering

■ No materials list is available for this plan

MAIN FLOOR — 1,544 SQ. FT.
BONUS ROOM — 284 SQ. FT.
GARAGE — 440 SQ. FT.

Refer to **Pricing Schedule B** on the order form for pricing information

Expandable Home

■ This plan features:

— Four bedrooms

— Three full baths

■ Front Entry into open Living Room highlighted by double window

■ Bright Dining Area with sliding glass door to optional Patio

■ Compact, efficient Kitchen with peninsula serving/snackbar, laundry closet and outdoor access

■ Two first floor bedrooms with ample closet share a full bath

■ Second floor Master Bedroom and additional bedroom feature dormer windows, private baths and walk-in closets

FIRST FLOOR — 957 SQ. FT.
SECOND FLOOR — 800 SQ. FT.

TOTAL LIVING AREA:
1,757 SQ. FT.

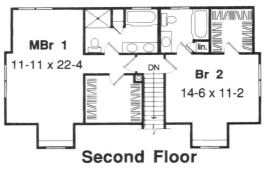

MBr 1
11-11 x 22-4

DN

Br 2
14-6 x 11-2

lin.

Second Floor

Entry

UP
Slab/crawlspace option

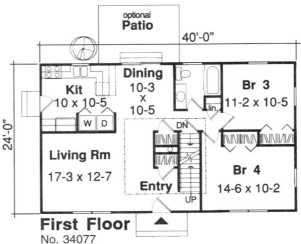

optional **Patio**

40'-0"

Kit
10 x 10-5

Dining
10-3 x 10-5

Br 3
11-2 x 10-5

lin.

24'-0"

W D

Living Rm
17-3 x 12-7

DN

Entry

UP

Br 4
14-6 x 10-2

First Floor
No. 34077

To order your Blueprints, call 1-800-235-5700

Refer to **Pricing Schedule B** on the order form for pricing information

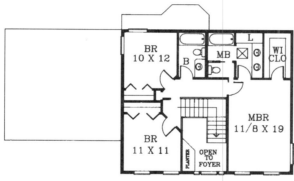

SECOND FLOOR PLAN
No. 91413

- BR 10 X 12
- B
- MB
- L
- WI CLO
- MBR 11/8 X 19
- BR 11 X 11
- OPEN TO FOYER
- PLANTER

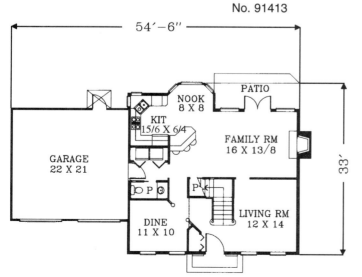

FIRST FLOOR PLAN

- 54'-6"
- PATIO
- NOOK 8 X 8
- KIT 15/6 X 6/4
- FAMILY RM 16 X 13/8
- GARAGE 22 X 21
- 33'
- P
- P
- DINE 11 X 10
- LIVING RM 12 X 14

Compact Classic

■ This plan features:

— Three bedrooms

— Two full and one half baths

■ A spacious Family Room with a cozy fireplace and direct access to the patio

■ A well-appointed Kitchen with an eating bar peninsula, double sink and sunny eating Nook

■ A formal Living Room and Dining Room located at the front of the house

■ A Master Suite equipped with a walk-in closet, a double vanity and a full Master Bath

■ An optional basement, crawl space or slab foundation — please specify when ordering

FIRST FLOOR — 963 SQ. FT.
SECOND FLOOR — 774 SQ. FT.

TOTAL LIVING AREA:
1,737 SQ. FT.

Refer to **Pricing Schedule A** on the order form for pricing information

Easy Maintenance

■ This plan features:

— Two bedroom

— Two three quarter baths

■ Abundant glass and a wrap-around Deck to enjoy the outdoors

■ A tiled entrance into a large Great Room with a fieldstone fireplace and dining area under a sloped ceiling

■ A compact tiled Kitchen open to Great Room and adjacent to the Utility area

■ Two bedrooms, one with a private bath, offer ample closet space

■ No materials list is available for this plan

MAIN AREA — 786 SQ. FT.

TOTAL LIVING AREA:
786 SQ. FT.

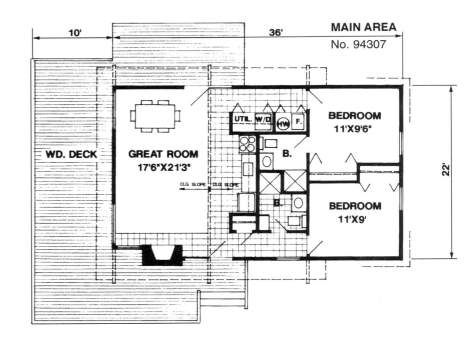

MAIN AREA
No. 94307

10' 36' 22'

WD. DECK

GREAT ROOM
17'6"X21'3"

CLG. SLOPE CLG. SLOPE

UTIL. W/D HW F.

B.

BEDROOM
11'X9'6"

B.

BEDROOM
11'X9'

An
EXCLUSIVE DESIGN
By Marshall Associates

Refer to **Pricing Schedule B** on
the order form for pricing information

TOTAL LIVING AREA:
1,782 SQ. FT.

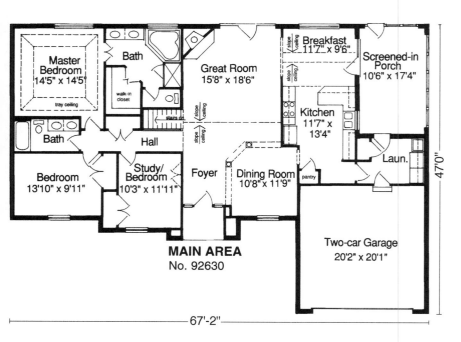

MAIN AREA
No. 92630

67'-2"

Charming Brick Ranch

■ This plan features:

— Three bedrooms

— Two full baths

■ Sheltered entrance leads into open Foyer and Dining Room defined by columns

■ Vaulted ceiling spans Foyer, Dining Room, and Great Room with corner fireplace and atrium door to rear year

■ Central Kitchen with separate Laundry and pantry easily serves Dining Room, Breakfast area and Screened Porch

■ Luxurious Master bedroom offers tray ceiling and French doors to double vanity, walk-in closet and whirlpool tub

■ Two additional bedrooms, one easily converted to a Study, share a full bath

■ No materials list available for this plan

MAIN FLOOR —1,782 SQ. FT.
GARAGE — 407 SQ. FT.
BASEMENT — 1,735 SQ. FT.

Refer to **Pricing Schedule B** on the order form for pricing information

© Frank E. Betz

With Room to Expand

■ This plan features:

— Three bedrooms

— Two full and one half baths

■ An impressive two-story Foyer

■ The Kitchen is equipped with ample cabinet and counter space

■ Spacious Family Room flows from the Breakfast Bay and is highlighted by a fireplace and a French door to the rear yard

■ The Master Suite is topped by a tray ceiling and is enhanced by a vaulted, five-piece master bath

■ Two additional bedrooms share the full bath in the hall

■ An optional basement/crawl space or slab foundation — please specify when ordering

FIRST FLOOR — 882 SQ. FT.
SECOND FLOOR — 793 SQ. FT.
BONUS ROOM — 416 SQ. FT.
BASEMENT — 882 SQ. FT.
GARAGE — 510 SQ. FT.

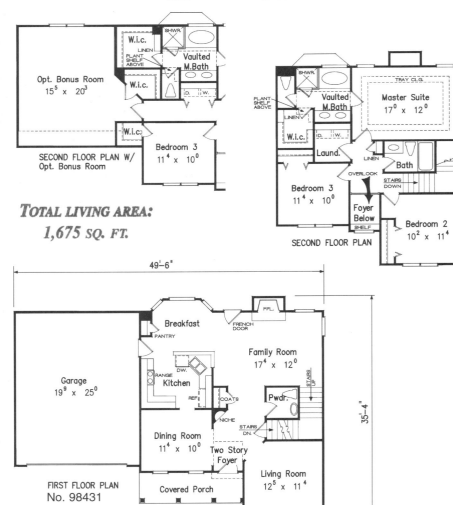

TOTAL LIVING AREA: 1,675 SQ. FT.

SECOND FLOOR PLAN W/ Opt. Bonus Room

Opt. Bonus Room 15⁵ x 20³

W.i.c. LINEN PLANT SHELF ABOVE W.i.c. SHWR. Vaulted M.Bath D. W.

W.i.c. Bedroom 3 11⁴ x 10⁰

SECOND FLOOR PLAN

PLANT SHELF ABOVE SHWR. Vaulted M.Bath LINEN W.i.c. D. W. Laund. LINEN Bath STAIRS DOWN

TRAY CLG. Master Suite 17⁰ x 12⁰

Bedroom 3 11⁴ x 10⁰ OVERLOOK Foyer Below SHELF Bedroom 2 10² x 11⁴

FIRST FLOOR PLAN No. 98431

49'-6"

35'-4"

Breakfast PANTRY FPL. FRENCH DOOR

Family Room 17⁴ x 12⁰

Garage 19⁹ x 25⁰

RANGE DW. Kitchen REF. COATS NICHE Pwr. STAIRS UP

Dining Room 11⁴ x 10⁰ STAIRS DN. Two Story Foyer

Covered Porch Living Room 12⁵ x 11⁴

Refer to **Pricing Schedule A** on the order form for pricing information

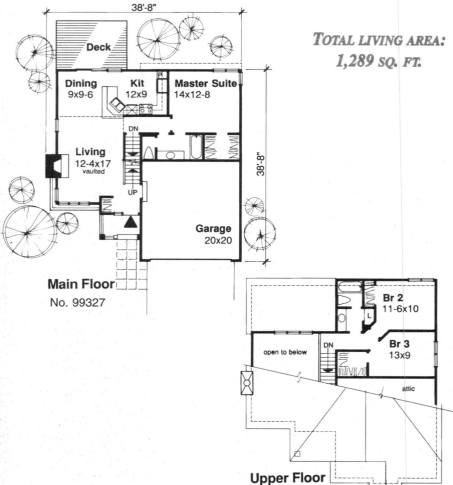

Deck

38'-8"

Dining
9x9-6

Kit
12x9

Master Suite
14x12-8

Living
12-4x17
vaulted

DN

UP

38'-8"

Garage
20x20

Main Floor
No. 99327

Br 2
11-6x10

Br 3
13x9

open to below

DN

attic

Upper Floor

TOTAL LIVING AREA:
1,289 SQ. FT.

Tradition Combined with Contemporary

■ This plan features:

— Three bedrooms

— Two full baths

■ A vaulted ceiling in the Entry

■ A formal Living Room with a fireplace and a half-round transom

■ A Dining Room with sliders to the deck and easy access to the Kitchen

■ A main floor Master Suite with corner windows, a closet and private bath access

■ Two additional bedrooms that share a full hall bath

FIRST FLOOR — 858 SQ. FT.
SECOND FLOOR — 431 SQ. FT.
BASEMENT — 858 SQ. FT.
GARAGE — 400 SQ. FT.

Refer to **Pricing Schedule A** on the order form for pricing information

For First Time Buyers

■ This plan features:

— Three bedrooms

— Two full baths

■ An efficiently designed Kitchen with a corner sink and ample counter space

■ A sunny Breakfast Room with a convenient hide-away laundry center

■ An expansive Family Room that includes a corner fireplace and direct access to the Patio

■ A private Master Suite with a walk-in closet and a double vanity bath

■ Two additional bedrooms, both with walk-in closets, share a full hall bath

■ No materials list available for this plan

MAIN FLOOR — 1,310 SQ. FT.
GARAGE — 449 SQ. FT.

© Larry E. Belk

WIDTH 49–10

TOTAL LIVING AREA:
1,310 SQ. FT.

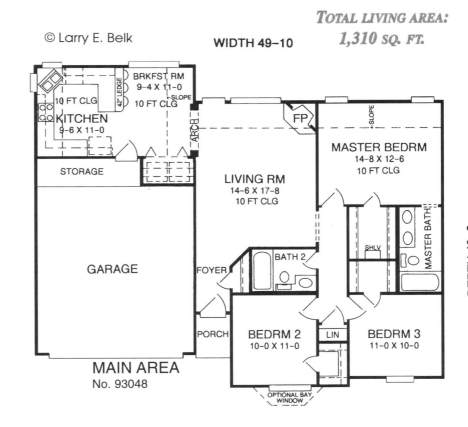

BRKFST RM
9-4 X 11-0
10 FT CLG

10 FT CLG

KITCHEN
9-6 X 11-0

STORAGE

GARAGE

MASTER BEDRM
14-8 X 12-6
10 FT CLG

LIVING RM
14-6 X 17-8
10 FT CLG

MASTER BATH

BATH 2

SHLV

FOYER

DEPTH 40-6

PORCH

BEDRM 2
10-0 X 11-0

LIN

BEDRM 3
11-0 X 10-0

OPTIONAL BAY WINDOW

MAIN AREA
No. 93048

To order your Blueprints, call 1-800-235-5700

TOTAL LIVING AREA:
1,367 SQ. FT.

One Story Country Home

■ This plan features:

— Three bedrooms

— Two full baths

■ A Living Room with an imposing, high ceiling that slopes down to a normal height of eight feet, focusing on the decorative heat-circulating fireplace at the rear wall

■ An efficient Kitchen that adjoins the Dining Room that views the front Porch

■ A Dinette Area for informal eating in the Kitchen that can comfortably seat six people

■ A Master Suite arranged with a large dressing area that has a walk-in closet plus two linear closets and space for a vanity

■ Two family bedrooms that share a full hall bath

MAIN AREA — 1,367 SQ. FT.
BASEMENT — 1,267 SQ. FT.
GARAGE — 431 SQ. FT.

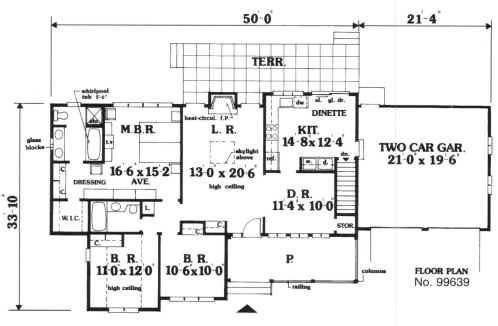

FLOOR PLAN
No. 99639

Refer to **Pricing Schedule A** on the order form for pricing information

No Wasted Space

■ This plan features:

— Three bedrooms

— Two full baths

■ A centrally located Great Room with a cathedral ceiling, exposed wood beams, and large areas of fixed glass

■ The Living and Dining areas separated by a massive stone fireplace

■ A secluded Master Suite with a walk-in closet and private Master Bath

■ An efficient Kitchen with a convenient laundry area

■ An optional basement, slab or crawl space foundation — please specify when ordering

MAIN AREA — 1,454 SQ. FT.

TOTAL LIVING AREA:
1,454 SQ. FT.

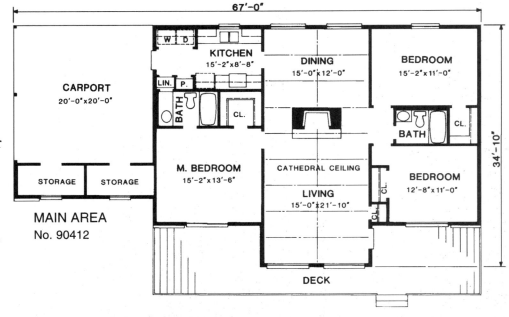

MAIN AREA
No. 90412

67'-0"

34'-10"

CARPORT
20'-0"x20'-0"

STORAGE   STORAGE

W D

KITCHEN
15'-2"x8'-8"

LIN.   P.

BATH

CL.

DINING
15'-0"x12'-0"

BEDROOM
15'-2"x11'-0"

BATH   CL.

M. BEDROOM
15'-2"x13'-6"

CATHEDRAL CEILING

LIVING
15'-0"x21'-10"

CL.

CL.

BEDROOM
12'-8"x11'-0"

DECK

Refer to **Pricing Schedule C** on the order form for pricing information

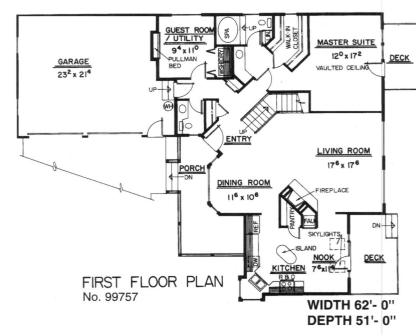

GARAGE
23² x 21⁴

GUEST ROOM / UTILITY
9⁴ x 11⁰
PULLMAN BED

SPA

WSH/DRY

UP

WH

UP

ENTRY

WALK-IN CLOSET

LIN

MASTER SUITE
12⁰ x 17²
VAULTED CEILING

DECK

LIVING ROOM
17⁶ x 17⁶

PORCH
DN

DINING ROOM
11⁶ x 10⁶

FIREPLACE

PANTRY

FAU

SKYLIGHTS

REF

DW

ISLAND

KITCHEN
R BO

NOOK
7⁶ x 11⁶

DECK

DN

FIRST FLOOR PLAN
No. 99757

WIDTH 62'- 0"
DEPTH 51'- 0"

DN

LINEN

OPEN TO BELOW

LANDING

BEDROOM 2
13⁴ x 10²

BEDROOM 3
11⁰ x 10²

SECOND FLOOR PLAN

The Ultimate Kitchen

■ This plan features:

— Three bedrooms

— Two full and one half baths

■ Front Porch leads into an open Entry with an angled staircase

■ Living Room with a wall of windows and an island fireplace opens to Dining Room

■ Kitchen with a work island, walk-in pantry, garden window over sink, skylit Nook and nearby Deck

■ Corner Master Suite enhanced by Deck access, vaulted ceiling, a large walk-in closet and spa bath

■ Guest/Utility Room offers a pullman bed and laundry

■ Two second floor bedrooms with large closets share a full bath

FIRST FLOOR —1,472 SQ. FT.
SECOND FLOOR — 478 SQ. FT.
GARAGE — 558 SQ. FT.

TOTAL LIVING AREA:
1,950 SQ. FT.

Refer to **Pricing Schedule C** on the order form for pricing information

Country Living in Any Neighborhood

■ This plan features:

— Three bedrooms

— Two full and two half baths

■ An expansive Family Room with fireplace

■ A Dining Room and Breakfast Nook lit by flowing natural light from bay windows

■ A first floor Master Suite with a double vanity bath that wraps around his-n-her closets

■ An optional basement, slab or crawl space foundation — please specify when ordering

FIRST FLOOR — 1,477 SQ. FT.
SECOND FLOOR — 704 SQ. FT.
BASEMENT — 1,374 SQ. FT.
GARAGE — 528 SQ. FT.

TOTAL LIVING AREA:
2,181 SQ. FT.

SECOND FLOOR

- CLOSET
- DRESS. BATH DRESS.
- STORAGE 13'-0"x9'-6"
- CLOSET
- BEDROOM 15'-4"x13'-6"
- DOWN
- BEDROOM 13'-0"x13'-6"

WOOD DECK 20'-0"x10'-0"

LINEN

STOR. 6'-4"x7'-2"

BREAKFAST 10'-6"x9'-0"

KITCHEN 13'-4"x10'-6"

M. BATH

CLOSET

PDR. RM.

CLOSET

GARAGE 21'-0"x20'-10"

FAMILY ROOM 16'-0"x25'-0"

DINING RM. 13'-4"x13'-6"

DOWN

M. BEDROOM 13'-4"x18'-6"

42'-8"

PORCH 26'-8"x8'-0"

69'-0"

FIRST FLOOR
No. 90436

To order your Blueprints, call 1-800-235-5700

Refer to **Pricing Schedule C** on the order form for pricing information

© 1991 Donald A. Gardner Architects, Inc.

PLAN NO. 99851

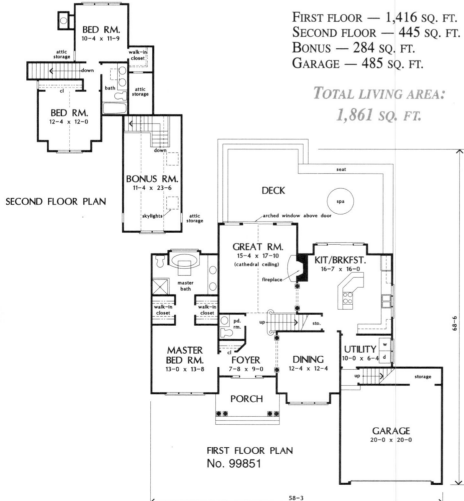

SECOND FLOOR PLAN

BED RM. 10-4 x 11-9
attic storage
walk-in closet
bath
attic storage
down
cl
BED RM. 12-4 x 12-0
down
BONUS RM. 11-4 x 23-6
skylights
attic storage

FIRST FLOOR — 1,416 SQ. FT.
SECOND FLOOR — 445 SQ. FT.
BONUS — 284 SQ. FT.
GARAGE — 485 SQ. FT.

TOTAL LIVING AREA:
1,861 SQ. FT.

DECK
seat
spa
arched window above door
GREAT RM. 15-4 x 17-10 (cathedral ceiling)
fireplace
KIT/BRKFST. 16-7 x 16-0
master bath
walk-in closet
walk-in closet
pd. rm.
up
sto.
cl
MASTER BED RM. 13-0 x 13-8
FOYER 7-8 x 9-0
DINING 12-4 x 12-4
UTILITY 10-0 x 6-4
w d
up
storage
PORCH
GARAGE 20-0 x 20-0

FIRST FLOOR PLAN
No. 99851

58-3
68-9

Dramatic Windows and Gables

- This plan features:
- — Three bedrooms
- — Two full and one half baths
- The barrel vaulted entrance is flanked by columns
- Interior columns add elegance while visually dividing the Foyer from the Dining Room and the Great Room from the Kitchen
- The Great Room is enlarged by its cathedral ceiling and a bank of windows
- An angled center island and breakfast counter in the Kitchen
- The first floor Master Suite has his-n-her closets plus a garden tub with skylight above
- An optional basement or crawl space foundation — please specify when ordering

125

Refer to **Pricing Schedule A** on the order form for pricing information

An EXCLUSIVE DESIGN
By Marshall Associates

Champagne Style on a Soda-Pop Budget

■ This plan features:

— Three bedrooms

— One full and one three quarter baths

■ Multiple gables, circle-top windows, and a unique exterior setting this delightful Ranch apart in any neighborhood

■ Living and Dining Rooms flowing together to create a very roomy feeling

■ Sliding doors leading from the Dining Room to a covered patio

■ A Master Bedroom with a private Bath

MAIN AREA — 988 SQ. FT.
BASEMENT — 988 SQ. FT.
GARAGE — 280 SQ. FT
OPTIONAL 2-CAR GARAGE — 384 SQ. FT.

TOTAL LIVING AREA:
988 SQ. FT.

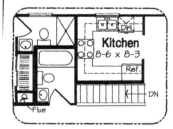

Optional Basement Plan

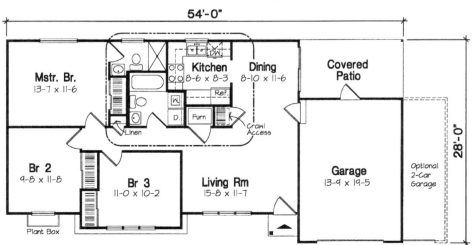

Main Floor
No. 24302

To order your Blueprints, call 1-800-235-5700

Refer to **Pricing Schedule B** on
the order form for pricing information

TOTAL LIVING AREA:
1,271 SQ. FT.

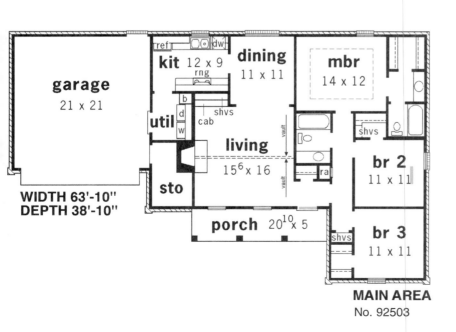

WIDTH 63'-10"
DEPTH 38'-10"

garage 21 x 21

kit 12 x 9
dining 11 x 11
mbr 14 x 12
util
sto
living 15⁶ x 16
br 2 11 x 11
br 3 11 x 11
porch 20¹⁰ x 5

MAIN AREA
No. 92503

Charming Southern Traditional

■ This plan features:

— Three bedrooms

— Two full baths

■ A covered front porch with striking columns, brick quoins, and dentil molding

■ A spacious Great Room with vaulted ceilings, a fireplace, and built-in cabinets

■ A Utility Room adjacent to the Kitchen which leads to the two- car Garage and Storage Rooms

■ A Master Bedroom including a large walk-in closet and a compartmentalized bath

■ This plan is available with a crawl space or slab foundation — please specify when ordering

MAIN AREA — 1,271 SQ. FT.
GARAGE — 506 SQ. FT.

Refer to **Pricing Schedule C** on the order form for pricing information

Distinctive Design

■ This plan features:

— Three bedrooms

— Two full and one half baths

■ Living Room is distinguished by warmth of bayed window and French doors leading to Family Room

■ Built-in curio cabinet adds interest to formal Dining Room

■ Well-appointed Kitchen with island cooktop and Breakfast area designed to save you steps

■ Family Room with fireplace for informal gatherings

■ Spacious Master Bedroom suite with vaulted ceiling over decorative window and plush dressing area with double walk-in closet, dual vanity and a corner whirlpool tub

■ Secondary bedrooms share a double vanity bath

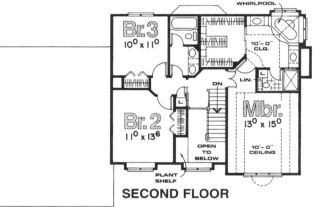

WHIRLPOOL

Br. 3
10⁰ x 11⁰

10'-0"
CLG.

LIN.

Br. 2
11⁰ x 13⁶

DN

Mbr.
13⁰ x 15⁰

OPEN TO BELOW

10'-0" CEILING

PLANT SHELF

SECOND FLOOR

FIRST FLOOR — 1,093 SQ. FT.
SECOND FLOOR — 905 SQ. FT.
BASEMENT — 1,093 SQ. FT.
GARAGE — 527 SQ. FT.

TOTAL LIVING AREA:
1,998 SQ. FT.

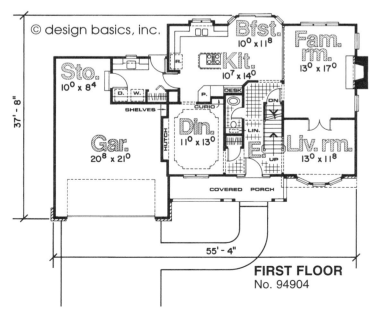

© design basics, inc.

Bfst.
10⁰ x 11⁸

Fam. rm.
13⁰ x 17⁰

Sto.
10⁰ x 8⁴

Kit.
10⁷ x 14⁰

DESK

D. W.

SHELVES

CURIO

P.

LIN.

37' - 8"

Gar.
20⁸ x 21⁰

HUTCH

Din.
11⁰ x 13⁰

DN

UP

Liv. rm.
13⁰ x 11⁸

COVERED PORCH

55' - 4"

FIRST FLOOR
No. 94904

To order your Blueprints, call 1-800-235-5700

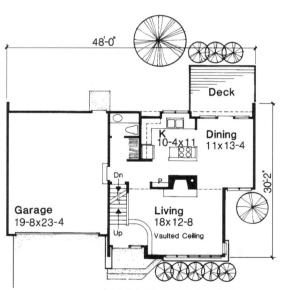

48'-0"

30'-2"

Deck

K 10-4x11   Dining 11x13-4

Dn

P

Garage 19-8x23-4

Living 18x12-8
Vaulted Ceiling

Up

MAIN FLOOR PLAN

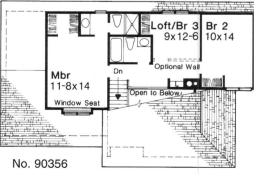

Loft/Br 3 9x12-6   Br 2 10x14

Dn

Optional Wall

Mbr 11-8x14

Open to Below

Window Seat

No. 90356

UPPER FLOOR PLAN

Balcony Overlooks Living Room Below

▪ This plan features:

— Three bedrooms

— Two full and one half baths

▪ A vaulted ceiling Living Room with a balcony above and a fireplace

▪ An efficient, well-equipped Kitchen with stovetop island and easy flow of traffic into the Dining Room

▪ A deck accessible from the Living Room

▪ A luxurious Master Suite with a bay window seat, walk-in closet, dressing area, and a private shower

▪ Two additional bedrooms that share a full hall bath

MAIN FLOOR — 674 SQ. FT.
UPPER FLOOR — 677 SQ. FT.

TOTAL LIVING AREA:
1,351 SQ. FT.

Refer to **Pricing Schedule A** on the order form for pricing information

For an Established Neighborhood

■ This plan features:

— Three bedrooms

— Two full baths

■ A covered entrance sheltering and welcoming visitors

■ A Living Room enhanced by natural light streaming in from the large front window

■ A bayed formal Dining Room with direct access to the Sun Deck and the Living Room

■ An efficient, galley Kitchen

■ An informal Breakfast Room with direct access to the Sun Deck

■ A large Master Suite equipped with a walk-in closet and a full private Bath

■ Two additional bedrooms that share a full hall bath

MAIN AREA — 1,276 SQ. FT.
FINISHED STAIRCASE — 16 SQ. FT.
BASEMENT — 392 SQ. FT.
GARAGE — 728 SQ. FT.

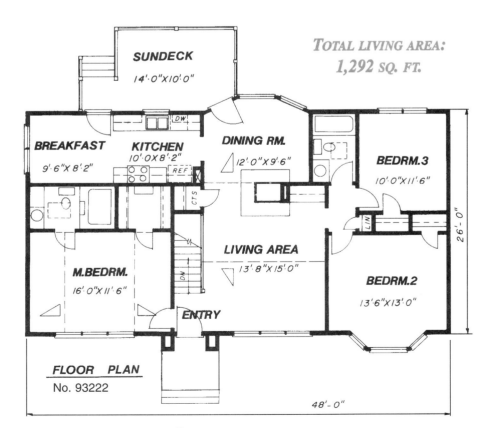

TOTAL LIVING AREA: 1,292 SQ. FT.

SUNDECK 14'-0"X10'-0"

BREAKFAST 9'-6"X8'-2"

KITCHEN 10'-0X8'-2"

DINING RM. 12'-0"X9'-6"

BEDRM.3 10'-0"X11'-6"

REF

CTS

DW

LIVING AREA 13'-8"X15'-0"

M.BEDRM. 16'-0"X11'-6"

BEDRM.2 13'-6"X13'-0"

ENTRY

26'-0"

48'-0"

FLOOR PLAN No. 93222

An EXCLUSIVE DESIGN
By Jannis Vann & Associates, Inc.

130

To order your Blueprints, call 1-800-235-5700

WIDTH 58'-0"
DEPTH 44'-0"

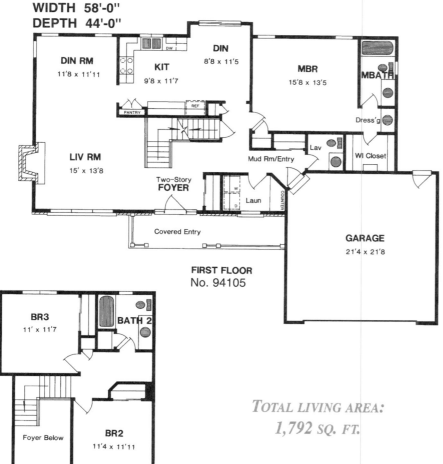

DIN RM
11'8 x 11'11

KIT
9'8 x 11'7

DIN
8'8 x 11'5

MBR
15'8 x 13'5

MBATH

DW

PANTRY

REF

Dress'g

LIV RM
15' x 13'8

Mud Rm/Entry

Lav

WI Closet

Two-Story
FOYER

W
D

Laun

COUNTER

Covered Entry

GARAGE
21'4 x 21'8

FIRST FLOOR
No. 94105

BR3
11' x 11'7

BATH 2

Foyer Below

BR2
11'4 x 11'11

SECOND FLOOR

TOTAL LIVING AREA:
1,792 SQ. FT.

Classic Style and Comfort

▪ This plan features:

— Three bedrooms

— Two full and one half bath

▪ Covered Entry leads into two-story Foyer with a dramatic landing staircase brightened by decorative window

▪ Spacious Living/Dining Room combination with hearth fireplace and decorative windows

▪ Hub Kitchen with built-in pantry and informal Dining area with sliding glass door to rear yard

▪ First floor Master Bedroom offers a walk-in closet, dressing area and full bath

▪ Two additional bedrooms on second floor share a full bath

▪ No materials list is available for this plan

FIRST FLOOR — 1,281 SQ. FT.
SECOND FLOOR —511 SQ. FT.
GARAGE — 481 SQ. FT.

Gingerbread Charm

■ This plan features:

— Three bedrooms

— Two and one half baths

■ A wrap-around porch and rear deck adding lots of outdoor living space

■ A formal Parlor and Dining Room just off the central entry

■ A Family Room with a fireplace

■ A Master Suite complete with a five-sided sitting nook, walk-in closets and a sunken tub

FIRST FLOOR — 1,260 SQ. FT.
SECOND FLOOR — 1,021 SQ. FT.
BASEMENT — 1,186 SQ. FT.
GARAGE — 851 SQ. FT.

TOTAL LIVING AREA:
2,281 SQ. FT.

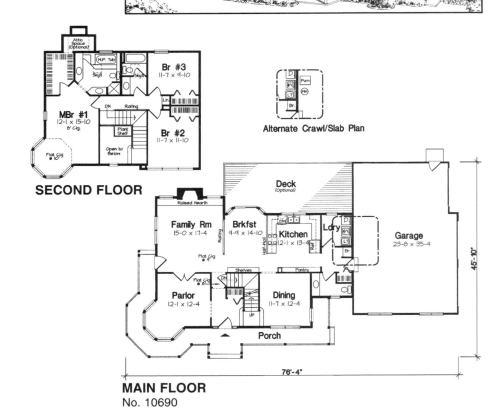

SECOND FLOOR

Alternate Crawl/Slab Plan

MAIN FLOOR
No. 10690

TOTAL LIVING AREA:
1,613 SQ. FT.

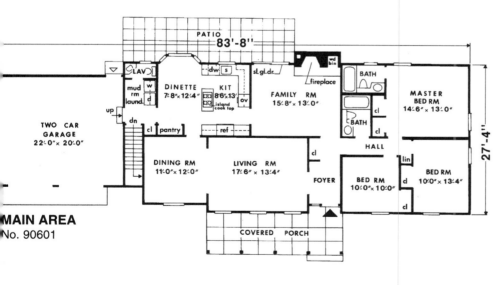

MAIN AREA
No. 90601

Varied Roof Heights Create Interesting Lines

This plan features:

— Three bedrooms

— Two full and one half baths

A spacious Family Room with a heat-circulating fireplace, which is visible from the Foyer

A large Kitchen with a cooktop island, opening into the dinette bay

A Master Suite with his-n-her closets and a private Master Bath

Two additional bedrooms which share a full hall bath

Formal Dining and Living Rooms, flowing into each other for easy entertaining

MAIN FLOOR — 1,613 SQ. FT.
BASEMENT — 1,060 SQ. FT.
GARAGE — 461 SQ. FT.

Refer to **Pricing Schedule B** on the order form for pricing information

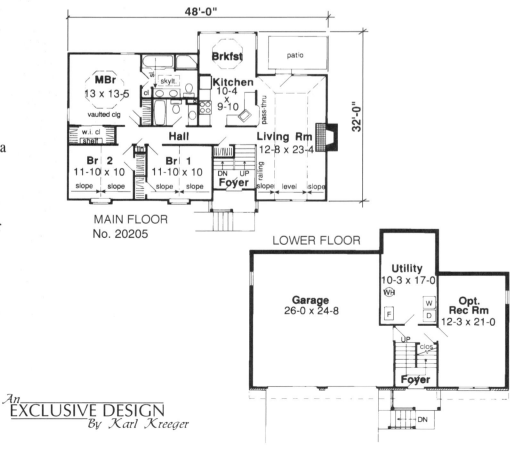

Small But Room To Grow

■ This plan features:

— Three Bedrooms

— Two full Baths

■ A Master Suite with a vaulted ceiling and its own skylit Bath

■ A fireplaced Living Room with a sloped ceiling

■ Efficient Kitchen with a Breakfast Nook

■ Options for growth on the lower level

MAIN FLOOR — 1,321 SQ. FT.
LOWER FLOOR — 286 SQ. FT.
GARAGE — 655 SQ. FT.

TOTAL LIVING AREA:
1,607 SQ. FT.

MAIN FLOOR
No. 20205

48'-0"
32'-0"

MBr 13 x 13-5 vaulted clg

w.i. cl shelf

skylt.

Brkfst

patio

Kitchen 10-4 x 9-10

pass-thru

Hall

Br 2 11-10 x 10 slope slope

Br 1 11-10 x 10 slope slope

DN UP **Foyer** railing

Living Rm 12-8 x 23-4 slope level slope

LOWER FLOOR

Garage 26-0 x 24-8

Utility 10-3 x 17-0 WH

F

W D

Opt. Rec Rm 12-3 x 21-0

UP clos

DN

Foyer

An EXCLUSIVE DESIGN *By Karl Kreeger*

© 1996 Donald A Gardner Architects, Inc.

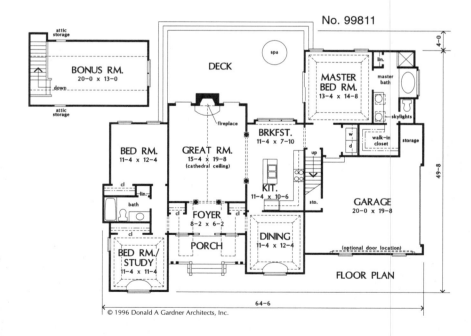

No. 99811

FLOOR PLAN

© 1996 Donald A Gardner Architects, Inc.

TOTAL LIVING AREA:
1,699 SQ. FT.

Cathedral Ceiling Enlarges Great Room

■ This plan features:

— Three bedrooms

— Two full baths

■ Two dormers add volume to the Foyer

■ Great Room, topped by a cathedral ceiling, is open to the Kitchen and Breakfast area

■ Accent columns define the Foyer, Great Room, Kitchen and Breakfast area

■ Private Master Suite crowned in a tray ceiling and highlighted by a skylit bath

■ Front bedroom topped by a tray ceiling

MAIN FLOOR — 1,699 SQ. FT.
GARAGE — 498 SQ. FT.
BONUS — 336 SQ. FT.

Refer to **Pricing Schedule B** on the order form for pricing information

Family Room With Fireplace

■ This plan features:

— Four bedrooms

— One full, one half, and one three quarter baths

■ A lovely Front Porch shading the entrance

■ A spacious Living Room that opens into the Dining Area which flows into the efficient Kitchen

■ A Family Room equipped with a cozy fireplace and sliding glass doors to a Patio

■ A Master Suite with a large walk-in closet and a private bath with a step-in shower

■ Three additional bedrooms that share a full hall bath

FIRST FLOOR — 692 SQ. FT.
SECOND FLOOR — 813 SQ. FT.
BASEMENT — 699 SQ. FT.
GARAGE — 484 SQ. FT.

TOTAL LIVING AREA:
1,505 SQ. FT.

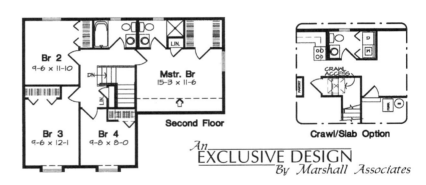

Br 2
9-6 x 11-10

Mstr. Br
15-3 x 11-6

Br 3
9-6 x 12-1

Br 4
9-8 x 8-0

Second Floor

CRAWL ACCESS

Crawl/Slab Option

An
EXCLUSIVE DESIGN
By Marshall Associates

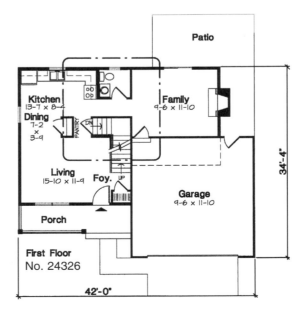

Patio

Kitchen
13-7 x 8-4

Dining
7-2 x 3-9

Family
9-6 x 11-10

Living
15-10 x 11-9

Foy.

Garage
9-6 x 11-10

Porch

34'-4"

First Floor
No. 24326

42'-0"

To order your Blueprints, call 1-800-235-5700

© Frank E. Betz

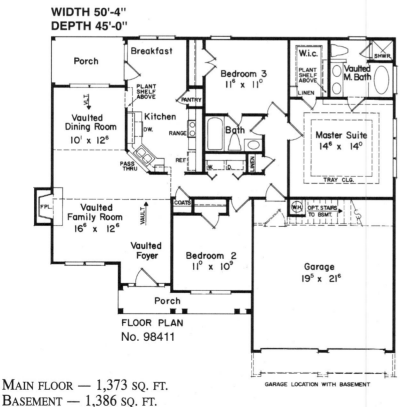

WIDTH 50'-4"
DEPTH 45'-0"

Porch

Breakfast

Bedroom 3
11⁶ x 11⁰

W.i.c.

PLANT SHELF ABOVE

LINEN

SHWR

Vaulted M. Bath

PLANT SHELF ABOVE

VLT

Vaulted Dining Room
10¹ x 12⁶

PANTRY

Kitchen

DW.

RANGE

REF

Bath

Master Suite
14⁶ x 14⁰

PASS THRU

W. D.

LINEN

TRAY CLG.

FPL.

VAULT

Vaulted Family Room
16⁶ x 12⁶

COATS

W.H.

OPT. STAIRS TO BSMT.

Vaulted Foyer

Bedroom 2
11⁰ x 10⁹

Garage
19⁵ x 21⁶

Porch

FLOOR PLAN
No. 98411

GARAGE LOCATION WITH BASEMENT

MAIN FLOOR — 1,373 SQ. FT.
BASEMENT — 1,386 SQ. FT.

TOTAL LIVING AREA:
1,373 SQ. FT.

Style and Convenience

■ This plan features:

— Three bedrooms

— Two full baths

■ Large front windows, dormers and an old-fashioned porch giving a pleasing style to the home

■ A vaulted ceiling topping the Foyer flowing into the Family Room which is highlighted by a fireplace

■ A Formal Dining Room flowing from the Family Room crowned in an elegant vaulted ceiling

■ An efficient Kitchen enhanced by a pantry, a pass through to the Family Room and direct access to the Dining Room and Breakfast Room

■ A decorative tray ceiling, a five-piece private bath and a walk-in closet in the Master Suite

■ An optional basement or crawl space foundation — please specify when ordering

Refer to **Pricing Schedule B** on the order form for pricing information

Convenient Country

■ This plan features:

— Three bedrooms

— Two full and one half baths

■ Full front Porch provides comfortable visiting area and a sheltered entrance

■ Expansive Living Room with an inviting fireplace opens to bright Dining Room and Kitchen

■ U-shaped Kitchen with peninsula serving counter, Dining Room and nearby Pantry, Laundry and Garage entry

■ Secluded Master Bedroom with two closets and a double vanity bath

■ Two second floor bedrooms with ample closets and dormer windows, share a full bath

■ No materials list is available for this plan

FIRST FLOOR — 1,108 SQ. FT.
SECOND FLOOR — 659 SQ. FT.
BASEMENT — 875 SQ. FT.

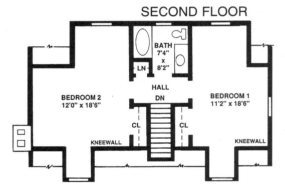

SECOND FLOOR

BEDROOM 2
12'0" x 18'6"

BATH
7'4" x 8'2"

LN

HALL
DN

BEDROOM 1
11'2" x 18'6"

CL   CL

KNEEWALL   KNEEWALL

WIDTH 67'-0"
DEPTH 30'-0"

2 CAR GARAGE
21'2" x 22'2"

PANTRY   PR   DW   REF

DINING ROOM
8'1" x 11'4"

WIC
6'2" x 7'2"

MASTER BATH
8'10" x 10'4"

HALL

KITCHEN
8'11" x 11'4"

CL   CL

LAUNDRY
7'6" x 7'8"

L
W
D

RANGE

LIVING ROOM
13'2" x 20'2"

FIREPLACE

DN

UP

LN   CL

MASTER BEDROOM
13'2" x 13'8"

PORCH

TOTAL LIVING AREA: 1,767 SQ. FT.

FIRST FLOOR
No. 99045

To order your Blueprints, call 1-800-235-5700

PLAN NO. 92238

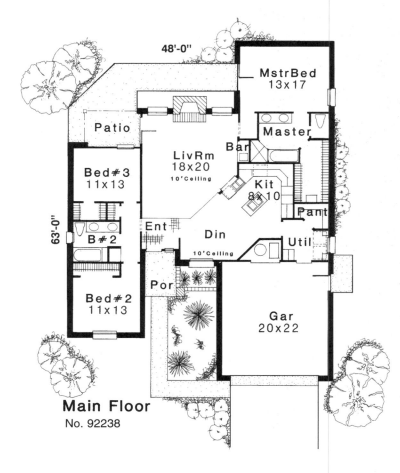

48'-0"

63'-0"

MstrBed
13x17

Patio

LivRm
18x20
10'Ceiling

Bar

Master

Bed #3
11x13

Kit
8x10

Pant

Ent

B # 2

Din
10'Ceiling

Util

Bed #2
11x13

Por

Gar
20x22

Main Floor
No. 92238

TOTAL LIVING AREA:
1,664 sq. ft.

Easy Everyday Living

◼ This plan features:

— Three bedrooms

— Two full baths

◼ Front entrance accented by segmented arches, sidelight and transom windows

◼ Open Living Room with focal point fireplace, wetbar and access to Patio

◼ Dining area open to both the Living Room and Kitchen

◼ Efficient Kitchen with a cooktop island, walk-in pantry and Utility area with a Garage entry

◼ Large walk-in closet, double vanity bath and access to Patio featured in the Master Bedroom

◼ Two additional bedrooms share a double vanity bath

◼ No materials list is available for this plan

MAIN FLOOR — 1,664 SQ. FT.
BASEMENT — 1,600 SQ. FT.
GARAGE — 440 SQ. FT

Refer to **Pricing Schedule A** on the order form for pricing information

Lovely Second Home

■ This plan features:

— Three bedrooms

— One full and one three-quarter baths

■ Firedrum fireplace warming both entryway and Living Room

■ Dining and Living Rooms opening onto the deck, which surrounds the house on three sides

FIRST FLOOR — 808 SQ. FT.
SECOND FLOOR — 288 SQ. FT.

TOTAL LIVING AREA:
1,096 SQ. FT.

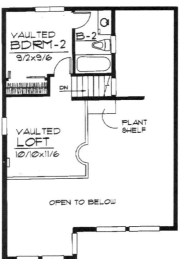

UPPER FLOOR PLAN

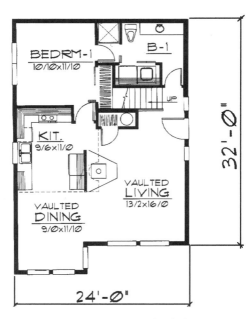

MAIN FLOOR PLAN
No. 91002

To order your Blueprints, call 1-800-235-5700

Refer to **Pricing Schedule A** on the order form for pricing information

An EXCLUSIVE DESIGN
By Westhome Planners, Ltd.

MAIN AREA
No. 90905

TOTAL LIVING AREA:
1,314 SQ. FT.

Compact Home is Surprisingly Spacious

■ This plan features:

— Three bedrooms

— One full and one three quarter baths

■ A spacious Living Room warmed by a fireplace

■ A Dining Room flowing off the Living Room, with sliding glass doors to the deck

■ An efficient, well-equipped Kitchen with a snack bar, double sink, and ample cabinet and counter space

■ A Master Suite with a walk-in closet and private full bath

■ Two additional, roomy bedrooms with ample closet space and protection from street noise from the two-car garage

MAIN AREA — 1,314 SQ. FT.
BASEMENT — 1,488 SQ. FT.
GARAGE — 484 SQ. FT.
WIDTH — 50'-0"
DEPTH — 54'-0"

Refer to **Pricing Schedule C** on the order form for pricing information

Special Details

■ This plan features:

— Four bedrooms

— Two full and one half baths

■ Two-story Foyer with a plant shelf and lovely railing staircase

■ Great Room with corner fireplace and access to rear yard topped by two-story ceiling

■ Kitchen with peninsula counter, walk-in pantry, Breakfast bay and access to Deck, Laundry, Garage entry and formal Dining Room

■ Secluded Master Bedroom offers a sloped ceiling and lavish bath

■ Three bedrooms on second floor share a double vanity bath

■ No materials list is available for this plan

FIRST FLOOR — 1,511 SQ. FT.
SECOND FLOOR — 646 SQ. FT.
BASEMENT — 1,479 SQ. FT.
GARAGE — 475 SQ. FT.

TOTAL LIVING AREA:
2,157 SQ. FT.

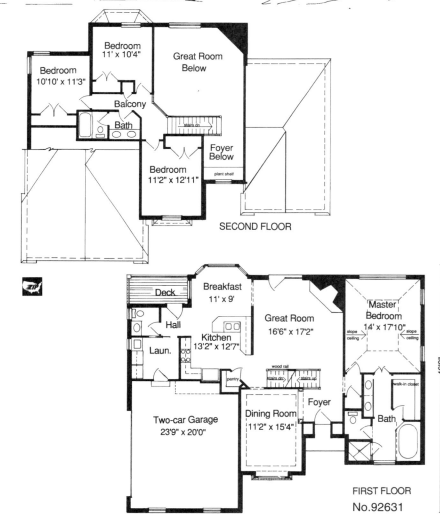

SECOND FLOOR

Bedroom 11' x 10'4"
Bedroom 10'10' x 11'3"
Great Room Below
Balcony
Bath
Bedroom 11'2" x 12'11"
Foyer Below
plant shelf
stairs dn.

FIRST FLOOR
No. 92631

Deck
Breakfast 11' x 9'
Great Room 16'6" x 17'2"
Master Bedroom 14' x 17'10"
slope ceiling
Hall
Kitchen 13'2" x 12'7"
Laun.
wood rail
stairs dn. stairs up.
pantry
Two-car Garage 23'9" x 20'0"
Dining Room 11'2" x 15'4"
Foyer
walk-in closet
Bath

54'8"
49'8"

To order your Blueprints, call 1-800-235-5700

Second Floor
No. 19422

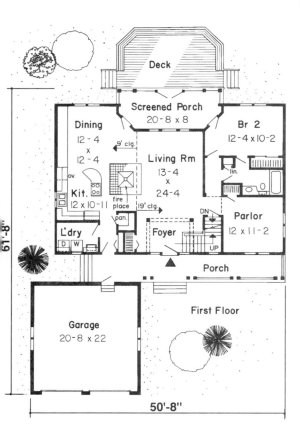

First Floor

FIRST FLOOR — 1,290 SQ. FT.
SECOND FLOOR — 405 SQ. FT.
SCREENED PORCH — 152 SQ. FT.
GARAGE — 513 SQ. FT.

TOTAL LIVING AREA:
1,695 SQ. FT.

Master Retreat Crowns Spacious Home

■ This plan features:

— Two bedrooms

— Two full baths

■ An open Foyer leading up an landing staircase with windows above and into a two-story Living Room

■ A unique four-sided fireplace separates the Living Room, Dining area and Kitchen

■ A well-equipped Kitchen featuring a cook island, a walk-in pantry and easy access to Dining area and Laundry room

■ A three season Screened Porch and Deck beyond adjoining Dining Room, Living Room, and second Bedroom

■ An private Master Suite on the second floor offering a cozy, dormer window seat, private balcony, and window tub in the spacious Bath

Refer to **Pricing Schedule C** on the order form for pricing information

© 1997 Donald A. Gardner Architects, Inc.

B. NATHAN

Casual Country Charmer

■ This plan features:

— Three bedrooms

— Two full baths

■ Columns and arches frame the front Porch

■ The open floor plan combines the Great Room, Kitchen and Dining Room

■ The Kitchen offers a convenient breakfast bar for meals on the run

■ The Master Suite features a private bath oasis

■ Secondary bedrooms share a full bath with a dual vanity

MAIN FLOOR — 1,770 SQ. FT.
BONUS — 401 SQ. FT.
GARAGE — 630 SQ. FT.

TOTAL LIVING AREA:
1,770 SQ. FT.

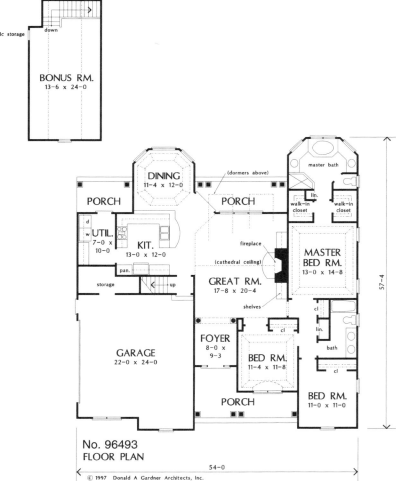

To order your Blueprints, call 1-800-235-5700

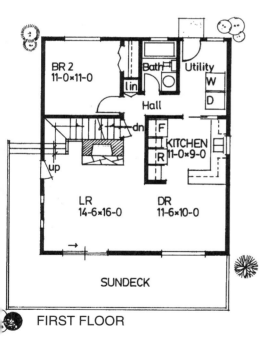

SUNDECK

FIRST FLOOR

BR 2 11-0×11-0

Bath

Utility

W

D

Lin

Hall

dn

F

R

KITCHEN 11-0×9-0

up

LR 14-6×16-0

DR 11-6×10-0

An EXCLUSIVE DESIGN *By Westhome Planners, Ltd.*

WIDTH 27'-0"
DEPTH 32'-0"

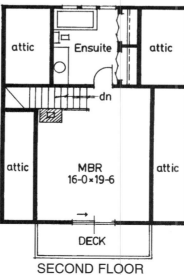

attic

Ensuite

attic

dn

attic

MBR 16-0×19-6

attic

DECK

SECOND FLOOR
No. 90847

Versatile Chalet

■ This plan features:

— Two bedrooms

— Two full baths

■ A Sun deck entry into a spacious Living Room/Dining Room with a fieldstone fireplace, a large window and a sliding glass door

■ A well-appointed Kitchen with extended counter space and easy access to the Dining Room and the Utility area

■ A first floor bedroom adjoins a full hall bath

■ A spacious Master Bedroom, with a private Deck, a Suite bath and plenty of storage

FIRST FLOOR — 864 SQ. FT.
SECOND FLOOR — 496 SQ. FT.
BASEMENT — 864 SQ. FT.

TOTAL LIVING AREA:
1,360 SQ. FT.

Refer to **Pricing Schedule B** on the order form for pricing information

© 1995 Donald A Gardner Architects, Inc.

Amenities of a Larger Home

■ This plan features:
— Three bedrooms
— Two full baths

■ A continuous cathedral ceiling in the Great Room, Kitchen, and Dining Room giving a spacious feel to this efficient plan

■ Skylighted Kitchen with a seven foot high wall by the Great Room and a popular plant shelf

■ Master Bedroom opens up with a cathedral ceiling and contains walk-in and linen closets and a private bath with garden tub and dual vanity

■ Cathedral ceiling as the crowing touch to the front bedrooms/study

MAIN FLOOR — 1,253 SQ. FT.
GARAGE & STORAGE — 420 SQ. FT.

TOTAL LIVING AREA:
1,253 SQ. FT.

DECK

SCREEN PORCH
10-0 x 11-4

DINING
10-0 x 11-0
(cathedral ceiling)

sto.

master bath

MASTER BED RM.
11-8 x 14-4
(cathedral ceiling)

GARAGE
19-4 x 20-4

skylight

KIT.
11-8 x 9-4

pan.

UTIL.
d   w

lin.

walk-in closet

cl   cl

plant shelf above

(cathedral ceiling)

GREAT RM.
15-8 x 15-4

fireplace

BED RM.
13-4 x 10-0

bath

skylight

PORCH

BED RM./ STUDY
11-0 x 11-4
(cathedral ceiling)

cl

10-0

48-0

60-0

FLOOR PLAN
No. 99858

© 1995   Donald A Gardner Architects, Inc.

To order your Blueprints, call 1-800-235-5700

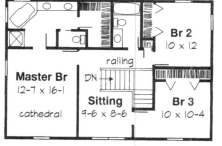

SECOND FLOOR
No. 24400

Master Br
12-7 x 16-1
cathedral

Br 2
10 x 12

railing

DN

Sitting
9-6 x 8-6

Br 3
10 x 10-4

crawl access → Dining Furn. w/h

An
EXCLUSIVE DESIGN
By Upright Design

Living
21-2 x 12-4
decor clg.

Kitchen
14-11 x 12-4

Storage/Shop
16-2 x 12-7

Den/
Guest
10 x 10

Dining
10 x 12-3
decor clg.

Garage
23-2 x 19-3

39'-6"

67'-6"

FIRST FLOOR

National Treasure

◾ This plan features:

— Three bedrooms

— Two full and one half baths

◾ A wrap-around Covered Porch

◾ Decorative vaulted ceilings in the fireplaced Living room

◾ A large Kitchen with central island/breakfast bar

◾ A sun-lit Sitting Area

FIRST FLOOR — 1,034 SQ. FT.
SECOND FLOOR — 944 SQ. FT.
BASEMENT — 944 SQ. FT.
GARAGE & STORAGE — 675 SQ. FT.

TOTAL LIVING AREA:
1,978 SQ. FT.

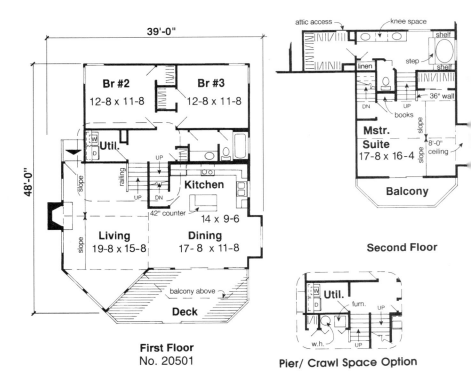

Refer to **Pricing Schedule C** on the order form for pricing information

Home on a Hill

- This plan features:

— Three bedrooms

— Two full baths

- Window walls combining with sliders to unite active areas with a huge outdoor deck

- Interior spaces flowing together for an open feeling, that is accentuated by the sloping ceilings and towering fireplace in the Living Room

- An island Kitchen with easy access to the Dining Room

- A Master Suite complete with a garden spa, abundant closet space and a balcony

FIRST FLOOR — 1,316 SQ. FT.
SECOND FLOOR — 592 SQ. FT.

TOTAL LIVING AREA:
1,908 SQ. FT.

First Floor
No. 20501

39'-0"
48'-0"

Br #2
12-8 x 11-8

Br #3
12-8 x 11-8

Util.

Kitchen
14 x 9-6

42" counter

Living
19-8 x 15-8

Dining
17-8 x 11-8

balcony above

Deck

Second Floor

attic access
knee space
shelf
linen
step
shelf
books
36" wall

Mstr.
Suite
17-8 x 16-4

8'-0"
ceiling

Balcony

Pier/ Crawl Space Option

Util.
furn.
w.h.

To order your Blueprints, call 1-800-235-5700

Refer to **Pricing Schedule C** on the order form for pricing information

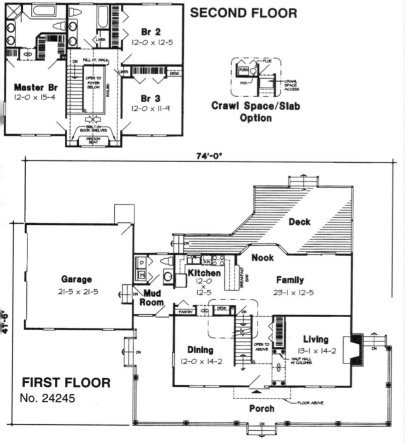

SECOND FLOOR

Master Br
12-0 x 15-4

Br 2
12-0 x 12-5

Br 3
12-0 x 11-9

OPEN TO FOYER BELOW

FULL HT. WALLS

LINEN

DESK

BUILT-IN BOOK SHELVES

WINDOW SEAT

Crawl Space/Slab Option

FURN

FLUE

CRAWL SPACE ACCESS

74'-0"

41'-6"

Garage
21-5 x 21-5

Mud Room

Deck

Nook

Kitchen
12-0 x 12-5

Family
23-1 x 12-5

BREAKFAST BAR

PANTRY

DESK

OPEN TO ABOVE

Dining
12-0 x 14-2

Living
13-1 x 14-2

HALF WALL W/ COLUMNS

FLOOR ABOVE

Porch

FIRST FLOOR
No. 24245

Old-Fashioned Wrap-Around Porch

■ This plan features:

— Three bedrooms

— Two full and one half baths

■ Formal areas flanking the entry hall

■ A Living Room that includes a fireplace

■ Direct access from the formal Dining Room to the Kitchen

■ A U-shaped Kitchen including a breakfast bar, built-in Pantry and a planning desk

■ A Mudroom entry

■ An expansive Family Room with direct access to the rear deck

■ A Master Suite highlighted by a walk-in closet and a private Master Bath

FIRST FLOOR — 1,113 SQ. FT.
SECOND FLOOR — 970 SQ. FT.
GARAGE — 480 SQ. FT.
BASEMENT — 1,113 SQ. FT.

TOTAL LIVING AREA:
2,083 SQ. FT.

To order your Blueprints, call 1-800-235-5700

PLAN NO. 20220

Refer to **Pricing Schedule B** on the order form for pricing information

Traditional Ranch

■ This plan features:

— Three bedrooms

— Two full baths

■ A large front palladium window that gives this home great curb appeal, and allows a view of the front yard from the Living Room

■ A vaulted ceiling in the Living Room, adding to the architectural interest and the spacious feel of the room

■ Sliding glass doors in the Dining Room that lead to a wood deck

■ A built-in pantry, double sink and breakfast bar in the efficient Kitchen

■ A Master Suite that includes a walk-in closet and a private bath with a double vanity

■ Two additional bedrooms that share a full hall bath

MAIN AREA —1,568 SQ. FT.
BASEMENT — 1,568 SQ. FT.
GARAGE — 509 SQ. FT.

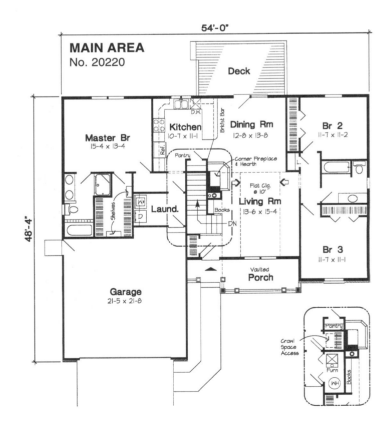

MAIN AREA
No. 20220

54'-0"

48'-4"

Master Br 15-4 x 13-4

Kitchen 10-7 x 11-1

Dining Rm 12-8 x 13-8

Br 2 11-7 x 11-2

Laund.

Living Rm 13-6 x 15-4

Br 3 11-7 x 11-2

Garage 21-5 x 21-8

Vaulted Porch

Deck

An EXCLUSIVE DESIGN *By Karl Kreeger*

TOTAL LIVING AREA: *1,568* SQ. FT.

To order your Blueprints, call 1-800-235-5700

© 1996 Donald A Gardner Architects, Inc.

P L A N N O . 9 9 8 1 2

Sunny Dormer Brightens Foyer

- ■ This plan features:
  - —Three bedrooms
  - —Two full baths
- ■ Today's comforts with cost effective construction
- ■ Open Great room, Dining Room, and Kitchen topped by a cathedral ceiling emphasizing spaciousness
- ■ Adjoining Deck providing extra living or entertaining room
- ■ Front bedroom crowned in cathedral ceiling and pampered by a private bath with garden tub, dual vanity and a walk-in closet
- ■ Skylit Bonus Room above the garage offering flexibility and opportunity for growth

MAIN FLOOR — 1,386 SQ. FT.
GARAGE — 517 SQ. FT.
BONUS ROOM — 314 SQ. FT.

TOTAL LIVING AREA:
1,386 SQ. FT.

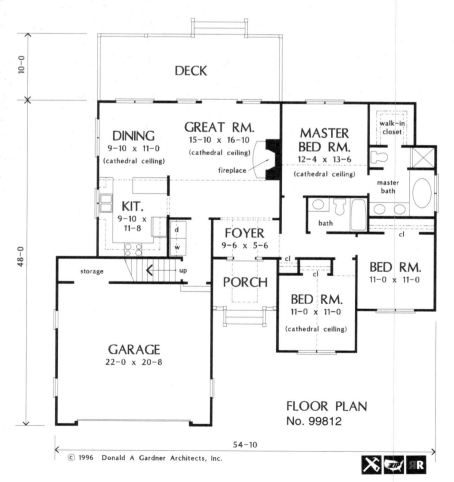

DECK

DINING
9–10 x 11–0
(cathedral ceiling)

GREAT RM.
15–10 x 16–10
(cathedral ceiling)

fireplace

MASTER
BED RM.
12–4 x 13–6
(cathedral ceiling)

walk-in closet

master bath

KIT.
9–10 x 11–8

d
w

FOYER
9–6 x 5–6

bath

cl

storage

up

PORCH

cl
cl

BED RM.
11–0 x 11–0

GARAGE
22–0 x 20–8

BED RM.
11–0 x 11–0
(cathedral ceiling)

10–0

48–0

54–10

FLOOR PLAN
No. 99812

© 1996   Donald A Gardner Architects, Inc.

To order your Blueprints, call 1-800-235-5700

Refer to **Pricing Schedule B** on the order form for pricing information

Keystone Arches and Decorative Windows

© design basics, inc.

■ This plan features:

— Three bedrooms

— One full and one three quarter baths

■ Brick and stucco enhance the dramatic front elevation and volume entrance

■ Inviting Entry leads into expansive Great Room with hearth fireplace framed by transom window

■ Bay window Dining Room topped by decorative ceiling convenient to the Great Room and the Kitchen/Breakfast area

■ Corner Master Suite enjoys a tray ceiling, roomy walk-in closet and a plush bath with a double vanity and whirlpool window tub

■ Two additional bedrooms with large closets, share a full bath

MAIN FLOOR — 1,666 SQ. FT.
BASEMENT — 1,666 SQ. FT.
GARAGE — 496 SQ. FT.

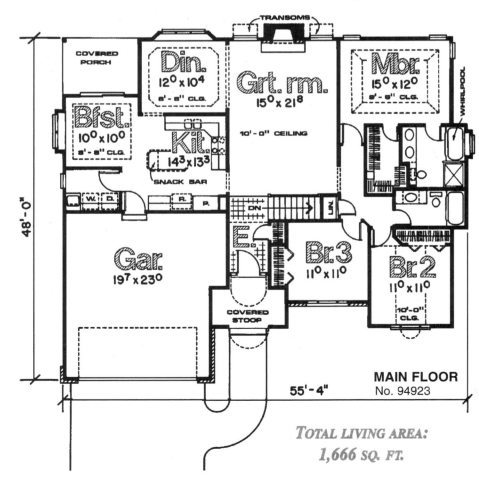

TRANSOMS

Din.
12⁰ x 10⁴
8'-8" CLG.

Grt. rm.
15⁰ x 21⁸
10'-0" CEILING

Mbr.
15⁰ x 12⁰
8'-8" CLG.

COVERED PORCH

Bfst.
10⁰ x 10⁰
8'-8" CLG.

Kit.
14³ x 13³

SNACK BAR

WHIRLPOOL

W. D.

R. P.

DN

LIN

Gar.
19⁷ x 23⁰

Br.3
11⁰ x 11⁰

Br.2
11⁰ x 11⁰
10'-0" CLG.

COVERED STOOP

48'-0"

55'-4"

MAIN FLOOR
No. 94923

TOTAL LIVING AREA:
1,666 SQ. FT.

To order your Blueprints, call 1-800-235-5700

Refer to **Pricing Schedule B** on the order form for pricing information

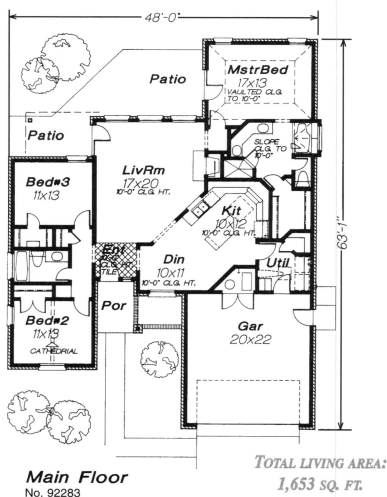

Main Floor
No. 92283

48'-0"

63'-1"

Patio

MstrBed
17x13
VAULTED CLG.
TO 10'-0"

SLOPE
CLG. TO
10'-0"

Patio

LivRm
17x20
10'-0" CLG. HT.

Bed#3
11x13

Kit
10x12
10'-0" CLG. HT.

Ent
CLG
TILE

Din
10x11
10'-0" CLG. HT.

Util

Por

Bed#2
11x13
CATHEDRIAL

Gar
20x22

TOTAL LIVING AREA:
1,653 SQ. FT.

Style and Convenience

■ This plan features:

— Three bedrooms

— Two full baths

■ A sheltered Porch leads into an easy-care tiled Entry

■ Spacious Living Room offers a cozy fireplace, triple window and access to Patio

■ An efficient Kitchen with a skylight, work island, Dining area, walk-in pantry and Utility/Garage entry

■ Secluded Master Bedroom highlighted by a vaulted ceiling, access to Patio and a lavish bath

■ Two additional bedrooms, one with a cathedral ceiling, share a full bath

■ No materials list available for this plan

MAIN FLOOR — 1,653 SQ. FT.
GARAGE — 420 SQ. FT.

Refer to **Pricing Schedule A** on
the order form for pricing information

Inviting Porch Adorns Affordable Home

■ This plan features:

— Three bedrooms

— Two full baths

■ A large and spacious Living Room that adjoins the Dining Room for ease in entertaining

■ A private bedroom wing offering a quiet atmosphere

■ A Master Bedroom with his-n-her closets and a private bath

■ An efficient Kitchen with a walk-in pantry

MAIN AREA — 1,160 SQ. FT.
LAUNDRY/MUDROOM — 83 SQ. FT.

TOTAL LIVING AREA:
1,243 SQ. FT.

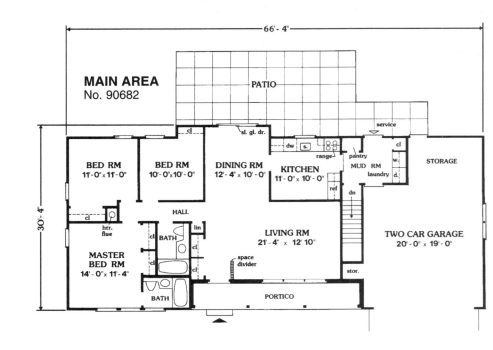

MAIN AREA
No. 90682

To order your Blueprints, call 1-800-235-5700

FIRST FLOOR — 905 SQ. FT.
SECOND FLOOR — 863 SQ. FT.
BASEMENT — 905 SQ. FT.
GARAGE — 487 SQ. FT.

TOTAL LIVING AREA:
1,768 SQ. FT.

© design basics, inc.

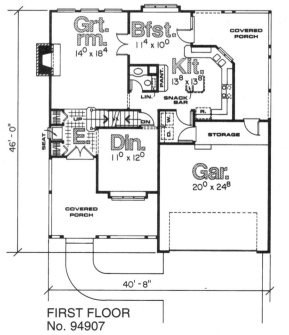

FIRST FLOOR
No. 94907

SECOND FLOOR

Victorian Accents

■ This plan features:

— Three bedrooms

— Two full and one half baths

■ Covered Porch and double doors lead into Entry accented by a window seat and curved banister staircase

■ Decorative windows overlooking the backyard and a large fireplace highlight Great Room

■ A hub Kitchen with an island/snack bar and large pantry acesses the formal Dining Room and Breakfast area

■ Powder room, laundry area, Garage entry and storage nearby to Kitchen

■ Cathedral ceiling crowns Master Bedroom with two walk-in closets, dual vanity and a whirlpool tub

■ Two additional bedrooms, one with a vaulted ceiling above a window seat, share a full bath

Bathed in Natural Light

- This plan features:
  - — Three bedrooms
  - — Two full and one half baths
- A high arched window illuminates the Foyer and adds style to the exterior of the home
- Vaulted ceilings in the formal Dining Room, Breakfast Room and Great Room create volume
- The Master Suite is crowned with a decorative tray ceiling
- The Master Bath has a double vanity, oval tub, separate shower and a walk-in closet
- Two additional bedrooms, a full bath and a loft highlight the second floor
- The Loft has the option of becoming a fourth bedroom
- An optional basement or a crawl space foundation available — please specify when ordering

FIRST FLOOR — 1,133 SQ. FT.
SECOND FLOOR — 486 SQ. FT.
BASEMENT — 1,133 SQ. FT.
BONUS — 134 SQ. FT.
GARAGE — 406 SQ. FT.

TOTAL LIVING AREA:
1,619 SQ. FT.

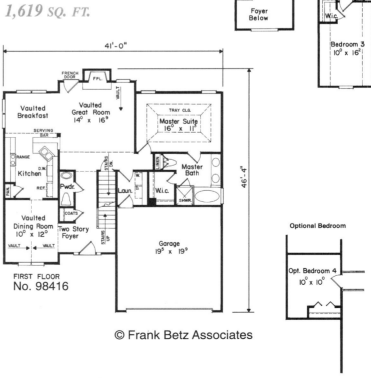

© Frank Betz Associates

To order your Blueprints, call 1-800-235-5700

Cathedral Ceiling in Living Room and Master Suite

■ This plan features:

— Three bedrooms

— Two full baths

■ A spacious Living Room with a cathedral ceiling and elegant fireplace

■ A Dining Room that adjoins both the Living Room and the Kitchen

■ An efficient Kitchen, with double sinks, ample cabinet space and peninsula counter that doubles as an eating bar

■ A convenient hallway laundry center

■ A Master Suite with a cathedral ceiling and a private Master Bath

MAIN AREA — 1,346 SQ. FT.
GARAGE — 449 SQ. FT.

TOTAL LIVING AREA:
1,346 SQ. FT.

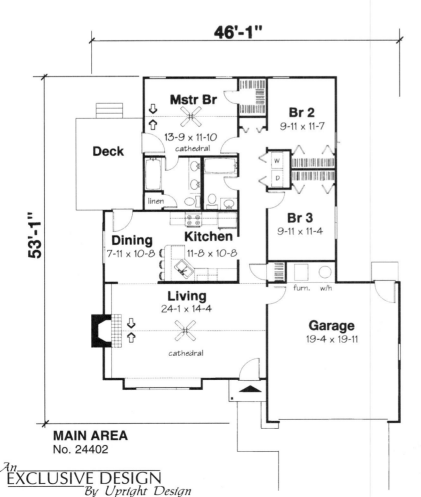

46'-1"

53'-1"

Deck

Mstr Br
13-9 x 11-10
cathedral

Br 2
9-11 x 11-7

w
D

linen

Br 3
9-11 x 11-4

Dining
7-11 x 10-8

Kitchen
11-8 x 10-8

furn.   w/h

Living
24-1 x 14-4
cathedral

Garage
19-4 x 19-11

MAIN AREA
No. 24402

An
EXCLUSIVE DESIGN
By Upright Design

Refer to **Pricing Schedule A** on the order form for pricing information

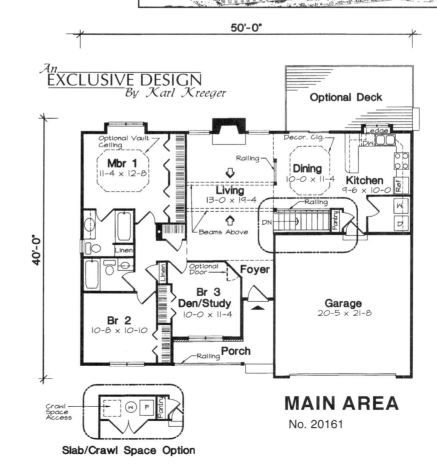

Delightful Doll House

■ This plan features:

— Three bedrooms

— Two full baths

■ A sloped ceiling in the Living Room which also has a focal point fireplace

■ An efficient Kitchen with a peninsula counter and a built-in pantry

■ A decorative ceiling and sliding glass doors to the deck in the Dining Room

■ A Master Suite with a decorative ceiling, ample closet space and a private full bath

■ Two additional bedrooms that share a full hall bath

MAIN FLOOR — 1,307 SQ. FT.
BASEMENT — 1,298 SQ. FT.
GARAGE — 462 SQ. FT.

TOTAL LIVING AREA:
1,307 SQ. FT.

An
EXCLUSIVE DESIGN
By Karl Kreeger

50'-0"

40'-0"

Optional Deck

Optional Vault Ceiling

Mbr 1
11-4 × 12-8

Living
13-0 × 19-4

Decor. Clg.

Railing

Dining
10-0 × 11-4

Kitchen
9-6 × 10-0

Ref

DW

Railing

DN

Pantry

Beams Above

Linen

Linen

Optional Door

Foyer

Br 3
Den/Study
10-0 × 11-4

Br 2
10-8 × 10-10

Garage
20-5 × 21-8

Railing   **Porch**

MAIN AREA
No. 20161

Crawl Space Access

M   F   Pantry

Slab/Crawl Space Option

Refer to **Pricing Schedule A** on the order form for pricing information

Quaint Starter Home

■ This plan features:

— Three bedrooms

— Two full baths

■ A vaulted ceiling giving an airy feeling to the Dining and Living Rooms

■ A streamlined Kitchen with a comfortable work area, a double sink and ample cabinet space

■ A cozy fireplace in the Living Room

■ A Master Suite with a large closet, French doors leading to the patio and a private bath

■ Two additional bedrooms sharing a full bath

■ No materials list available for this plan

MAIN FLOOR — 1,050 SQ. FT.
GARAGE — 261 SQ. FT.

TOTAL LIVING AREA:
1,050 SQ. FT.

36

42

PATIO

MASTER BEDROOM
11 X 12

BEDROOM
9 X 12

W D

BEDROOM
9 X 10

GARAGE
12 x 24

KITCHEN
9 X 11

VAULT

VAULT

DINING
9 x 10

LIVING
14 x 14

MAIN AREA
No. 92400

Refer to **Pricing Schedule B** on the order form for pricing information

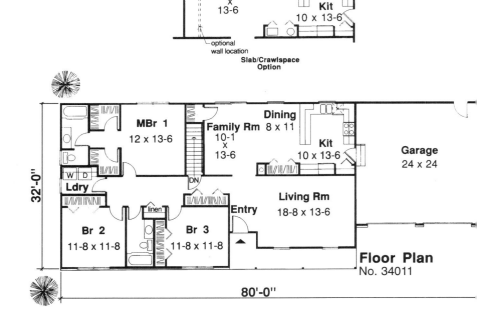

Windows Add Warmth To All Living Areas

■ This plan features:

— Three bedrooms

— Two full baths

■ A Master Suite with huge his-n-her walk-in closets and private bath

■ A second and third bedroom with ample closet space

■ A Kitchen equipped with an island counter, and flowing easily into the Dining and Family Rooms

■ A Laundry Room conveniently located near all three bedrooms

■ An optional garage

MAIN AREA— 1,672 SQ. FT.

OPTIONAL GARAGE — 566 SQ. FT.

TOTAL LIVING AREA:
1,672 SQ. FT.

Family Rm 13-7 x 13-6   **Dining** 8 x 11   **Kit** 10 x 13-6

optional wall location

Slab/Crawlspace Option

MBr 1 12 x 13-6   **Family Rm** 10-1 x 13-6   **Dining** 8 x 11   **Kit** 10 x 13-6   **Garage** 24 x 24

Ldry   W D   DN   **Living Rm** 18-8 x 13-6

Br 2 11-8 x 11-8   linen   **Br 3** 11-8 x 11-8   Entry

32'-0"   80'-0"

Floor Plan No. 34011

To order your Blueprints, call 1-800-235-5700

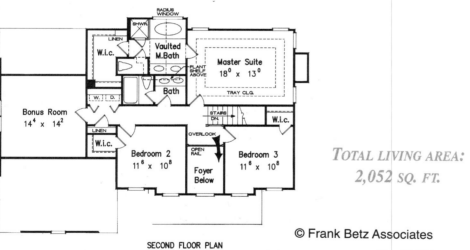

SECOND FLOOR PLAN

RADIUS WINDOW

SHWR.

LINEN

W.i.c.

Vaulted M.Bath

PLANT SHELF ABOVE

Master Suite 18⁰ x 13⁰

TRAY CLG.

Bath

W. D.

Bonus Room 14⁴ x 14²

LINEN

W.i.c.

STAIRS DN.

W.i.c.

Bedroom 2 11⁶ x 10⁸

OVERLOOK

OPEN RAIL

Foyer Below

Bedroom 3 11⁶ x 10⁸

TOTAL LIVING AREA: 2,052 SQ. FT.

© Frank Betz Associates

No. 98407

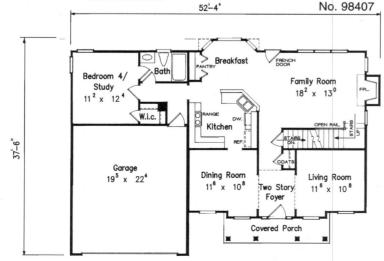

FIRST FLOOR PLAN

52'-4"

37'-6"

Bedroom 4/ Study 11² x 12⁴

W.i.c.

Bath

PANTRY

Breakfast

FRENCH DOOR

Family Room 18² x 13⁰

FPL.

RANGE

Kitchen

DW.

REF.

OPEN RAIL

STAIRS DN.

STAIRS UP

Garage 19⁵ x 22⁴

Dining Room 11⁶ x 10⁸

Two Story Foyer

COATS

Living Room 11⁶ x 10⁸

Covered Porch

Old Fashioned With Contemporary Interior

■ This plan features:

— Four bedrooms

— Three full baths

■ A two-story Foyer is flanked by the Living and Dining Rooms

■ The Family Room features a fireplace and a French door

■ The bayed Breakfast Nook and Pantry are adjacent to the Kitchen

■ Master Suite has a trayed ceiling, an attached Bath with a vaulted ceiling and radius window

■ Two additional Bedrooms, a full Bath, a laundry closet, and Bonus room complete the upstairs floor

■ An optional basement, crawl space or slab foundation available — please specify when ordering

FIRST FLOOR — 1,135 SQ. FT.
SECOND FLOOR — 917 SQ. FT.
BONUS — 216 SQ. FT.

Compact and Convenient Colonial

■ This plan features:

— Three bedrooms

— Two full and one half baths

■ Traditional Entry with landing staircase, closet and powder room

■ Living Room with focal point fireplace opens to formal Dining Room for ease in entertaining

■ Efficient, L-shaped Kitchen with built-in pantry, eating Nook and Garage entry

■ Corner Master Bedroom with private bath and attic access

■ Two additional bedrooms with ample closets share a double vanity bath

FIRST FLOOR — 624 SQ. FT.
SECOND FLOOR — 624 SQ. FT.
GARAGE — 510 SQ. FT.

TOTAL LIVING AREA:
1,248 SQ. FT.

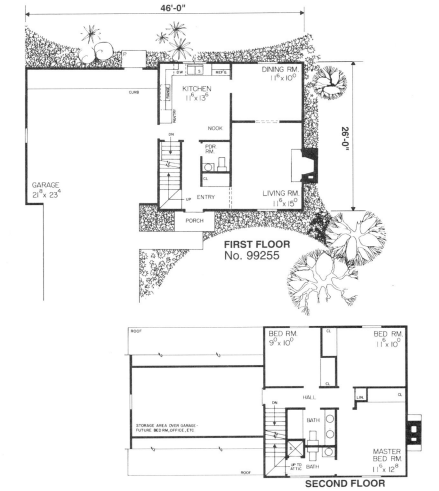

FIRST FLOOR
No. 99255

SECOND FLOOR

Refer to **Pricing Schedule A** on the order form for pricing information

FIRST FLOOR
No. 99238

28'-0"

28'-0"

40'-0"

BED RM.
10⁰ x 11⁶

KIT.
9⁴ x 15⁴

BATH
LIN.
CL.
CL.
P
REF.
RANGE

OPT. BSMT. STAIR
AIR COND.
UP

DINING

FIREPLACE

LIVING
27⁴ x 12⁰

DECK

SECOND FLOOR

DORMITORY
17⁴ x 9⁴

STOR.
CL.
BATH
DN.
STORAGE

STOR.
CL.
CL.
ROOF

MASTER
BED RM.
15⁰ x 12⁰

ROOF

BALCONY

Economical Vacation Home

■ This plan features:

— Three bedrooms

— Two full baths

■ A large rectangular Living Room with a fireplace at one end and plenty of room for separate activities at the other end

■ A galley-style Kitchen with adjoining Dining area

■ A second-floor Master Bedroom with a children's dormitory across the hall

■ A second-floor deck outside the Master Bedroom

FIRST FLOOR — 784 SQ. FT.
SECOND FLOOR — 504 SQ. FT.

TOTAL LIVING AREA:
1,288 SQ. FT.

© Frank E. Betz

Refer to **Pricing Schedule C** on the order form for pricing information

For the Growing Family

■ This plan features:

— Three bedrooms

— Three full baths

■ An open rail staircase adorning the living room while the Dining Room features easy access to the Kitchen

■ Kitchen equipped with a corner double sink and a wrap-around snack bar is open to the Family Room and Breakfast Area

■ Fireplace in the Family Room giving warmth and atmosphere to living space

■ Master Suite decorated by a tray ceiling in the bedroom and a vaulted ceiling in the master bath

■ An optional basement or crawl space foundation — please specify when ordering

■ No materials list is available for this plan

FIRST FLOOR — 1,103 SQ. FT.
SECOND FLOOR — 759 SQ. FT.
BASEMENT — 1,103 SQ. FT.
GARAGE — 420 SQ. FT.

TOTAL LIVING AREA:
1,862 SQ. FT.

SECOND FLOOR
No. 98473

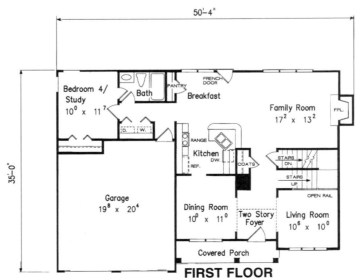

FIRST FLOOR

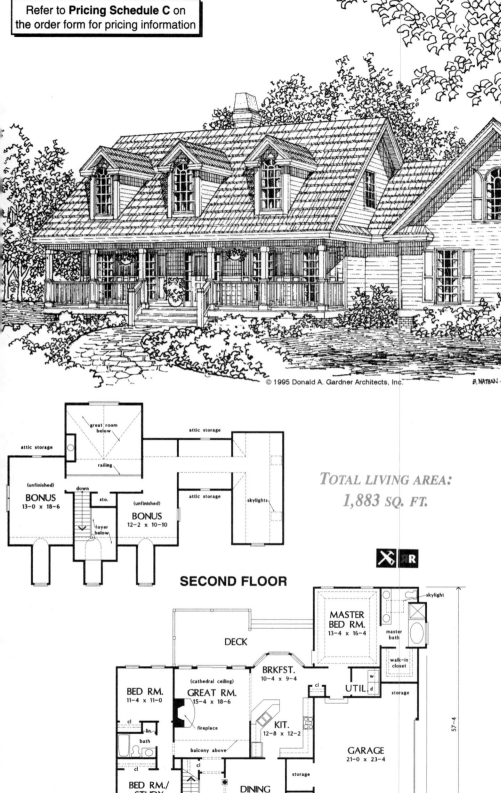

© 1995 Donald A. Gardner Architects, Inc.

B. NATHAN

SECOND FLOOR

TOTAL LIVING AREA:
1,883 SQ. FT.

FIRST FLOOR
No. 96479

© 1995 Donald A Gardner Architects, Inc.

Growing Families Take Note

■ This plan features:

— Three bedrooms

— Two full baths

■ Unlimited options for the second floor bonus area

■ Columns accenting the dining room, adjacent to the Foyer

■ Great room, open to the Kitchen and Breakfast Room, enlarged by a cathedral ceiling

■ Living and entertaining space expands to the deck

■ Master Suite topped by a tray ceiling and includes a walk-in closet, skylit bath with garden tub and a double vanity

■ Flexible bedroom/study shares a bath with another bedroom

FIRST FLOOR — 1,803 SQ. FT.
SECOND FLOOR — 80 SQ.FT.
GARAGE & STORAGE — 569 SQ. FT.
BONUS SPACE — 918 SQ. FT.

Refer to **Pricing Schedule A** on the order form for pricing information

Delightful, Compact Home

■ This plan features:

— Three bedrooms

— Two full baths

■ A fireplaced Living Room further enhanced by a wonderful picture window

■ A counter island featuring double sinks separating the Kitchen and Dining areas

■ A Master Bedroom that includes a private Master Bath and double closets

■ Two additional bedrooms with ample closet spacethat share a full bath

MAIN AREA — 1,146 SQ. FT.

TOTAL LIVING AREA:
1,146 SQ. FT.

slab/crawlspace option

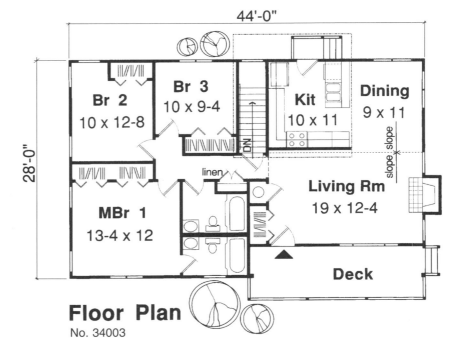

44'-0"

28'-0"

Br 2
10 x 12-8

Br 3
10 x 9-4

Kit
10 x 11

Dining
9 x 11

MBr 1
13-4 x 12

linen

Living Rm
19 x 12-4

slope : slope

DN

Deck

Floor Plan
No. 34003

To order your Blueprints, call 1-800-235-5700

© 1994 Donald A. Gardner Architects, Inc.

PLAN NO. 99826

Perfect for Family Gatherings

■ This plan features:

—Three bedrooms

—Two full baths

■ An open layout between the Great Room, Kitchen and Breakfast Bay, linked by a cathedral ceiling

■ Master Suite with a soaring cathedral ceiling, direct access to the deck and a well appointed bath with a large walk-in closet

■ Additional bedrooms sharing a full bath in the hall

■ Centrally located utility and storage spaces

MAIN FLOOR — 1,346 SQ. FT.
GARAGE AND STORAGE — 462 SQ. FT.

TOTAL LIVING AREA:
1,346 SQ. FT.

Floor Plan

MASTER BED RM.
14-8 x 13-0

DECK

GREAT RM.
15-8 x 15-0

DINING
11-4 x 11-0

GARAGE
21-0 x 21-0

master bath

walk-in closet

(cathedral ceiling)

fireplace

w d

UTIL.

lin. sto.

bath

cl

FOYER
6-8 x 5-8

KIT.
11-4 x 12-4

cl

BED RM.
10-0 x 10-4

BED RM.
10-0 x 10-4

PORCH

44-2

65-0

FLOOR PLAN
No. 99826

To order your Blueprints, call 1-800-235-5700

Refer to **Pricing Schedule A** on the order form for pricing information

Formal Balance

■ This plan features:

— Three bedrooms

— Two full baths

■ A cathedral ceiling in the Living Room with a heat-circulating fireplace as the focal point

■ A bow window in the Dining Room that adds elegance as well as natural light

■ A well-equipped Kitchen that serves both the Dinette and the formal Dining Room efficiently

■ A Master Bedroom with three closets and a private Master Bath with sliding glass doors to the Master Deck with a hot tub

MAIN FLOOR — 1,476 SQ. FT.
BASEMENT — 1,361 SQ. FT.
GARAGE — 548 SQ. FT.

TOTAL LIVING AREA:
1,476 SQ. FT.

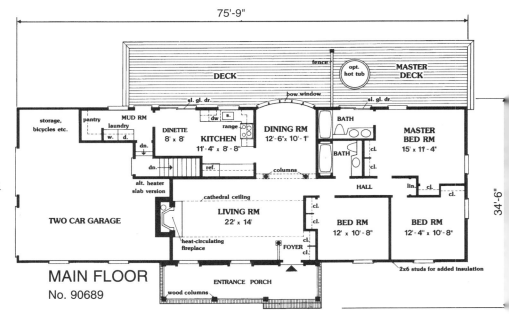

MAIN FLOOR
No. 90689

© 1992 Donald A Gardner Architects, Inc.

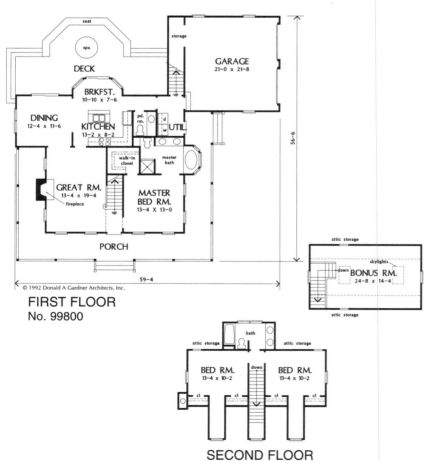

FIRST FLOOR
No. 99800

© 1992 Donald A Gardner Architects, Inc.

SECOND FLOOR

Classic Country Farmhouse

■ This plan features:

— Three bedrooms

— Two full and one half baths

■ Covered Porch gives classic country farmhouse look

■ Clerestory dormer window bathes the two-story Foyer in light

■ Great Room with fireplace opens to the Dining/Breakfast/Kitchen area, which leads to a Deck with optional spa and seating for indoor/outdoor entertaining

■ Master Bedroom offers a separate shower, whirlpool tub, and a double vanity

FIRST FLOOR — 1,145 SQ. FT.
SECOND FLOOR — 518 SQ. FT.
BONUS ROOM — 380 SQ. FT.
GARAGE & STORAGE — 509 SQ. FT.

TOTAL LIVING AREA:
1,663 SQ. FT.

Refer to **Pricing Schedule A** on the order form for pricing information

Country Charmer

■ This plan features:

—Three bedrooms

—Two full baths

■ Quaint front Porch is perfect for sitting and relaxing

■ Great Room opening into Dining area and Kitchen

■ Corner deck in rear of home accessed from Kitchen and Master Suite

■ Master Suite with a private bath, walk-in closet and built-in shelves

■ Two large secondary bedrooms in the front of the home share a hall bath

■ Two car garage located in the rear of the home

MAIN FLOOR — 1,438 SQ. FT.
GARAGE — 486 SQ. FT.

TOTAL LIVING AREA:
1,438 SQ. FT.

MAIN FLOOR
No. 96509

54'

57'

GARAGE
22 × 22

DECK

PANTRY

REFG

DINING
12 × 11

KITCHEN
12 × 10

RNG

D/W

BATH

MASTER SUITE
13 × 15

WASH   DRY

BATH

SHELVES

STOR

CLOSET

GREAT RM
17 × 18

F/P

A/C

CLOS

CLOS

BEDRM
14 × 11

CLOS

CLOS

BEDRM
11 × 13

FOYER

PORCH

To order your Blueprints, call 1-800-235-5700

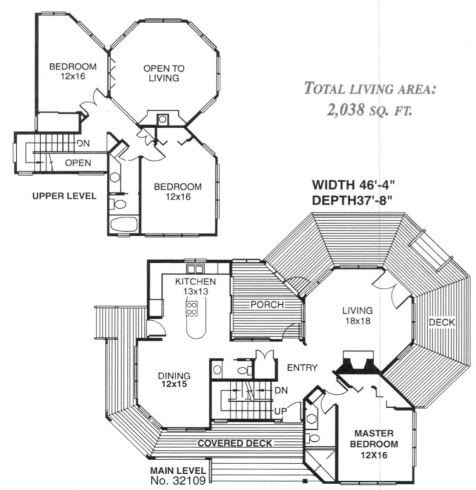

BEDROOM 12x16

OPEN TO LIVING

DN

OPEN

UPPER LEVEL

BEDROOM 12x16

TOTAL LIVING AREA: 2,038 SQ. FT.

WIDTH 46'-4"
DEPTH 37'-8"

KITCHEN 13x13

PORCH

LIVING 18x18

DECK

DINING 12x15

ENTRY

DN

UP

COVERED DECK

MASTER BEDROOM 12X16

MAIN LEVEL
No. 32109

Prairie Style Retreat

No. 32109

■ This plan features:

— Three bedrooms

— Two full and one half baths

■ Shingle siding, tall expanses of glass and wrapping decks accent the exterior

■ The octagonal shaped Living Room has a two-story ceiling and French doors

■ The Kitchen is enhanced by a cook top island

■ The first floor Master Suite offers a private bath

■ Two additional, second floor bedrooms share the full bath in the hall

■ No materials list is available for this plan

MAIN FLOOR — 1,213 SQ. FT.
UPPER FLOOR — 825 SQ. FT.
BASEMENT — 1,213 SQ. FT.

Refer to **Pricing Schedule C** on the order form for pricing information

© 1994 Donald A. Gardner Architects, Inc.

Sunny Two-story Foyer

■ This plan features:

— Three bedrooms

— Two full and one half baths

■ The two-story Foyer off the formal Dining Room sets an elegant mood in this one-and-a-half story, dormered home

■ The Great Room and Breakfast Area are both topped by a vaulted ceiling

■ The screened porch has a relaxing atmosphere

■ The Master Suite on the first floor includes a cathedral ceiling and an elegant bath with whirlpool tub and separate shower

■ There is plenty of attic and garage storage space available

FIRST FLOOR — 1,335 SQ. FT.
SECOND FLOOR — 488 SQ. FT.
GARAGE & STORAGE — 465 SQ. FT.

TOTAL LIVING AREA:
1,823 SQ. FT.

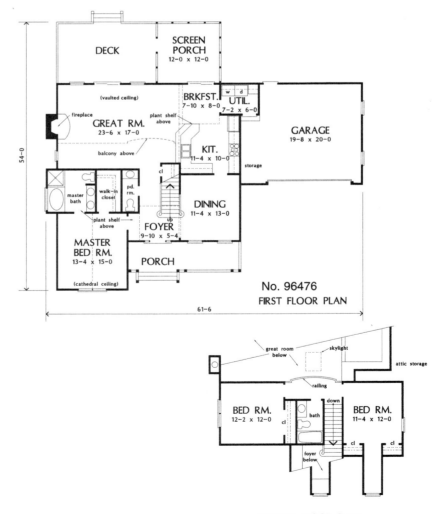

No. 96476
FIRST FLOOR PLAN

SECOND FLOOR PLAN

To order your Blueprints, call 1-800-235-5700

Main Floor
No. 24319

28'-0"
32'-0"

Broom
Ref
Kitchen
11-1 X 7-7
Linen
Flue
Brkfst Bar
Dining
11-11 X 8-7
DN
Br 1
12-0 X 11-3
Loft
Above
Fireplace
Railing
UP
Living
15-1 X 14-10
Deck
DN

An
EXCLUSIVE DESIGN
By Marshall Associates

Loft/
Br 3
11-7 X 16-6
Clg @ 9'-6"
DN
Mbr
11-8 X 14-0
Railing
Open to Below
Clerestory Windows Above
Roof
Balcony
Upper Floor

Util Rm
10-11 X 5-9
Wet Bar
Garage
11-8 X 19-0
Storage
Rec Rm
11-1 X 20-2
Optional
Hot
Tub
Step
UP
Lower Floor

Home With Many Views

- This plan features:
  — Three bedrooms
  — Two full baths
- Large Decks and windows taking full advantage of the view
- A fireplace that divides the Living Room from the Dining Room
- A Kitchen flowing into the Dining Room
- A Master Bedroom with full master bath
- A Recreation Room sporting a whirlpool tub and a bar

MAIN FLOOR — 728 SQ. FT.
UPPER FLOOR — 573 SQ. FT.
LOWER FLOOR — 409 SQ. FT.
GARAGE — 244 SQ. FT.

TOTAL LIVING AREA:
1,710 SQ. FT.

Refer to **Pricing Schedule C** on the order form for pricing information

© 1997 Donald A. Gardner Architects, Inc.

Private Master Suite

■ This plan features:

— Three bedrooms

— Two full baths

■ Working at the Kitchen island focuses your view to the Great Room with it's vaulted ceiling and a fireplace

■ Clerestory dormers emanate light into the Great Room

■ Both the Dining Room and Master Bedroom are enhanced by tray ceilings

■ Skylights floods natural light into the Bonus space

■ The private Master Suite has its own bath and an expansive walk-in closet

MAIN FLOOR — 1,515 SQ. FT.
BONUS — 288 SQ. FT.
GARAGE — 476 SQ. FT.

TOTAL LIVING AREA:
1,515 SQ. FT.

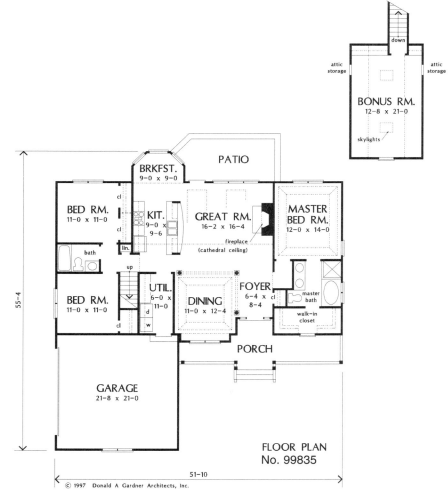

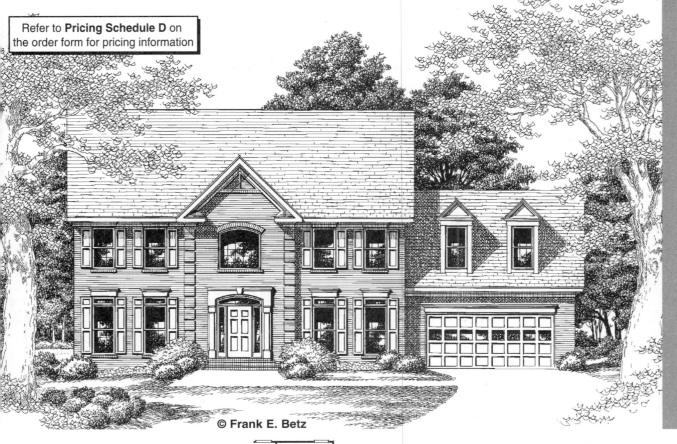

© Frank E. Betz

TOTAL LIVING AREA: 2,389 SQ. FT.

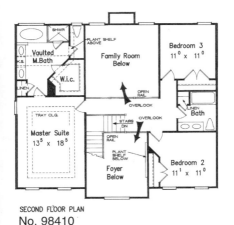

SECOND FLOOR PLAN
No. 98410

Bedroom 3
11⁰ x 12⁴

Bath

Bonus Room
12¹⁰ x 20⁵

Bedroom 2
13⁵ x 12³

LINEN

SECOND FLOOR W/ BONUS ROOM

FIRST FLOOR — 1,428 SQ. FT.
SECOND FLOOR — 961 SQ. FT.
BASEMENT — 1,428 SQ. FT.
GARAGE — 507 SQ. FT.
BONUS — 472 SQ. FT.

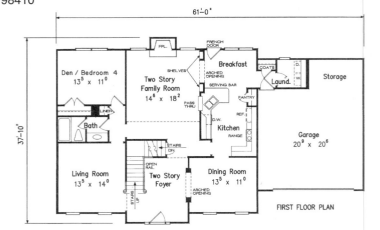

FIRST FLOOR PLAN

A Magnificent Manor

No. 98410

■ This plan features:

— Three bedrooms

— Three full baths

■ The two-story Foyer is dominated by a lovely staircase

■ The formal Living Room is located directly off the Foyer

■ An efficient Kitchen accesses the formal Dining Room for ease in serving

■ The Breakfast area is separated from the Kitchen by an extended counter/serving bar

■ The two-story Family Room is highlighted by a fireplace that is framed by windows

■ A tray ceiling crowns the Master Bedroom while a vaulted ceiling tops the master bath

■ An optional basement or crawl space foundation — please specify when ordering

Refer to **Pricing Schedule C** on the order form for pricing information

Enhanced by a Columned Porch

■ This plan features:

— Three bedrooms

— Two full baths

■ A Great Room with a fireplace and decorative ceiling

■ A large efficient Kitchen with Breakfast area

■ A Master Bedroom with a private Master Bath and walk-in closet

■ A formal Dining Room located near the Kitchen

■ Two additional bedrooms with walk-in closets and use of full hall bath

■ An optional crawl space or slab foundation — please specify when ordering

MAIN FLOOR — 1,754 SQ. FT.
GARAGE — 552 SQ. FT.

TOTAL LIVING AREA:
1,754 SQ. FT.

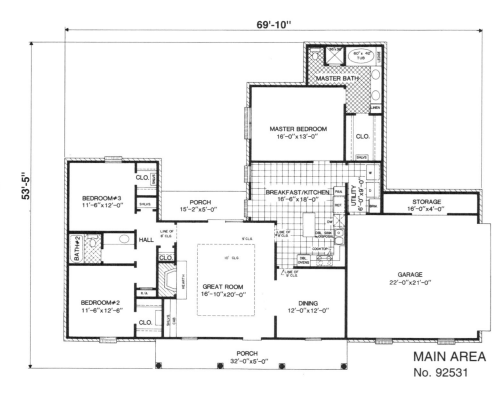

MAIN AREA
No. 92531

To order your Blueprints, call 1-800-235-5700

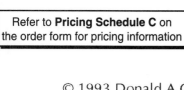

© 1993 Donald A Gardner Architects, Inc.

TOTAL LIVING AREA:
1,576 SQ. FT.

FLOOR PLAN

No. 99802

© 1993 Donald A Gardner Architects, Inc.

Traditional Beauty

■ This plan features:

— Three bedrooms

— Two full baths

■ Traditional beauty with large arched windows, round columns, covered porch, brick veneer and an open floor plan

■ Clerestory dormers above covered porch lighting the Foyer

■ Cathedral ceiling and fireplace enhancing the Great Room

■ Island Kitchen with Breakfast area accessing the large Deck with an optional spa

■ Columns defining spaces

■ Tray ceiling over the Master Bedroom, Dining Room and Bedroom/Study

■ Dual vanity, separate shower, and whirlpool tub in the Master Bath

MAIN FLOOR — 1,576 SQ. FT.
GARAGE — 465 SQ. FT.

Refer to **Pricing Schedule B** on the order form for pricing information

Skylight Brightens Master Bedroom

■ This plan features:

— Three bedrooms

— Two full baths

■ A covered Porch entry

■ A foyer separating the Dining Room from the Breakfast Area and Kitchen

■ A Living Room enhanced by a vaulted beam ceiling and a fireplace

■ A Master Bedroom with a decorative ceiling and a skylight in the private bath

■ An optional Deck accessible through sliding doors off the Master Bedroom

MAIN FLOOR — 1,686 SQ. FT.
BASEMENT — 1,676 SQ. FT.
GARAGE — 484 SQ. FT.

TOTAL LIVING AREA:
1,686 SQ. FT.

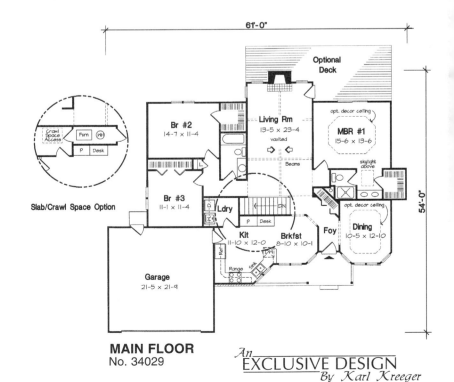

MAIN FLOOR
No. 34029

An
EXCLUSIVE DESIGN
By Karl Kreeger

To order your Blueprints, call 1-800-235-5700

Refer to **Pricing Schedule B** on the order form for pricing information

TOTAL LIVING AREA:
1,761 SQ. FT.

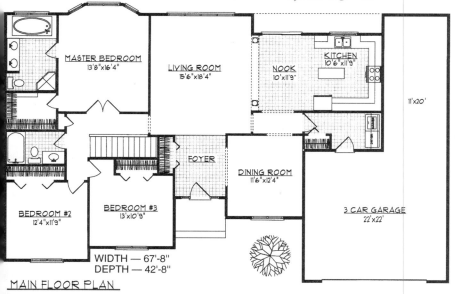

MASTER BEDROOM
13'8"x16'4"

LIVING ROOM
15'6"x18'4"

NOOK
10'x11'9"

KITCHEN
10'6"x11'9"

11'x20'

FOYER

DINING ROOM
11'6"x12'4"

3 CAR GARAGE
22'x22'

BEDROOM #2
12'4"x11'9"

BEDROOM #3
13'x10'9"

WIDTH — 67'-8"
DEPTH — 42'-8"

MAIN FLOOR PLAN
No. 93133

An
EXCLUSIVE DESIGN
By Ahmann Design Inc.

Triple Tandem Garage

■ This plan features:

— Three bedrooms

— Two full baths

■ A large Foyer leading to the bright and spacious Living Room

■ A large open Kitchen with a central work island

■ A handy Laundry Room with a pantry and garage access

■ A Master Suite with a bay windowed sitting area and French doors, as well as a private Master Bath with a oversized tub, corner shower and room-sized walk-in closet

■ Two additional front bedrooms that share a full bath

■ A triple tandem garage with space for a third car, boat or just extra work and storage space

■ No materials list available for this plan

MAIN FLOOR — 1,761 SQ. FT.
BASEMENT — 1,761 SQ. FT.
GARAGE — 658 SQ. FT.

Refer to **Pricing Schedule C** on the order form for pricing information

Moderate Ranch Has Features of Much Larger Plan

■ This plan features:

— Three bedrooms

— Two full baths

■ A large Great Room with a vaulted ceiling and a stone fireplace with bookshelves on either side

■ A spacious Kitchen with ample cabinet space conveniently located next to the large Dining Room

■ A Master Suite having a large bath with a garden tub, double vanity and a walk-in closet

■ Two other large bedrooms, each with a walk-in closet and access to the full bath

■ An optional basement, slab or crawl space foundation — please specify when ordering

MAIN FLOOR — 1,811 SQ. FT.

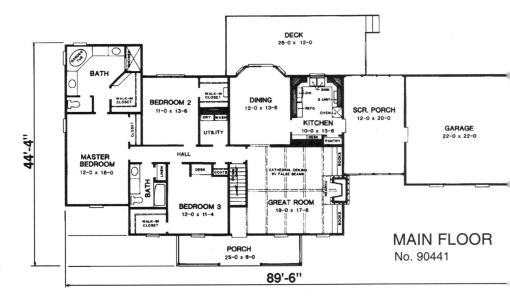

MAIN FLOOR
No. 90441

44'-4"

89'-6"

TOTAL LIVING AREA:
1,811 SQ. FT.

To order your Blueprints, call 1-800-235-5700

Refer to **Pricing Schedule D** on the order form for pricing information

An EXCLUSIVE DESIGN
By Upright Design

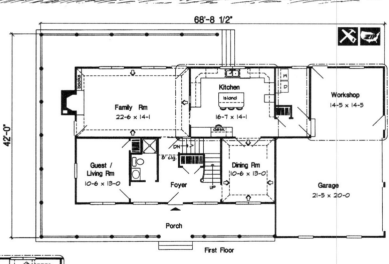

68'-8 1/2"

42'-0"

Kitchen
16-7 x 14-1
Island

Family Rm
22-6 x 14-1

Workshop
14-5 x 14-5

Guest / Living Rm
10-6 x 13-0

Foyer

Dining Rm
10-6 x 13-0

Garage
21-5 x 20-0

Porch

First Floor

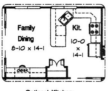

Family Dining
8-10 x 14-1

Kit.
10-0 x 14-1

Optional Kitchen

FIRST FLOOR — 1,236 SQ. FT.
SECOND FLOOR — 1,120 SQ. FT.

TOTAL LIVING AREA:
2,356 SQ. FT.

Workshop
14-5 x 14-5

Crawl Space / Slab Option

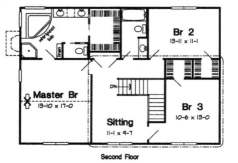

Master Br
13-10 x 17-0

Br 2
13-11 x 11-1

Br 3
10-6 x 13-0

Sitting
11-1 x 9-7

Second Floor

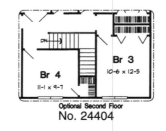

Br 4
11-1 x 9-7

Br 3
10-6 x 12-5

Optional Second Floor
No. 24404

Yesteryear Flavor

■ This plan features:

— Three or four bedrooms

— Three full baths

■ Wrap-around Porch invites visiting and access into gracious Foyer with landing staircase

■ Formal Living Room doubles as a Guest Room

■ Huge Family Room highlighted by a decorative ceiling, cozy fireplace, book shelves and Porch access

■ Country-size Kitchen with island snackbar, built-in desk and nearby Dining Room, laundry/Workshop and Garage access

■ Corner Master Bedroom enhanced by a large walk-in closet and plush bath with a whirlpool tub

■ Two additional bedrooms with walk-in closets, share a full bath and Sitting Area

Refer to **Pricing Schedule B** on the order form for pricing information

A-Frame for Year-Round Living

■ This plan features:

— Three bedrooms

— One full and one three quarter baths

■ A vaulted ceiling in the Living Room with a massive fireplace

■ A wrap-around sun deck that gives you a lot of outdoor living space

■ A luxurious Master Suite complete with a walk-in closet, full bath and private Deck

■ Two additional bedrooms that share a full hall bath

MAIN FLOOR — 1,238 SQ. FT.
LOFT — 464 SQ. FT.
BASEMENT — 1,175 SQ. FT.
WIDTH — 34'-0"
DEPTH — 56'-0"

An
EXCLUSIVE DESIGN
By Westhome Planners, Ltd.

TOTAL LIVING AREA:
1,702 SQ. FT.

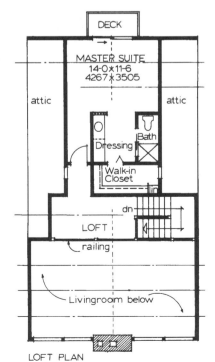

DECK

MASTER SUITE
14-0 x 11-6
4267 x 3505

attic   attic

Dressing   Bath

Walk-in
Closet

dn

LOFT
railing

Livingroom below

LOFT PLAN

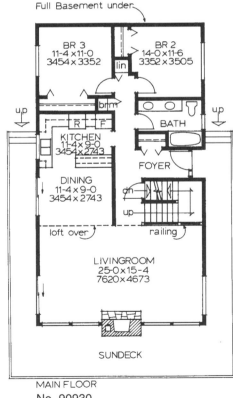

Full Basement under

BR 3
11-4 x 11-0
3454 x 3352

BR 2
14-0 x 11-6
3352 x 3505

lin

up   up

BATH

R   F

KITCHEN
11-4 x 9-0
3454 x 2743

FOYER

DINING
11-4 x 9-0
3454 x 2743

dn

up

loft over   railing

LIVINGROOM
25-0 x 15-4
7620 x 4673

SUNDECK

MAIN FLOOR
No. 90930

To order your Blueprints, call 1-800-235-5700

Refer to **Pricing Schedule C** on the order form for pricing information

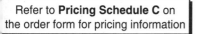

PLAN NO. 90606

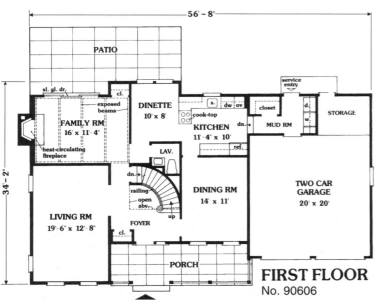

FIRST FLOOR
No. 90606

56'- 8"

34'- 2"

PATIO

sl. gl. dr.   cl.
exposed beams

FAMILY RM
16' x 11'-4"

heat-circulating fireplace

DINETTE
10' x 8'

service entry

s.   dw   ov   closet

cook-top

KITCHEN
11'- 4" x 10'

dn.

MUD RM

d.
w.

STORAGE

LAV.

ref.

dn.

railing open abv.

up

DINING RM
14' x 11'

TWO CAR GARAGE
20' x 20'

LIVING RM
19'-6" x 12'-8"

FOYER
cl.

PORCH

SECOND FLOOR

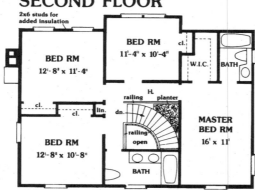

2x6 studs for added insulation

BED RM
12'-8" x 11'-4"

cl.

cl.   lin.

BED RM
12'-8" x 10'-8"

BED RM
11'-4" x 10'-4"

cl.

W.I.C.

BATH

dn.

railing   H.   planter

railing   open

MASTER BED RM
16' x 11'

BATH

Traditional Elements Combine in Friendly Colonial

■ This plan features:

— Four bedrooms

— Two full and one half baths

■ A beautiful circular stair ascending from the central Foyer and flanked by the formal Living Room and Dining Room

■ Exposed beams, wood paneling, and a brick fireplace wall in the Family Room

■ A separate Dinette opening to an efficient Kitchen

FIRST FLOOR — 1,099 SQ. FT.
SECOND FLOOR — 932 SQ. FT.
BASEMENT — 1,023 SQ. FT.
GARAGE — 476 SQ. FT.

TOTAL LIVING AREA:
2,031 SQ. FT.

Refer to **Pricing Schedule B** on the order form for pricing information

Classic Ranch

■ This plan features:

— Three bedrooms

— Two full baths

■ A fabulous Great Room with a step ceiling and a cozy fireplace

■ An elegant arched soffit connects the Great Room to the Dining Room

■ The Kitchen has wrap-around counters, a center island and a nook

■ The Master Bedroom is completed with a walk-in closet, and a private bath

■ Two additional bedrooms with ample closet space share a full bath

■ No materials list is available for this plan

MAIN FLOOR — 1,794 SQ. FT.
BASEMENT — 1,794 SQ. FT.

TOTAL LIVING AREA:
1,794 SQ. FT.

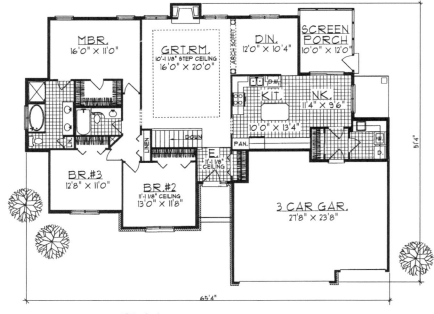

MAIN FLOOR PLAN
No. 97108

To order your Blueprints, call 1-800-235-5700

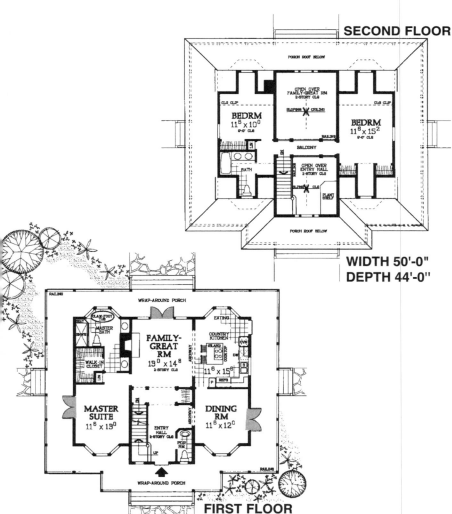

SECOND FLOOR

PORCH ROOF BELOW

OPEN OVER
FAMILY-GREAT RM
2-STORY CLG

CLG CLG

BEDRM
11⁶ x 10⁰
9'-0" CLG

SLOPING CEILING

BEDRM
11⁸ x 15²
9'-0" CLG

CLG CLG

RAILING

BATH

BALCONY

OPEN OVER
ENTRY HALL
2-STORY CLG

PORCH ROOF BELOW

WIDTH 50'-0"
DEPTH 44'-0"

WRAP-AROUND PORCH

RAILING

MASTER
BATH
CLAW-FOOT

WALK-IN
CLOSET

FAMILY-
GREAT
RM
13⁰ x 14⁸
2-STORY CLG

EATING

COUNTRY
KITCHEN

ISLAND

OV

DW
REF

ARCHWAY

MASTER SUITE
11⁶ x 13⁰

ENTRY
HALL
2-STORY CLG

DINING
RM
11⁶ x 12⁰

ARCHWAY

POR
RM

UP

RAILING

WRAP-AROUND PORCH

FIRST FLOOR
No. 99285

Southern Hospitality

■ This plan features:

— Three bedrooms

— Two full and one half baths

■ Porch surrounding and shading
entire home

■ Two-story Entry Hall with a
landing staircase and arched
window

■ Double doors access to Porch
from Family-Great Room, Dining
Room and Master Suite

■ Country Kitchen with cooktop
island/snackbar, Eating alcove
and archway to Family Room
with cozy fireplace

■ Master Suite with bay window,
walk-in closet and private bath

■ Upstairs, two double dormer
bedrooms share a full bath

FIRST FLOOR — 1171 SQ. FT.
SECOND FLOOR — 600 SQ. FT.

TOTAL LIVING AREA:
1,771 SQ. FT.

Refer to **Pricing Schedule B** on the order form for pricing information

Letting the Light In

■ This plan features:

— Four bedrooms

— Two full baths

■ Covered Porch leads into tile Entry with angled staircase

■ Decorative corner windows and cozy wood stove in Living Room

■ Sliding glass door to rear yard brightens Dining Room and adjoining Living Room

■ Efficient Kitchen with built-in pantry, and pass-through counter

■ Two first floor bedrooms with ample closets, share a full bath

■ French doors lead into private Master Bedroom with skylit bath

■ Loft/Bedroom overlooking Living Room offers many options

■ No materials list is available for this plan

FIRST FLOOR — 1076 SQ. FT.
SECOND FLOOR — 449 SQ. FT.
GARAGE — 495 SQ. FT.

TOTAL LIVING AREA:
1,525 SQ. FT.

SECOND FLOOR

FIRST FLOOR
No. 91081

To order your Blueprints, call 1-800-235-5700

Second Floor Balcony Overlooks Great Room

■ This plan features:

— Three bedrooms

— Two full and one half baths

■ A Great Room with a focal point fireplace and a two-story ceiling

■ Kitchen has an island, double sinks, built-in pantry and ample storage and counter space

■ A first floor Laundry Room

■ A Dining Room with easy access to the Kitchen and the outside

■ A Master Suite with a private master Bath and a walk-in closet

■ Two additional bedrooms with ample closet space that share a full hall bath

FIRST FLOOR — 891 SQ. FT.
SECOND FLOOR — 894 SQ. FT.
GARAGE — 534 SQ. FT.
BASEMENT — 891 SQ. FT.

TOTAL LIVING AREA:
1,785 SQ. FT.

An
EXCLUSIVE DESIGN
By Greg Stafford

Second Floor

Br 2
11-6 x 11-4

linen

Br 3
11 x 11-4

open to below

1/2 wall

railing

DN

Mstr Br
13-4 x 15

46'-8"

Dining
12-1 x 11-4

Kitchen
13 x 11-4

W
D

pantry

Great Rm
14 x 21-8

DN

UP

Garage
22 x 23-4

open to above

35'-8"

First Floor
No. 24610

Refer to **Pricing Schedule B** on the order form for pricing information

Easy Living Plan

■ This plan features:

— Three bedrooms

— Two full and one half baths

■ Kitchen, Breakfast Bay, and Family Room blend into a spacious open living area

■ Convenient Laundry Center is tucked into the rear of the Kitchen

■ Luxurious Master Suite is topped by a tray ceiling while a vaulted ceiling is in the bath

■ Two roomy secondary bedrooms share the full bath in the hall

■ Please specify a basement, crawl space or slab foundation when ordering

FIRST FLOOR — 828 SQ. FT.
SECOND FLOOR — 772 SQ. FT.
BASEMENT — 828 SQ. FT.
GARAGE — 473 SQ. FT.

TOTAL LIVING AREA:
1,600 SQ. FT.

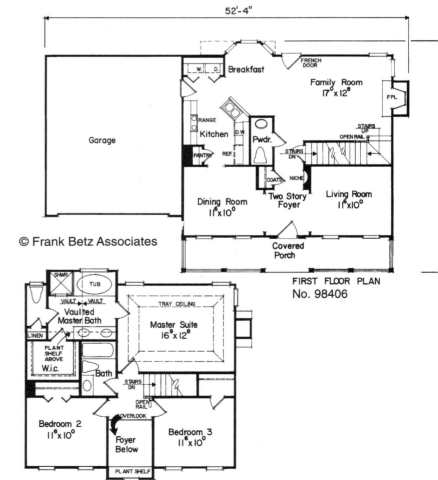

© Frank Betz Associates

FIRST FLOOR PLAN
No. 98406

SECOND FLOOR PLAN

To order your Blueprints, call 1-800-235-5700

PLAN NO. 96408

© 1994 Donald A. Gardner Architects, Inc.

B. NATHAN

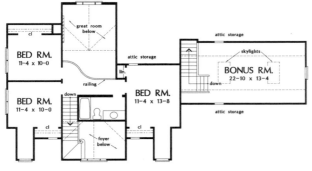

great room below

cl

BED RM.
11-4 x 10-0

attic storage

attic storage

skylights

BONUS RM.
22-10 x 13-4

lin.

railing

down

BED RM.
11-4 x 10-0

down

BED RM.
11-4 x 13-8

attic storage

foyer below

cl

cl

SECOND FLOOR PLAN

Four Bedroom Country Classic

▨ This plan features:

— Four bedrooms

— Two full and one half baths

▨ Foyer open to the dining room creating a hall with a balcony over the vaulted Great Room

▨ Great Room opens to the deck and to the island Kitchen with convenient pantry

▨ Nine foot ceilings on the first floor expand volume

▨ Master Suite pampered by a whirlpool tub, double vanity, separate shower and access to the deck

▨ Bonus room to be finished now or later

FIRST FLOOR — 1,499 SQ. FT.
SECOND FLOOR — 665 SQ. FT.
GARAGE & STORAGE — 567 SQ. FT.
BONUS ROOM — 380 SQ. FT.

14-0

spa

DECK

MASTER BED RM.
14-10 x 17-1

GREAT RM.
15-4 x 20-1

BRKFST.
9-0 x 8-11

w d

UTILITY
7-6 x 7-9

up

GARAGE
21-4 x 22-0

pan.

KITCHEN
11-4 x 13-4

balcony above

walk-in closet

40-6

cl

pd. rm.

storage

master bath

FOYER
9-10 x 8-3

DINING
11-4 x 13-9

up

PORCH

No. 96408
FIRST FLOOR PLAN

© 1994 Donald A Gardner Architects, Inc.

69-8

TOTAL LIVING AREA:
2,164 SQ. FT.

Refer to **Pricing Schedule A** on the order form for pricing information

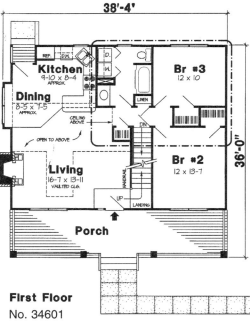

Large Front Porch Adds a Country Touch

■ This plan features:

— Three bedrooms

— Two full baths

■ A country-styled Front Porch

■ Vaulted ceiling in the Living Room which includes a fireplace

■ An efficient Kitchen with double sinks and peninsula counter that may double as an eating bar

■ Two first floor bedrooms with ample closet space

■ A second floor Master Suite with sloped ceiling, walk-in closet and private Master Bath

FIRST FLOOR — 1,007 SQ. FT.
SECOND FLOOR — 408 SQ. FT.
BASEMENT — 1,007 SQ. FT.

TOTAL LIVING AREA:
1,415 SQ. FT.

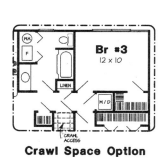

Crawl Space Option

Br #3
12 x 10

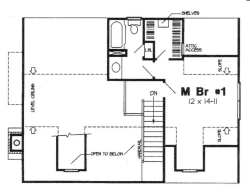

Second Floor

M Br #1
12 x 14-11

38'-4'

36'-0"

Kitchen
9-10 x 8-4
APPROX.

Dining
8-5 x 7-5
APPROX.

Br #3
12 x 10

Br #2
12 x 13-7

Living
16-7 x 13-11
VAULTED CLG.

Porch

First Floor
No. 34601

To order your Blueprints, call 1-800-235-5700

PLAN NO. 94911

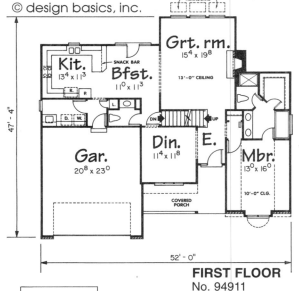

© design basics, inc.

TRANSOMS

Grt. rm.
15⁴ x 19⁸

13'-0" CEILING

Kit.
13⁴ x 11³

SNACK BAR

Bfst.
11⁰ x 11³

47'-4"

Gar.
20⁸ x 23⁰

Din.
11⁴ x 11⁸

E.

DN UP

Mbr.
13⁰ x 16⁰

10'-0" CLG.

COVERED PORCH

52'-0"

FIRST FLOOR
No. 94911

FIRST FLOOR — 1,405 SQ. FT.
SECOND FLOOR — 453 SQ. FT.
BONUS ROOM — 300 SQ. FT.
BASEMENT — 1,405 SQ. FT.
GARAGE — 490 SQ. FT.

TOTAL LIVING AREA:
1,858 SQ. FT.

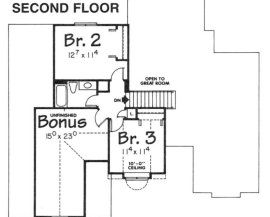

SECOND FLOOR

Br. 2
12⁷ x 11⁴

OPEN TO GREAT ROOM

DN

UNFINISHED

Bonus
15⁰ x 23⁰

Br. 3
11⁴ x 11⁴

10'-0" CEILING

Fieldstone Facade and Arched Windows

■ This plan features:

— Three bedrooms

— Two full and one half baths

■ Inviting Covered Porch shelters entrance

■ Expansive Great Room enhanced by warm fireplace and three transom windows

■ Breakfast area adjoins Great Room giving a feeling of more space

■ An efficient Kitchen with counter snack bar and nearby laundry and Garage entry

■ A first floor Master Bedroom suite with an arched window below a sloped ceiling and a double vanity bath

■ Two additional bedrooms share a Bonus area and a full bath on the second floor

To order your Blueprints, call 1-800-235-5700

Refer to **Pricing Schedule B** on the order form for pricing information

A Modern Slant On A Country Theme

■ This plan features:

— Three bedrooms

— Two full and one half baths

■ Country styled front porch highlighting exterior enhanced by dormer windows

■ Modern open floor plan for a more spacious feeling

■ Great Room accented by a quaint, corner fireplace and a ceiling fan

■ Dining Room flowing from the Great Room for easy entertaining

■ Kitchen graced by natural light from near by bay window and a convenient snackbar for meals on the go

■ Master suite secluded in separate wing for total privacy

■ Two additional bedrooms sharing full bath in the hall

FIRST FLOOR — 1,648 SQ. FT.
GARAGE — 479 SQ. FT.

TOTAL LIVING AREA:
1,648 SQ. FT.

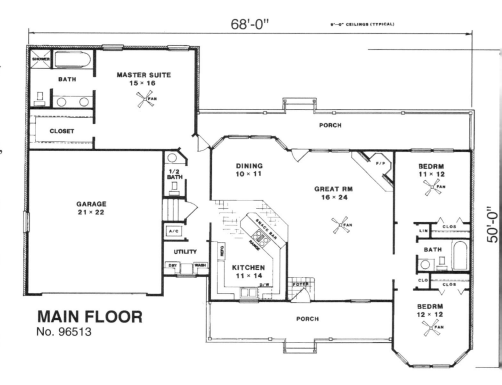

MAIN FLOOR
No. 96513

To order your Blueprints, call 1-800-235-5700

PLAN NO. 94944

WHIRLPOOL

Mbr.
14⁰ x 13⁰

9'- 0" CEILING

Br. 2
10³ x 11⁰

LIN.

DN

Br. 3
11⁷ x 10⁰

Br. 4
11⁷ x 10⁰

OPEN TO BELOW

PLANT SHELF

SECOND FLOOR

© design basics, inc.

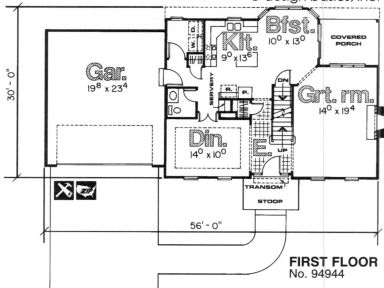

Gar.
19⁸ x 23⁴

30' - 0"

Bfst.
10⁰ x 13⁰

COVERED PORCH

Kit.
9⁰ x 13⁶

W. D.

SERVERY

R. P.

Grt. rm.
14⁰ x 19⁴

DN

Din.
14⁰ x 10⁰

UP

E.

TRANSOM

STOOP

56' - 0"

FIRST FLOOR
No. 94944

Spectacular Sophistication

■ This plan features:

— Four bedrooms

— Two full and one half baths

■ Open Foyer with circular window and a plant shelf leads into the Dining Room

■ Great Room with an inviting fireplace and windows front and back

■ Open Kitchen has a work island and accesses the Breakfast area

■ Master Bedroom suite features a nine-foot boxed ceiling, a walk-in closet and whirlpool bath

■ Three additional bedrooms share a full bath with a double vanity

FIRST FLOOR — 941 SQ. FT.
SECOND FLOOR — 992 SQ. FT.
BASEMENT — 941 SQ. FT.
GARAGE — 480 SQ. FT.

TOTAL LIVING AREA:
1,933 SQ. FT.

Refer to **Pricing Schedule A** on the order form for pricing information

Perfect for a Woodland Setting

■ This plan features:

— Two bedrooms

— One full bath

■ A sloped ceiling adding to the cozy feeling of the home

■ A built-in entertainment center in the Living Room adding convenience

■ An L-shaped Kitchen that includes a double sink and Dining area

■ A full hall Bath easily accessible from either bedroom

■ A Loft and Balcony that over-looks the Living Room and the Dining area

■ Storage on either side of the Loft

FIRST FLOOR — 763 SQ. FT.
SECOND FLOOR — 264 SQ. FT.

TOTAL LIVING AREA:
1,027 SQ. FT.

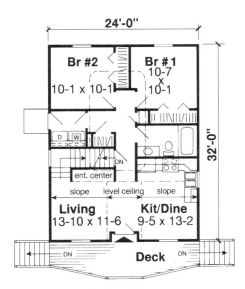

First Floor
No. 35007

Slab/ Crawl Space Option

To order your Blueprints, call 1-800-235-5700

Refer to **Pricing Schedule A** on the order form for pricing information

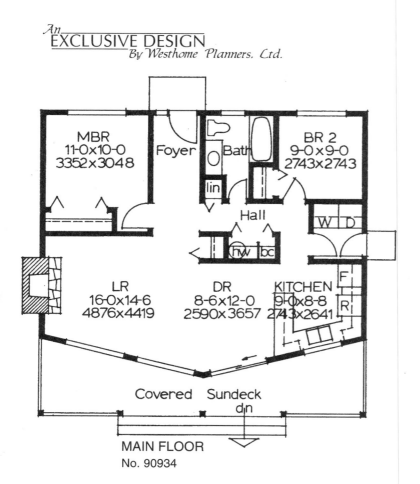

An
EXCLUSIVE DESIGN
By Westhome Planners, Ltd.

MBR
11-0x10-0
3352x3048

Foyer

Bath

BR 2
9-0x9-0
2743x2743

lin

Hall

W D

LR
16-0x14-6
4876x4419

DR
8-6x12-0
2590x3657

KITCHEN
9-0x8-8
2743x2641

F
R

Covered   Sundeck
dn

MAIN FLOOR
No. 90934

A Nest for Empty-Nesters

- ■ This plan features:
- — Two bedrooms
- — One full bath
- ■ An economical design
- ■ A covered sun deck adding outdoor living space
- ■ A mudroom/laundry area inside the side door, trapping dirt before it can enter the house
- ■ An open layout between the Living Room with fireplace, Dining Room and Kitchen

MAIN FLOOR — 884 SQ. FT.
WIDTH — 34'-0"
DEPTH — 28'-0"

TOTAL LIVING AREA:
884 SQ. FT.

Refer to **Pricing Schedule B** on the order form for pricing information

Amenity-Packed Affordability

■ This plan features:

— Three bedrooms

— Two full baths

■ A sheltered entrance inviting your guests onward

■ A fireplace in the Den offering a focal point, while the decorative ceiling adds definition to the room

■ A well-equipped Kitchen flowing with ease into the Breakfast Bay or Dining Room

■ A Master Bedroom, having two closets and a private master bath

■ An optional crawl space or slab foundation — please specify when ordering

MAIN AREA — 1,484 SQ. FT.
GARAGE — 544 SQ. FT.

TOTAL LIVING AREA:
1,484 SQ. FT.

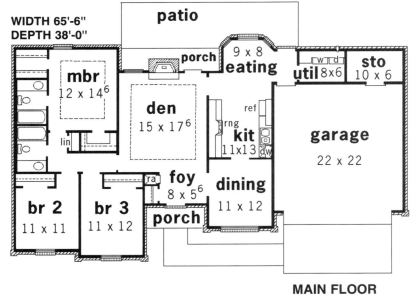

WIDTH 65'-6"
DEPTH 38'-0"

patio

porch

mbr
12 x 14⁶

eating
9 x 8

util 8x6

sto
10 x 6

den
15 x 17⁶

kit
11x13

garage
22 x 22

lin

foy
8 x 5⁶

dining
11 x 12

br 2
11 x 11

br 3
11 x 12

porch

MAIN FLOOR
No. 92525

To order your Blueprints, call 1-800-235-5700

TOTAL LIVING AREA:
1,654 SQ. FT.

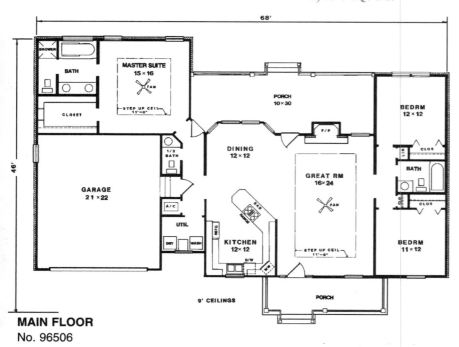

MAIN FLOOR
No. 96506

Attractive Ceiling Treatments and Open Layout

■ This plan features:

— Three bedrooms

— Two full and one half baths

■ Great Room and Master Suite with step-up ceiling treatments

■ A cozy fireplace providing warm focal point in the Great Room

■ Open layout between Kitchen, Dining and Great Room lending a more spacious feeling

■ Five-piece, private bath and walk-in closet in the pampering Master Suite

■ Two additional bedrooms located at opposite end of home

MAIN FLOOR — 1,654 SQ. FT.
GARAGE — 480 SQ. FT.

Refer to **Pricing Schedule B** on the order form for pricing information

Perfect Plan for Busy Family

■ This plan features:

— Three bedrooms

— Two full baths

■ Covered Entry opens to vaulted Foyer

■ Spacious Family Room with another vaulted ceiling, a central fireplace and expansive backyard views

■ Angular and efficient Kitchen with an eating bar, built-in desk, Dining area with outdoor access, and nearby laundry and Garage entry

■ Secluded Master Bedroom with a large walk-in closet and double vanity bath

■ Two additional bedrooms with ample closets and easy access to a full bath

■ No materials list is available for this plan

MAIN FLOOR — 1,756 SQ. FT.
BASEMENT — 1,756 SQ. FT.

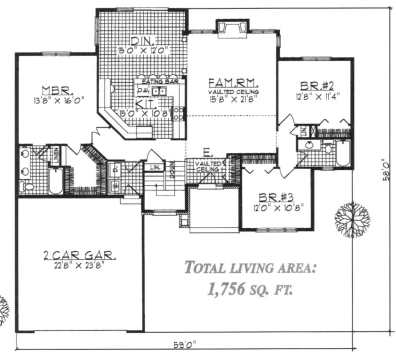

TOTAL LIVING AREA:
1,756 SQ. FT.

MAIN FLOOR PLAN
No. 93191

To order your Blueprints, call 1-800-235-5700

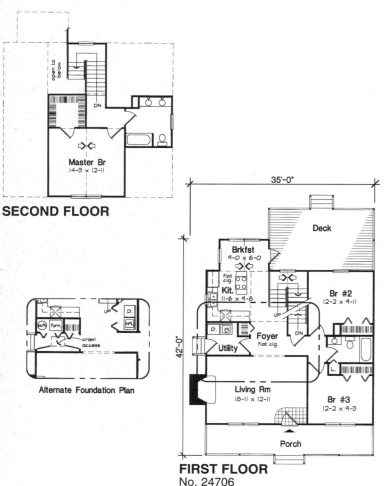

SECOND FLOOR

Master Br
14-3 x 12-11

open to below

DN

Alternate Foundation Plan

crawl access

35'-0"

42'-0"

Deck

Brkfst
9-0 x 6-0

Kit.
11-6 x 9-2

flat clg.

Br #2
12-2 x 9-11

UP

Foyer
flat clg.

DN

Utility

Living Rm
18-11 x 12-11

Br #3
12-2 x 9-3

Porch

FIRST FLOOR
No. 24706

Country Porch Topped by Dormer

■ This plan features:

— Three bedrooms

— Two full baths

■ Front Porch offers outdoor living and leads into tiled entry and spacious Living Room with focal point fireplace

■ Side entrance leads into Utility Room and central Foyer with a landing staircase

■ Country-size Kitchen with cook-top island, bright Breakfast area and access to Deck

■ Second floor Master Bedroom offers lovely dormer window, vaulted ceiling, walk-in closet and double vanity bath

FIRST FLOOR — 1,035 SQ. FT.
SECOND FLOOR — 435 SQ. FT.
BASEMENT — 1,018 SQ. FT.

TOTAL LIVING AREA:
1,470 SQ. FT.

Family Get-Away

◾ This plan features:

— Three bedrooms

— Two and one half baths

◾ A Wrap-around Porch for views and visiting provides access into the Great Room and Dining area

◾ A spacious Great Room with a two-story ceiling and dormer window above a massive fireplace

◾ A combination Dining/Kitchen with an island work area and breakfast bar opening to a Great Room and adjacent to the laundry/storage and half-bath area

◾ A private two-story Master Bedroom with a dormer window, walk-in closet, double vanity bath and optional deck with hot tub

◾ Two second floor bedrooms sharing a full bath

FIRST FLOOR — 1,061 SQ. FT.
SECOND FLOOR — 499 SQ. FT.
BASEMENT — 1,061 SQ. FT.

TOTAL LIVING AREA: *1,560 SQ. FT.*

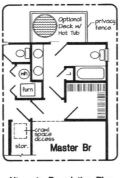

Alternate Foundation Plan

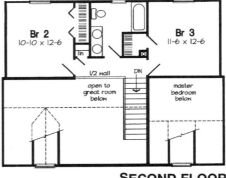

SECOND FLOOR

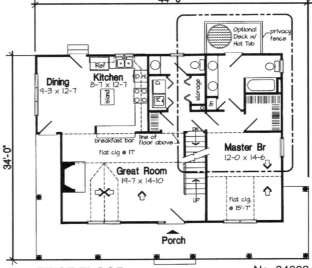

FIRST FLOOR No. 34602

To order your Blueprints, call 1-800-235-5700

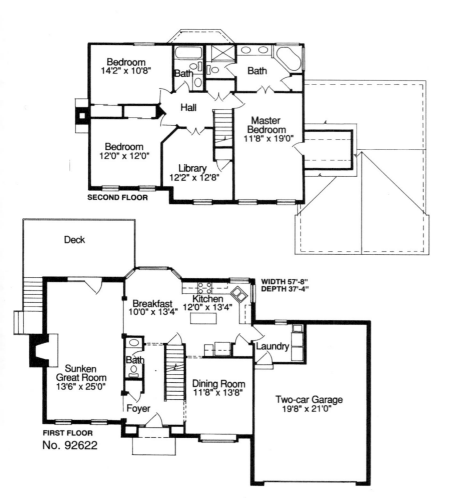

SECOND FLOOR

Bedroom 14'2" x 10'8"

Bath

Bath

Hall

Bedroom 12'0" x 12'0"

Master Bedroom 11'8" x 19'0"

Library 12'2" x 12'8"

Deck

Breakfast 10'0" x 13'4"

Kitchen 12'0" x 13'4"

WIDTH 57'-8"
DEPTH 37'-4"

Laundry

Sunken Great Room 13'6" x 25'0"

Bath

Dining Room 11'8" x 13'8"

Foyer

Two-car Garage 19'8" x 21'0"

FIRST FLOOR
No. 92622

Simple Elegance

- This plan features:
  - — Three bedrooms
  - — Two full and one half baths
- A sunken Great Room, large enough for family gatherings, that is enhanced by a fireplace
- A bay window in the Dining Room that has direct access to the Kitchen
- A Master Bedroom Suite with a garden bath and walk-in closet
- A second floor Library that can double as a fourth bedroom
- Two additional bedrooms share a full hall bath
- No materials list is available for this plan

FIRST FLOOR — 1,134 SQ. FT.
SECOND FLOOR — 1,083 SQ. FT.
BASEMENT — 931 SQ. FT.
GARAGE — 554 SQ. FT.

TOTAL LIVING AREA:
2,217 SQ. FT.

Refer to **Pricing Schedule D** on the order form for pricing information

Spacious Family Living

■ This plan features:

— Four bedrooms

— Two full and one half baths

■ Front Porch welcomes friends and family home

■ Entry opens to spacious Living Room with a tiered ceiling and Dining Room beyond

■ Hub Kitchen easily serves the Dining Room, the Breakfast bay and the Family Room

■ Corner Master Bedroom has access to a private bath

■ Three additional bedrooms share a double vanity bath

FIRST FLOOR — 1,269 SQ. FT.
SECOND FLOOR — 1,034 SQ. FT.
BASEMENT — 1,269 SQ. FT.
GARAGE — 485 SQ. FT.

TOTAL LIVING AREA:
2,303 SQ. FT.

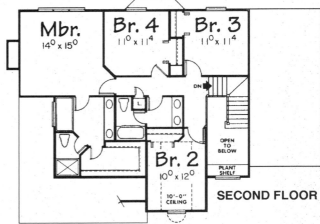

SECOND FLOOR

Mbr. 14⁰ x 15⁰
Br. 4 11⁰ x 11⁴
Br. 3 11⁰ x 11⁴
Br. 2 10⁰ x 12⁰
10'-0" CEILING
DN
OPEN TO BELOW
PLANT SHELF

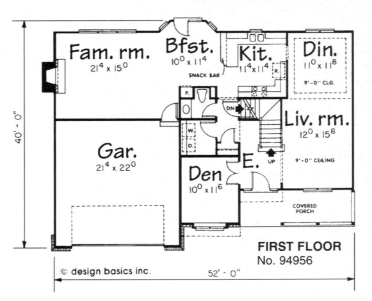

FIRST FLOOR
No. 94956

Fam. rm. 21⁴ x 15⁰
Bfst. 10⁰ x 11⁴
Kit. 11⁴ x 11⁴
Din. 11⁰ x 11⁸
9'-0" CLG.
SNACK BAR
Liv. rm. 12⁰ x 15⁸
9'-0" CEILING
Gar. 21⁴ x 22⁰
Den 10⁰ x 11⁶
E.
UP
DN
COVERED PORCH

40' - 0"
52' - 0"

© design basics inc.

To order your Blueprints, call 1-800-235-5700

©1994 Donald A. Gardner Architects, Inc.

Sense of Spaciousness

- This plan features:
- — Three bedrooms
- — Two full and one half baths
- Creative use of natural lighting gives a feeling of spaciousness to this country home
- Traffic flows easily from the bright Foyer into the Great Room which has a vaulted ceiling and skylights
- The open floor plan is efficient for Kitchen/Breakfast area and the Dining Room
- Master Bedroom suite features a walk-in closet and a private bath with whirlpool tub
- Two second floor bedrooms with storage access, share a full bath

FIRST FLOOR — 1,180 SQ. FT.
SECOND FLOOR — 459 SQ. FT.
BONUS ROOM — 385 SQ. FT.
GARAGE & STORAGE — 533 SQ. FT.

TOTAL LIVING AREA:
1,639 SQ. FT.

SECOND FLOOR PLAN

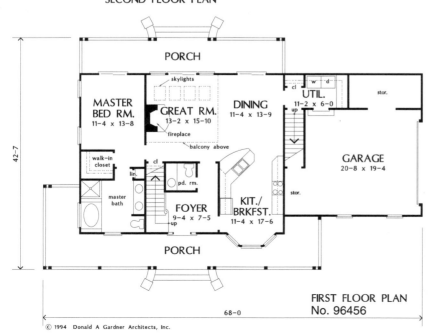

FIRST FLOOR PLAN
No. 96456

68-0

© 1994 Donald A Gardner Architects, Inc.

To order your Blueprints, call 1-800-235-5700

Refer to **Pricing Schedule B** on the order form for pricing information

Open Plan is Full of Air & Light

■ This plan features:

— Three bedrooms

— Two full and one half baths

■ Foyer open to the Family Room and highlighted by a fireplace

■ Dining Room, with a sliding glass door to rear yard, adjoins Family Room

■ Kitchen and Nook in an efficient open layout

■ Second floor Master Suite topped by tray ceiling over the bedroom and a vaulted ceiling over the lavish bath

■ No materials list is available for this plan

■ When ordering this plan—please specify a basement or crawl space foundation

FIRST FLOOR — 767 SQ. FT.
SECOND FLOOR — 738 SQ. FT.
BONUS ROOM — 240 SQ. FT.
BASEMENT — 767 SQ. FT.
GARAGE — 480 SQ. FT.

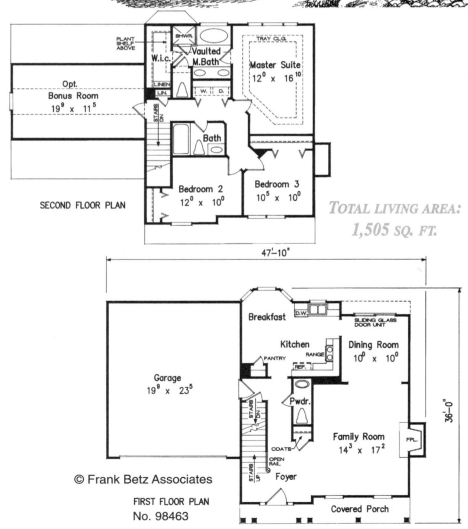

SECOND FLOOR PLAN

Opt.
Bonus Room
19^9 x 11^5

PLANT SHELF ABOVE

SHWR.
W.i.c.
Vaulted
M.Bath

TRAY CLG.
Master Suite
12^0 x 16^{10}

LINEN
LIN.
W. D.

STAIRS DN

Bath

Bedroom 2
12^0 x 10^0

Bedroom 3
10^5 x 10^0

TOTAL LIVING AREA:
1,505 SQ. FT.

47'-10"

36'-0"

Breakfast
D.W.
SLIDING GLASS DOOR UNIT

Kitchen
PANTRY
RANGE
REF.

Dining Room
10^0 x 10^0

Garage
19^9 x 23^5

Pwdr.

STAIRS DN

COATS
OPEN RAIL

STAIRS UP

Family Room
14^3 x 17^2

FPL

Foyer

Covered Porch

© Frank Betz Associates

FIRST FLOOR PLAN
No. 98463

To order your Blueprints, call 1-800-235-5700

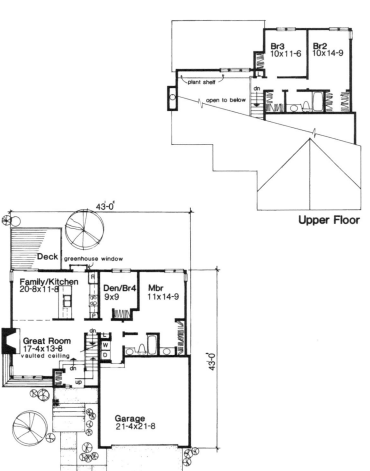

Upper Floor

Br3
10x11-6

Br2
10x14-9

plant shelf

open to below

dn

43-0"

Deck   greenhouse window

Family/Kitchen
20-8x11-8

Den/Br4
9x9

Mbr
11x14-9

Great Room
17-4x13-8
vaulted ceiling

Garage
21-4x21-8

43-0"

Main Floor
No. 90358

Four Bedroom 1-1/2 Story Design

■ This plan features:

— Three bedrooms

— Two full baths

■ A vaulted ceiling in the Great Room and a fireplace

■ An efficient Kitchen with a peninsula counter and double sink

■ A Family Room with easy access to the wood Deck

■ A Master Bedroom with private bath entrance

■ Convenient laundry facilities outside the Master Bedroom

■ Two additional bedrooms upstairs with walk-in closets and the use of the full hall bath

FIRST FLOOR — 1,062 SQ. FT.
SECOND FLOOR — 469 SQ. FT.

TOTAL LIVING AREA:
1,531 SQ. FT.

Refer to **Pricing Schedule B** on the order form for pricing information

An
EXCLUSIVE DESIGN
By Jannis Vann & Associates, Inc.

Old Fashioned Country Porch

■ This plan features:

— Three bedrooms

— Two full and one half baths

■ A Traditional front Porch, with matching dormers above and a garage hidden below, leading into a open, contemporary layout

■ A Living Area with a cozy fireplace visible from the Dining Room for warm entertaining

■ A U-shaped, efficient Kitchen featuring a corner, double sink and pass-thru to the Dining Room

■ A convenient half bath with a laundry center on the first floor

■ A spacious, first floor Master Suite with a lavish Bath including a double vanity, walk-in closet and an oval, corner window tub

■ Two large bedrooms with dormer windows, on the second floor, sharing a full hall bath

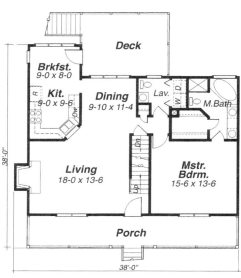

FIRST FLOOR
No. 93219

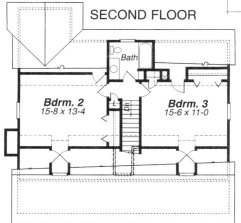

FIRST FLOOR — 1,057 SQ. FT.
SECOND FLOOR — 611 SQ. FT.
BASEMENT — 511 SQ. FT.
GARAGE — 546 SQ. FT.

TOTAL LIVING AREA:
1,668 SQ. FT.

To order your Blueprints, call 1-800-235-5700

An EXCLUSIVE DESIGN
By Westhome Planners, Ltd.

Surrounded with Sunshine

■ This plan features:

— Three bedrooms

— Two full and one half baths

■ An Italianate style, featuring columns and tile originally designed to sit on the edge of a golf course

■ Tile used from the Foyer, into the Kitchen and Nook, as well as in the Utility Room

■ A whirlpool tub in the elaborate and spacious Master Bedroom suite

■ A Great Room with a corner gas fireplace

■ A turreted Breakfast Nook and an efficient Kitchen with peninsula counter

■ Two family bedrooms that share a full hall bath

■ An optional basement or crawl space foundation available — please specify when ordering

TOTAL LIVING AREA:
1,731 SQ. FT.

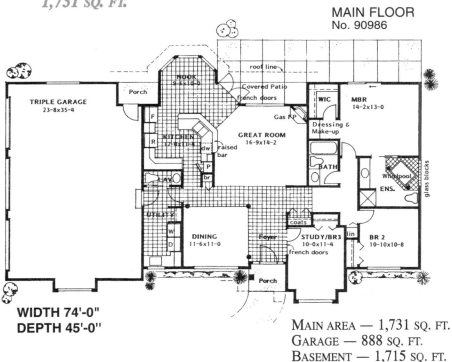

MAIN FLOOR
No. 90986

WIDTH 74'-0"
DEPTH 45'-0"

MAIN AREA — 1,731 SQ. FT.
GARAGE — 888 SQ. FT.
BASEMENT — 1,715 SQ. FT.

Refer to **Pricing Schedule B** on the order form for pricing information

Attractive Gables and Arches

This plan features:

— Three bedrooms

— Two full baths

■ Entry opens to formal Dining Room with arched window

■ Angles and transom windows add interest to the Great Room

■ Bright Hearth area expands Breakfast/Kitchen area and shares three-sided fireplace

■ Efficient Kitchen offers an angled snack bar, a large pantry and nearby laundry/Garage entry

■ Secluded Master Bedroom suite crowned by decorative ceiling, a large walk-in closet and a plush bath with a whirlpool tub

■ Secondary bedrooms located separately from master suite

MAIN FLOOR — 1,782 SQ. FT.
BASEMENT — 1,782 SQ. FT.
GARAGE — 466 SQ. FT.

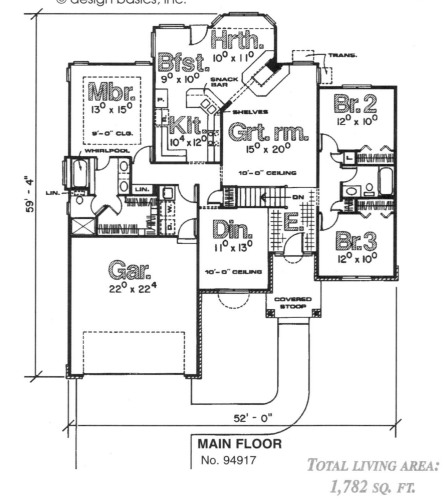

© design basics, inc.

MAIN FLOOR
No. 94917

TOTAL LIVING AREA:
1,782 SQ. FT.

To order your Blueprints, call 1-800-235-5700

Refer to **Pricing Schedule B** on the order form for pricing information

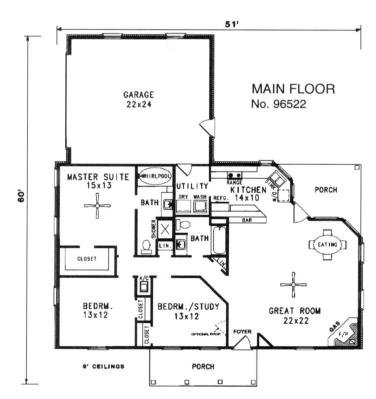

51'

GARAGE
22x24

MAIN FLOOR
No. 96522

60'

MASTER SUITE
15x13

WHIRLPOOL

UTILITY

RANGE

KITCHEN
14x10

PORCH

BATH

DRY WASH

REFG.

BAR

SHOWER

LIN.

BATH

EATING

CLOSET

A/C

BEDRM.
13x12

CLOSET
CLOSET

BEDRM./STUDY
13x12

GREAT ROOM
22x22

GAS
F/P

OPTIONAL DOOR

FOYER

9' CEILINGS

PORCH

Cozy Three Bedroom

No. 96522

▪ This plan features:

— Three bedrooms

— Two full baths

▪ The triple arched front Porch adds to the curb appeal of the home

▪ The expansive Great Room is accented by a cozy gas fireplace

▪ The efficient Kitchen includes an eating bar that separates it from the Great Room

▪ The Master Bedroom is highlighted by a walk-in closet and a whirlpool bath

▪ Two secondary bedrooms share use of the full hall bath

▪ The rear porch extends dining to the outdoors

MAIN FLOOR — 1,515 SQ. FT.
GARAGE — 528 SQ. FT.

TOTAL LIVING AREA:
1,515 SQ. FT.

Refer to **Pricing Schedule B** on the order form for pricing information

Beckoning Country Porch

■ This plan features:

— Three bedrooms

— Two full and one half baths

■ Country styled exterior with dormer windows above friendly front Porch

■ Vaulted ceiling and central fireplace accent the spacious Great Room

■ L-shaped Kitchen/Dining Room with work island and atrium door to back yard

■ First floor Master Suite with vaulted ceiling, walk-in closet, private bath and optional private Deck with hot tub

■ Two additional bedrooms on the second floor with easy access to full bath

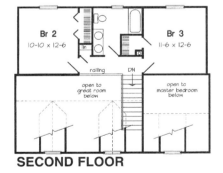

SECOND FLOOR

FIRST FLOOR — 1,061 SQ. FT.
SECOND FLOOR — 499 SQ. FT.
BASEMENT — 1,061 SQ. FT.

TOTAL LIVING AREA:
1,560 SQ. FT.

FIRST FLOOR
No. 34603

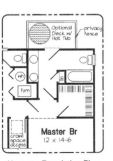

Alternate Foundation Plan

To order your Blueprints, call 1-800-235-5700

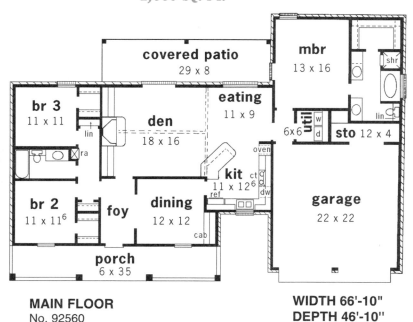

PLAN NO. 92560

TOTAL LIVING AREA:
1,660 SQ. FT.

covered patio
29 x 8

mbr
13 x 16

shr

eating
11 x 9

br 3
11 x 11

den
18 x 16

lin

util
6 x 6

w
d

lin

sto 12 x 4

ra

oven

kit
11 x 12⁶

ct

ref

dw

garage
22 x 22

br 2
11 x 11⁶

foy

dining
12 x 12

cab

porch
6 x 35

MAIN FLOOR
No. 92560

WIDTH 66'-10"
DEPTH 46'-10"

Covered Front and Rear Porches

■ This plan features:

—Three bedrooms

—Two full baths

■ Traditional country styling with front and rear covered porches

■ Peninsula counter/eating bar in Kitchen for meals on the go

■ Informal Breakfast area and formal Dining room with built-in cabinet

■ Vaulted ceiling and cozy fireplace highlighting Den

■ Master Bedroom in private corner pampered by five-piece bath

■ Split bedroom plan with additional bedrooms at the opposite of home sharing full bath

■ An optional slab or crawl space foundation — please specify when ordering

MAIN FLOOR — 1,660 SQ. FT.
GARAGE — 544 SQ. FT.

Refer to **Pricing Schedule A** on the order form for pricing information

Three Porches Offer Outdoor Charm

- This plan features:
- — Three bedrooms
- — Two full baths
- An oversized log burning fireplace in the spacious Living/Dining area which is two stories high with sliding glass doors
- Three Porches offering the maximum in outdoor living space
- A private bedroom located on the second floor
- An efficient Kitchen including an eating bar and access to the covered Dining Porch

FIRST FLOOR — 974 SQ. FT.
SECOND FLOOR — 300 SQ. FT.

TOTAL LIVING AREA:
1,274 SQ. FT.

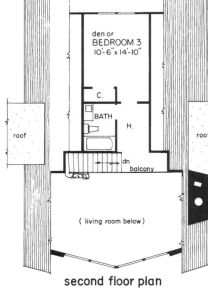

second floor plan

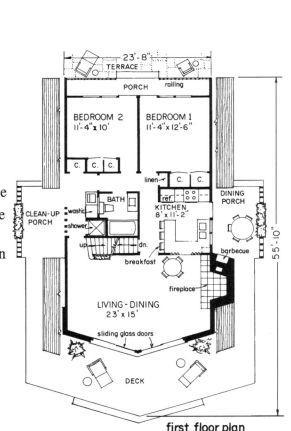

first floor plan
No. 90048

© 1996 Donald A. Gardner Architects, Inc.

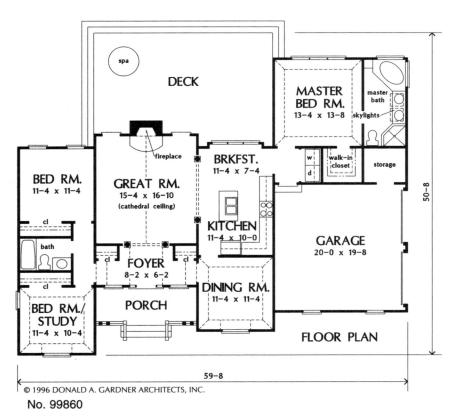

DECK

spa

MASTER BED RM.
13-4 x 13-8

master bath

skylights

fireplace

BRKFST.
11-4 x 7-4

w
d

walk-in closet

storage

BED RM.
11-4 x 11-4

GREAT RM.
15-4 x 16-10
(cathedral ceiling)

cl

bath

cl

KITCHEN
11-4 x 10-0

GARAGE
20-0 x 19-8

FOYER
8-2 x 6-2

cl   cl

BED RM./ STUDY
11-4 x 10-4

PORCH

DINING RM.
11-4 x 11-4

FLOOR PLAN

50-8

59-8

© 1996 DONALD A. GARDNER ARCHITECTS, INC.

No. 99860

TOTAL LIVING AREA:
1,498 SQ. FT

Home Builders on a Budget

■ This plan features:

— Three bedrooms

— Two full baths

■ Down-sized country plan for home builder on a budget

■ Columns punctuate open, one-level floor plan and connect Foyer with clerestory window dormers

■ Front Porch and large, rear Deck extend living space outdoors

■ Tray ceilings decorate Master Bedroom, Dining Room and Bedroom/Study

■ Private Master Bath features garden tub, double vanity, separate shower and skylights

MAIN FLOOR — 1,498 SQ. FT.
GARAGE & STORAGE — 427 SQ. FT.

Refer to **Pricing Schedule D** on the order form for pricing information

Arches Add Ambiance

■ This plan features:

— Four bedrooms

— Two full and one half baths

■ Arched two-story entrance highlighted by a lovely arched window

■ Expansive Den offers hearth fireplace between book shelves, raised ceiling and access to rear yard

■ Efficient Kitchen with peninsula counter, built-in pantry, Breakfast bay, Garage entry, Laundry and adjoining Dining room

■ Private Master Bedroom enhanced by a large walk-in closet and plush bath

■ Three second floor bedrooms with walk-in closets share a double vanity bath

■ An optional slab or crawl space foundation — please specify when ordering

FIRST FLOOR — 1,250 SQ. FT.
SECOND FLOOR — 783 SQ. FT
GARAGE AND STORAGE — 555 SQ. FT.

TOTAL LIVING AREA:
2,033 SQ. FT.

SECOND FLOOR

FIRST FLOOR
No. 92539

To order your Blueprints, call 1-800-235-5700

SECOND FLOOR

© Frank Betz Associates

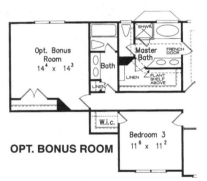

OPT. BONUS ROOM

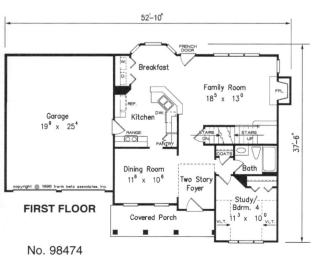

FIRST FLOOR

No. 98474

Triple Arched Porch

■ This plan features:

— Four bedrooms

— Three full baths

■ An impressive two-story Foyer adjoins the elegant Dining Room

■ The Family Room, Breakfast Room and Kitchen have an open layout

■ The Study is topped by a vaulted ceiling and is located close to a Full Bath

■ The Master Suite is topped by a tray ceiling while there is a vaulted ceiling over the Bath

■ An optional Bonus Room offers expansion for future needs

■ An optional basement or crawl space foundation — please specify when ordering

■ No materials list is available for this plan

FIRST FLOOR — 972 SQ. FT.
SECOND FLOOR — 772 SQ. FT.
BONUS ROOM — 358 SQ. FT.
BASEMENT — 972 SQ. FT.
GARAGE — 520 SQ. FT.

TOTAL LIVING AREA:
1,744 SQ. FT.

Refer to **Pricing Schedule B** on the order form for pricing information

Back Yard Views

■ This plan features:

— Three bedrooms

— Two full baths

■ Front Porch accesses open Foyer, and spacious Dining Room and Great Room with sloped ceilings

■ Corner fireplace, windows and atrium door to Patio enhance Great Room

■ Convenient Kitchen with a pantry, peninsula serving counter for bright Breakfast area and nearby Laundry/Garage entry

■ Luxurious bath, walk-in closet and back yard view offered in Master Bedroom

■ Two additional bedrooms, one with an arched window, share full bath

■ No materials list available for this plan

MAIN FLOOR — 1,746 SQ. FT.
GARAGE — 480 SQ. FT.
BASEMENT — 1,697 SQ. FT.

TOTAL LIVING AREA:
1,746 SQ. FT.

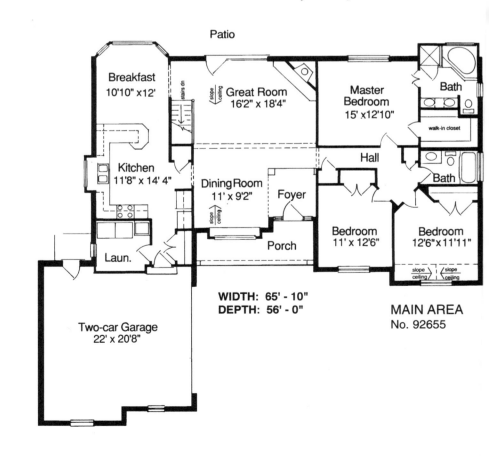

Patio

Breakfast
10'10" x12'

Great Room
16'2" x 18'4"

Master Bedroom
15' x12'10"

Bath

walk-in closet

Kitchen
11'8" x 14' 4"

Dining Room
11' x 9'2"

Foyer

Hall

Bath

Laun.

Porch

Bedroom
11' x 12'6"

Bedroom
12'6"x 11'11"

Two-car Garage
22' x 20'8"

WIDTH: 65' - 10"
DEPTH: 56' - 0"

MAIN AREA
No. 92655

To order your Blueprints, call 1-800-235-5700

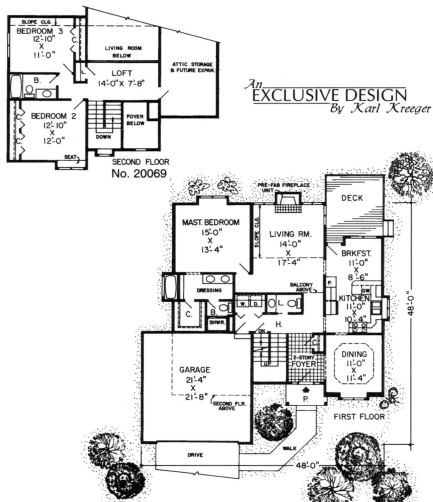

An EXCLUSIVE DESIGN
By Karl Kreeger

No. 20069

Stylish and Practical Plan

■ This plan features:

— Three bedrooms

— Two full and one half baths

■ A Kitchen with a Breakfast Area large enough for most informal meals

■ A spacious Living Room with a fireplace

■ A formal Dining Room with a decorative ceiling for comfortable entertaining

■ A first floor Master Bedroom providing a private retreat and lavish Master Bath

FIRST FLOOR — 1,345 SQ. FT.
SECOND FLOOR — 662 SQ. FT.
BASEMENT — 1,304 SQ. FT.
GARAGE — 477 SQ. FT.
BONUS — 122 SQ. FT.

TOTAL LIVING AREA:
2,007 SQ. FT.

Refer to **Pricing Schedule B** on the order form for pricing information

Hip Roof Ranch

■ This plan features:

— Three bedrooms

— Two full baths

■ Cozy front Porch leads into Entry with vaulted ceiling and sidelights

■ Open Living Room enhanced by a cathedral ceiling, a wall of windows and corner fireplace

■ Large and efficient Kitchen with an extended counter and a bright Dining area with access to Screen Porch

■ Convenient Utility area with access to Garage and Storage area

■ Spacious Master Bedroom with a walk-in closet and private bath

■ Two additional bedrooms with ample closets, share a full bath

■ No materials list available for this plan

MAIN FLOOR — 1,540 SQ. FT.
BASEMENT — 1,540 SQ. FT.

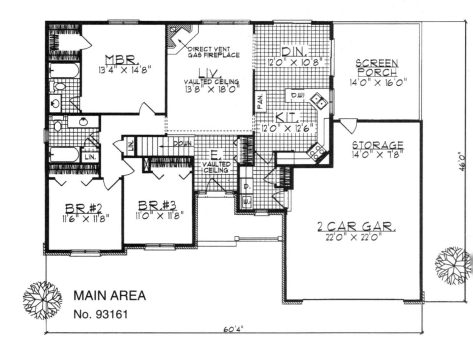

MBR.
13'4" × 14'8"

DIRECT VENT
GAS FIREPLACE

LIV.
VAULTED CEILING
13'8" × 18'0"

DIN.
12'0" × 10'8"

SCREEN
PORCH
14'0" × 16'0"

PAN.

KIT.
12'0" × 12'6"

STORAGE
14'0" × 7'8"

DOWN

E.
VAULTED
CEILING

LIN.

BR. #2
11'6" × 11'8"

BR. #3
11'0" × 11'8"

2 CAR GAR.
22'0" × 22'0"

46'0"

MAIN AREA
No. 93161

60'4"

TOTAL LIVING AREA:
1,540 SQ. FT.

Refer to **Pricing Schedule C** on the order form for pricing information

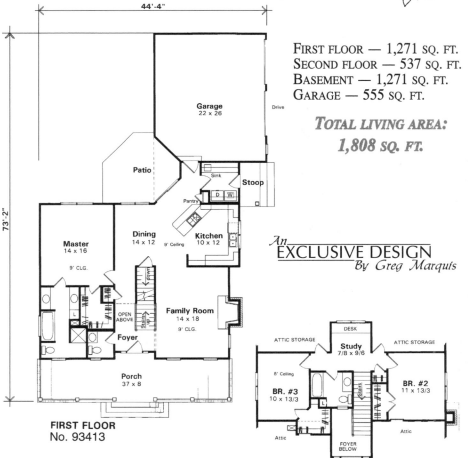

44'-4"

73'-2"

Garage
22 x 26

Drive

Patio

Sink   Stoop

D   W

Pantry

Master
14 x 16

9' CLG.

Dining
14 x 12

9' Ceiling

Kitchen
10 x 12

OPEN
ABOVE

Stairs   down   up

Family Room
14 x 18

9' CLG.

L

Foyer

Porch
37 x 8

FIRST FLOOR
No. 93413

DESK

Study
7/8 x 9/6

ATTIC STORAGE   ATTIC STORAGE

8' Ceiling

BR. #3
10 x 13/3

Stairs

BR. #2
11 x 13/3

L

Attic

Attic

FOYER
BELOW

SECOND FLOOR

FIRST FLOOR — 1,271 SQ. FT.
SECOND FLOOR — 537 SQ. FT.
BASEMENT — 1,271 SQ. FT.
GARAGE — 555 SQ. FT.

TOTAL LIVING AREA:
1,808 SQ. FT.

An
EXCLUSIVE DESIGN
By Greg Marquis

Open & Airy

- This plan features:
- — Three bedrooms
- — Two full and one half baths
- The Foyer is naturally lit by a dormer window above
- The Family Room is highlighted by two front windows and a fireplace
- The Kitchen includes an angled extended counter/snack bar and an abundance of counter/cabinet space
- The Dining area opens to the Kitchen, for a more spacious feeling
- The roomy Master Suite is located on the first floor and has a private five-piece bath plus a walk-in closet
- The Laundry Room doubles as a mud room from the side entrance
- No materials list is available for this plan

Refer to **Pricing Schedule B** on the order form for pricing information

© 1996 Donald A. Gardner Architects, I█

Compact Plan

■ This plan features:
— Three bedrooms
— Two full baths
■ A Great Room topped by a cathedral ceiling adjoins the Dining Room and Kitchen to create a spacious living area
■ A bay window enlarging the Dining Room and a palladian window allowing ample light into the Great Room
■ An efficient U-shaped Kitchen leading directly to the garage, convenient for unloading groceries
■ A Master Suite highlighted by ample closet space and a private skylit bath enhanced by a dual vanity and a separate tub and shower

MAIN FLOOR — 1,372 SQ. FT.
GARAGE & STORAGE — 537 SQ. FT.

TOTAL LIVING AREA:
1,372 SQ. FT.

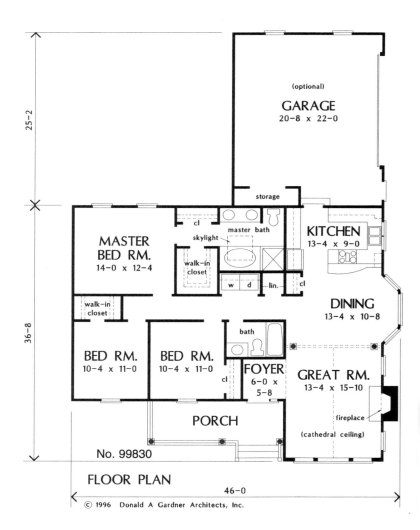

GARAGE
20-8 x 22-0
(optional)

25-2

storage

MASTER BED RM.
14-0 x 12-4

cl

master bath
skylight

walk-in closet

w | d | lin. | cl

KITCHEN
13-4 x 9-0

DINING
13-4 x 10-8

walk-in closet

36-8

BED RM.
10-4 x 11-0

BED RM.
10-4 x 11-0

cl

bath

FOYER
6-0 x 5-8

bath

GREAT RM.
13-4 x 15-10

fireplace
(cathedral ceiling)

PORCH

No. 99830

FLOOR PLAN

46-0

© 1996 Donald A Gardner Architects, Inc.

To order your Blueprints, call 1-800-235-5700

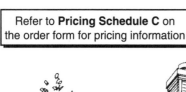

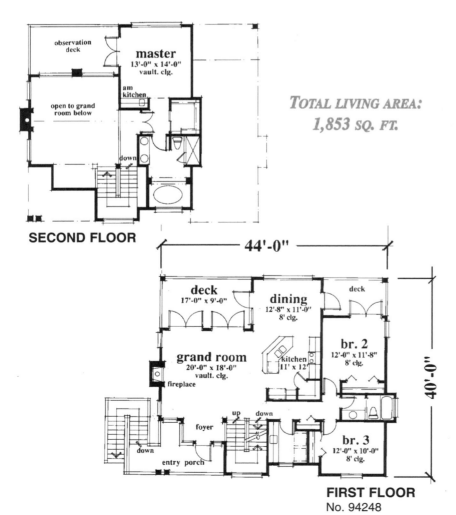

observation deck

master
13'-0" x 14'-0"
vault. clg.

am kitchen

open to grand room below

down

SECOND FLOOR

TOTAL LIVING AREA:
1,853 SQ. FT.

← 44'-0" →

deck
17'-0" x 9'-0"

dining
12'-8" x 11'-0"
8' clg.

deck

grand room
20'-0" x 18'-0"
vault. clg.

fireplace

kitchen
11' x 12'

br. 2
12'-0" x 11'-8"
8' clg.

40'-0"

up   down

foyer

down

entry porch

br. 3
12'-0" x 10'-0"
8' clg.

FIRST FLOOR
No. 94248

Delightful Home

■ This plan features:

— Three bedrooms

— Two full baths

■ Grand Room with a fireplace, vaulted ceiling and double French doors to the rear deck

■ Kitchen and Dining Room open to continue the overall feel of spaciousness

■ Kitchen has a large walk-in pantry, island with a sink and dishwasher creating a perfect triangular workspace

■ Dining Room with doors to both decks, has expanses of glass looking out to the rear yard

■ Master Bedroom features a double door entry, private bath, and a morning kitchen

■ No materials list is available for this plan

FIRST FLOOR — 1,342 SQ. FT.
SECOND FLOOR — 511 SQ. FT.
GARAGE — 1,740 SQ. FT.

Refer to **Pricing Schedule B** on the order form for pricing information

Wide Open and Convenient Plan

■ This plan features:

— Three bedrooms

— Two full baths

■ Vaulted ceilings in the Dining Room and Master Bedroom

■ A sloped ceiling in the fireplaced Living Room

■ A skylight illuminating the Master Bath

■ A large Master Bedroom with a walk-in closet

MAIN AREA — 1,737 SQ. FT.
BASEMENT — 1,727 SQ. FT.
GARAGE — 484 SQ. FT.

TOTAL LIVING AREA:
1,727 SQ. FT.

An
EXCLUSIVE DESIGN
By Karl Kreeger

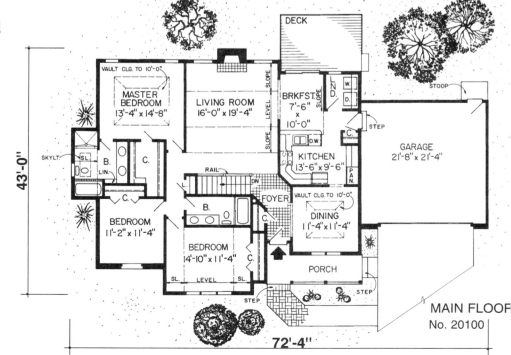

MAIN FLOOR
No. 20100

72'-4"
43'-0"

To order your Blueprints, call 1-800-235-5700

Refer to **Pricing Schedule A** on
the order form for pricing information

An
EXCLUSIVE DESIGN
By Westhome Planners, Ltd.

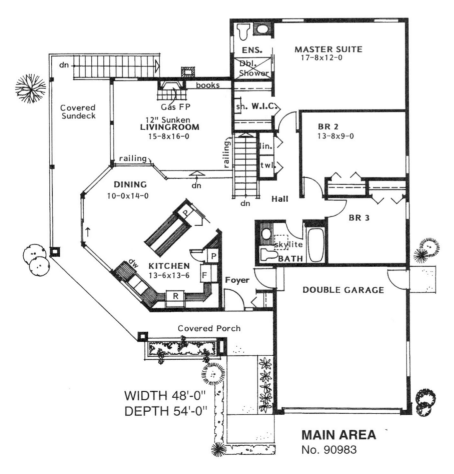

ENS.
Dbl.
Shower
books
Gas FP
sh. W.I.C.
12" Sunken
LIVINGROOM
15-8x16-0
lin.
twl.
railing
railing
DINING
10-0x14-0
dn
dn
Hall
dn
MASTER SUITE
17-8x12-0
BR 2
13-8x9-0
BR 3
skylite
BATH
DOUBLE GARAGE
P
P
dw
F
R
KITCHEN
13-6x13-6
Foyer
Covered
Sundeck
dn
Covered Porch

WIDTH 48'-0"
DEPTH 54'-0"

MAIN AREA
No. 90983

Attractive Roof Lines

■ This plan features:

— Three bedrooms

— One full and one three quarter
baths

■ An open floor plan shared by the
sunken Living Room, Dining and
Kitchen areas

■ An unfinished daylight Basement
which will provide future
bedrooms, a bathroom and
laundry facilities

■ A Master Suite with a big walk-
in closet and a private bath
featuring a double shower

FIRST FLOOR — 1,396 SQ. FT.
BASEMENT — 1,396 SQ. FT.
GARAGE — 389 SQ. FT.

TOTAL LIVING AREA:
1,396 SQ. FT.

Refer to **Pricing Schedule C** on the order form for pricing information

Plush Master Bedroom Wing

- ■ This plan features:
- — Three bedrooms
- — Two full baths
- ■ A raised, tiled Foyer with decorative window leading into an expansive Living Room, accented by a tiled fireplace and framed by French doors
- ■ An efficient Kitchen with a walk-in pantry and serving bar adjoining the Breakfast and Utility areas
- ■ A private Master Bedroom, crowned by a stepped ceiling, offering an atrium door to outside, a huge, walk-in closet and a luxurious bath
- ■ Two additional bedrooms with walk-in closets, share a full hall bath
- ■ No materials list is available for this plan

MAIN FLOOR — 1,849 SQ. FT.
GARAGE — 437 SQ. FT.

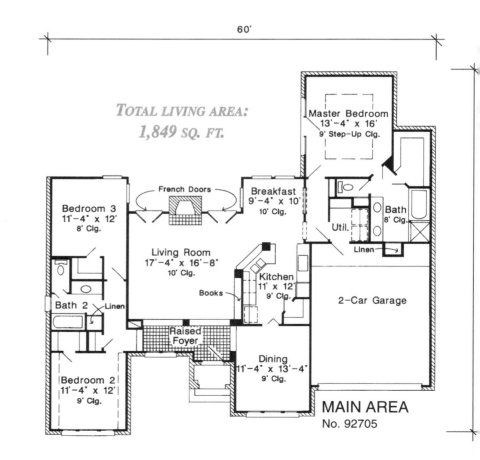

TOTAL LIVING AREA: 1,849 SQ. FT.

60'

Master Bedroom
13'-4" x 16'
9' Step-Up Clg.

Breakfast
9'-4" x 10'
10' Clg.

Bath
8' Clg.

Util.

Linen

French Doors

Bedroom 3
11'-4" x 12'
8' Clg.

Living Room
17'-4" x 16'-8"
10' Clg.

Kitchen
11' x 12'
9' Clg.

Books

2-Car Garage

Bath 2

Linen

Raised Foyer

Dining
11'-4" x 13'-4"
9' Clg.

Bedroom 2
11'-4" x 12'
9' Clg.

MAIN AREA
No. 92705

To order your Blueprints, call 1-800-235-5700

Refer to **Pricing Schedule B** on the order form for pricing information

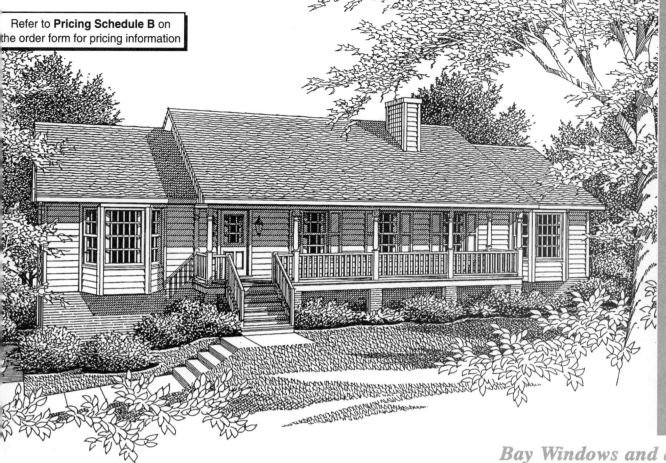

TOTAL LIVING AREA:
1,778 SQ. FT.

An
EXCLUSIVE DESIGN
By Jannis Vann & Associates, Inc.

Bay Windows and a Terrific Front Porch

■ This plan features:

— Three bedrooms

— Two full baths

■ A Country style front porch

■ An expansive Living Area that includes a fireplace

■ A Master Suite with a private Master Bath and a walk-in closet, as well as a bay window view of the front yard

■ An efficient Kitchen that serves the sunny Breakfast Area and the Dining Room with equal ease

■ A built-in pantry and a desk add to the conveniences in the Breakfast Area

■ Two additional bedrooms that share the full hall bath

■ A convenient main floor Laundry Room

MAIN AREA — 1,778 SQ. FT.
BASEMENT — 1,008 SQ. FT.
GARAGE — 728 SQ. FT.

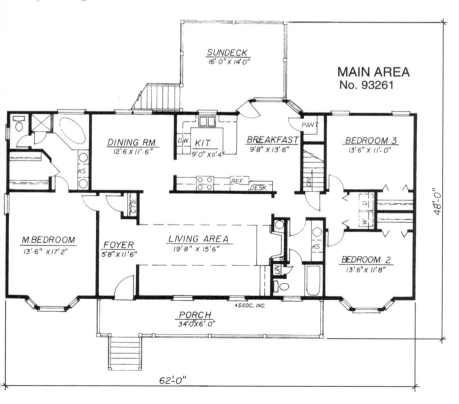

MAIN AREA
No. 93261

SUNDECK
16'0" X 14'0"

DINING RM.
12'6" X 11'6"

KIT.
9'0" X 11'4"

BREAKFAST
9'8" X 13'6"

PANT

BEDROOM 3
13'6" X 11'0"

REF. DESK

M. BEDROOM
13'6" X 17'2"

FOYER
5'8" X 11'6"

LIVING AREA
19'8" X 15'6"

BEDROOM 2
13'6" X 11'8"

PORCH
34'0" X 6'0"

ASSOC. INC.

48'-0"

62'-0"

Refer to **Pricing Schedule B** on the order form for pricing information

Covered Porch on Farm Style Traditional

■ This plan features:

— Three bedrooms

— Two and one half baths

■ A Dining Room with bay window and elevated ceiling

■ A Living Room complete with gas light fireplace

■ A two-car Garage

■ Ample storage space throughout the home

FIRST FLOOR — 909 SQ. FT
SECOND FLOOR — 854 SQ. FT.
BASEMENT — 899 SQ. FT.
GARAGE — 491 SQ. FT.

TOTAL LIVING AREA:
1,763 SQ. FT.

SECOND FLOOR

Master Br 14-3 x 17-5
Br 3 12-2 x 10-1
Br 2 13-11 x 11-9
Second Floor

Opt. Slab/ Crawl Space

An EXCLUSIVE DESIGN *By Karl Kreeger*

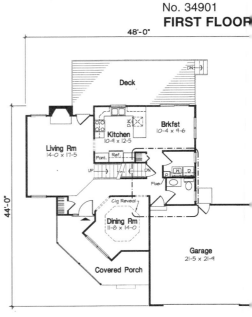

No. 34901
FIRST FLOOR

48'-0"
44'-0"
Deck
Brkfst 10-4 x 9-6
Kitchen 10-4 x 12-5
Living Rm 14-0 x 17-5
Dining Rm 11-8 x 14-0
Garage 21-5 x 21-4
Covered Porch

An EXCLUSIVE DESIGN *By Westhome Planners, Ltd.*

PLAN NO. 90990

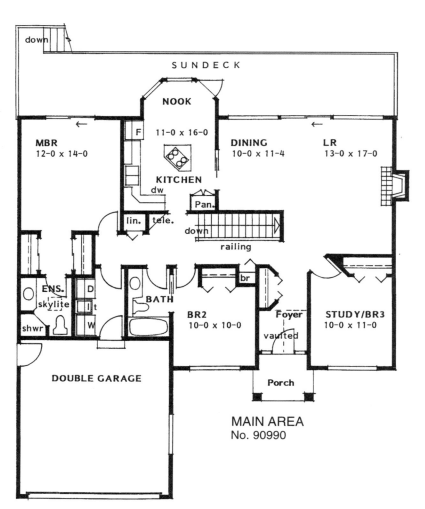

down

SUNDECK

NOOK
11-0 x 16-0

MBR
12-0 x 14-0

F

KITCHEN
dw

DINING
10-0 x 11-4

LR
13-0 x 17-0

Pan.

down
railing

lin. tele.

ENS.
skylite

D
l
t

W

BATH

br

BR2
10-0 x 10-0

Foyer
vaulted

STUDY/BR3
10-0 x 11-0

shwr

DOUBLE GARAGE

Porch

MAIN AREA
No. 90990

Comfort and Style

This plan features:

— Two bedrooms with possible third bedroom/den

— One full and one three quarter baths

An unfinished daylight basement, providing possible space for family recreation

A Master Suite complete with private bath and skylight

A large Kitchen including an eating nook

A sundeck that is easily accessible from the Master Suite, Nook and the Living/Dining area

MAIN AREA — 1,423 SQ. FT.
BASEMENT — 1,423 SQ. FT.
GARAGE — 399 SQ. FT.
WIDTH — 46'-0"
DEPTH — 52'-0"

TOTAL LIVING AREA:
1,423 SQ. FT.

No. 98432

Keystones and Arched Windows

■ This plan features:
— Three bedrooms
— Two full baths

■ A large arched window in the Dining Room offers eye-catching appeal

■ A decorative column helps to define the Dining Room from the Great Room

■ A fireplace and French door to the rear yard can be found in the Great Room

■ An efficient Kitchen includes a serving bar, Pantry and pass through to the Great Room

■ A vaulted ceiling over the Breakfast Room

■ A plush Master Suite includes a private bath and a walk-in closet

■ Two additional bedrooms share a full bath in the hall

■ An optional basement, slab or a crawl space foundation available — please specify when ordering

MAIN FLOOR — 1,670 SQ. FT.
GARAGE — 240 SQ. FT.

© Frank Betz Associates

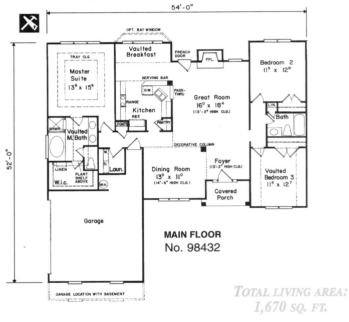

MAIN FLOOR
No. 98432

TOTAL LIVING AREA:
1,670 SQ. FT.

No. 9964

Recreation Room Houses Fireplace

■ This plan features:
— Four bedrooms
— Two full baths

■ A wood-burning fireplace warming the Living/Dining Room, which is accessible to the large wooden Sun Deck

■ Two first-floor bedrooms with access to a full hall bath

■ Two ample-sized second floor bedrooms

■ A Recreation Room with a cozy fireplace and convenient half bath

MAIN FLOOR — 906 SQ. FT.
UPPER FLOOR — 456 SQ. FT.
LOWER FLOOR — 594 SQ. FT.
BASEMENT — 279 SQ. FT.

TOTAL LIVING AREA:
1,956 SQ. FT.

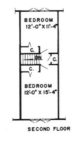

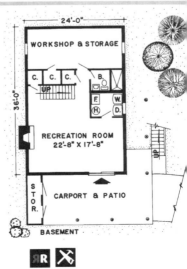

No. 9964

No. 94203

A Decorative Widows Walk

- This plan features:
  — Three bedrooms
  — Two full baths
- Living area above the Carport and Storage/Bonus areas offering a "piling" design for coastal, waterfront or low-lying terrain
- A covered Entry Porch leading into a spacious Great Room
- A Great Room with a vaulted ceiling, cozy fireplace and double glass door to the screened Veranda
- An efficient, L-shaped Kitchen with a work island and Dining area with a double door to a Sun Deck
- A Study and secondary Bedroom with ample closet space sharing a full bath and laundry area
- A private, second floor Master Suite with an oversized walk-in closet and luxurious bath
- No materials list is available for this plan

FIRST FLOOR — 1,136 SQ. FT.
SECOND FLOOR — 636 SQ. FT.
GARAGE — 526 SQ. FT.

TOTAL LIVING AREA:
1,772 SQ. FT.

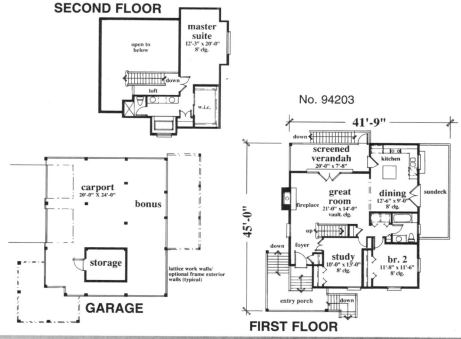

SECOND FLOOR

master suite
12'-3" x 20'-0"
8' clg.

open to below

down

loft

w.i.c.

carport
20'-0" X 24'-0"

bonus

storage

lattice work walls/
optional frame exterior
walls (typical)

GARAGE

No. 94203

41'-9"

45'-0"

down

screened verandah
20'-0" x 7'-8"

kitchen

great room
21'-6" x 14'-0"
vault. clg.

dining
12'-6" x 9'-0"
8' clg.

sundeck

fireplace

up

down

foyer

study
10'-0" x 13'-0"
8' clg.

br. 2
11'-8" x 11'-6"
8' clg.

entry porch

down

FIRST FLOOR

PRICE CODE B

No. 20070

Sheltered Porch is an Inviting Entrance

■ This plan features:
— Three bedrooms
— Two full and one half baths
■ A dramatic two-story Entry
■ A fireplaced Living Room
■ A modern Kitchen flowing easily into a sunny Breakfast Nook
■ A formal Dining Room with elegant decorative ceiling
■ A Master Bedroom highlighted by a sky lit bath

FIRST FLOOR — 877 SQ. FT.
SECOND FLOOR — 910 SQ. FT.
BASEMENT — 877 SQ. FT.
GARAGE — 458 SQ. FT.

TOTAL LIVING AREA:
1,787 SQ. FT.

An
EXCLUSIVE DESIGN
By Karl Kreeger

SECOND FLOOR

No. 20070

FIRST FLOOR

No. 94902

Abundance of Windows for Natural Lighting

■ This plan features:
— Four bedrooms
— Two full and a half baths
■ Interesting staircase with landing in volume Entry
■ Ten foot ceiling above transom windows and hearth fireplace accent the Great Room
■ Island counter/snack bar, Pantry and desk featured in Kitchen/Breakfast area
■ Kitchen conveniently accesses Laundry Area and Garage
■ Beautiful arched window under volume ceiling in Bedroom two
■ Master Bedroom suite features decorative ceiling to walk-in closets and double vanity bath with a whirlpool tub
■ Two additional bedrooms with ample closets share a full bath

SECOND FLOOR

© design basics, inc.

FIRST FLOOR — 944 SQ. FT.
SECOND FLOOR — 987 SQ. FT.
BASEMENT — 944 SQ. FT.
GARAGE — 557 SQ. FT.

TOTAL LIVING AREA:
1,931 SQ. FT.

FIRST FLOOR
No. 94902

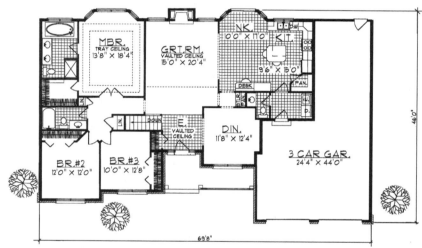

PRICE CODE C

No. 99115

A Very Distinctive Ranch

■ This plan features:

— Three bedrooms

— Two full and one half baths

■ This hip roofed ranch has an exterior mixing brick and siding

■ The recessed entrance has sidelights which work to create a formal entry

■ The formal Dining Room has a butler's Pantry for added convenience

■ The Great Room features a vaulted ceiling and a fireplace for added atmosphere

■ The large open Kitchen has ample cupboard space and a spacious Breakfast Area

■ The Master Suite includes a walk-in closet, private bath and an elegant bay window

■ A Laundry Room is on the main level between the three-car Garage and the Kitchen

■ No materials list is available for this plan

MAIN FLOOR — 1,947 SQ. FT.

BASEMENT — 1,947 SQ. FT.

TOTAL LIVING AREA:
1,947 SQ. FT.

MAIN FLOOR PLAN

No. 99115

PRICE CODE C

PRICE CODE C

Comfort and Charm

No. 96480

- This plan features:
— Three bedrooms
— Two full and one half baths
- The Foyer opens into the dormer's vaulted ceiling
- A cathedral ceiling in the Great Room soars up to a palladian window
- The Kitchen is equipped with an angled island peninsula
- Bay windows accent the formal Dining Room and Breakfast nook
- The Master Suite accesses the Deck and includes a private bath
- Upstairs find two bedrooms and a balcony that overlooks the Great Room

FIRST FLOOR — 1,480 SQ. FT.
SECOND FLOOR — 511 SQ. FT.
BONUS ROOM — 363 SQ. FT.
GARAGE — 621 SQ. FT.

TOTAL LIVING AREA:
1,991 SQ. FT.

SECOND FLOOR PLAN

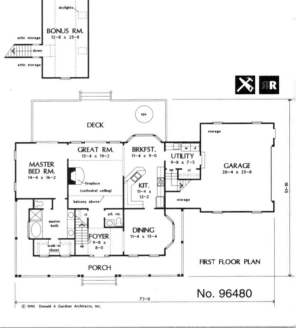

FIRST FLOOR PLAN

No. 96480

No. 91031
Snug Retreat With A View

- This plan features:
— One bedroom plus loft
— One full bath
- A large front Deck providing views and an expansive entrance
- A two-story Living/Dining area with double glass doors leading out to the Deck
- An efficient, U-shaped Kitchen with a pass through counter to the Dining area
- A first floor Bedroom, with ample closet space, located near a full shower bath
- A Loft/Bedroom on the second floor offering multiple uses

MAIN LEVEL — 572 SQ. FT.
LOFT — 308 SQ. FT.

TOTAL LIVING AREA:
880 SQ. FT.

LOFT/BDRM
308 SQ. FT.

DOWN

No. 91031

MAIN LEVEL

PRICE CODE C

No. 99859
Flexibility to Expand

■ This plan features:
— Three bedrooms
— Two full and one half baths

■ Three bedroom country cottage has lots of room to expand

■ Two-story Foyer contains palladian window in a clerestory dormer

■ Efficient Kitchen opens to Breakfast area and Deck for outdoor dining

■ Columns separating the Great Room and the dining Room that have nine foot ceilings

■ Master Bedroom suite is on the first level and features a skylight above the whirlpool tub

■ An optional basement or crawl space foundation available — please specify when ordering

FIRST FLOOR — 1,289 SQ. FT.

SECOND FLOOR — 542 SQ. FT.

BONUS ROOM — 393 SQ. FT.

GARAGE & STORAGE — 521 SQ. FT.

TOTAL LIVING AREA:
1,831 SQ. FT.

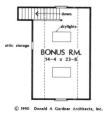

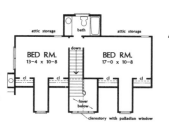

attic storage   bath   attic storage

BED RM.
13-4 x 10-8

BED RM.
17-0 x 10-8

cl   cl   cl   cl

down

foyer below

clerestory with palladian window

SECOND FLOOR PLAN

attic storage

BONUS RM.
14-4 x 23-8

down

skylights

© 1990 Donald A Gardner Architects, Inc.

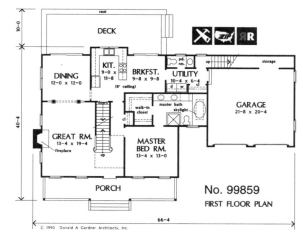

seat

DECK

DINING
12-0 x 12-0

KIT.
9-0 x
11-8

BRKFST.
9-8 x 9-8
(8' ceiling)

UTILITY
10-4 x 6-4

pd. rm.

up

storage

d w

10-0

40-4

GREAT RM.
13-4 x 19-4

fireplace

down

up

walk-in closet

master bath   skylight

MASTER
BED RM.
13-4 x 13-0

GARAGE
21-8 x 20-4

PORCH

No. 99859
FIRST FLOOR PLAN

66-4

© 1990 Donald A Gardner Architects, Inc.

PRICE CODE A

© 1996 Donald A. Gardner Architects, Inc.

PRICE CODE C

No. 99871
Charm and Personality

■ This plan features:
— Three bedrooms
— Two full baths

■ Charm and personality radiate through this country home

■ Interior columns dramatically open the Foyer and Kitchen to the spacious Great Room

■ Drama is heightened by the Great Room cathedral ceiling and fireplace

■ Master Suite with a tray ceiling combines privacy with access to the rear deck with spa, while the skylight bath has all the amenities expected in a quality home

■ Tray ceilings with round-top picture windows bring a special elegance to the Dining Room and the front swing room

■ An optional basement, or crawl space foundation available — please specify when ordering

MAIN FLOOR — 1,655 SQ. FT.
GARAGE — 434 SQ. FT.

TOTAL LIVING AREA:
1,655 SQ. FT.

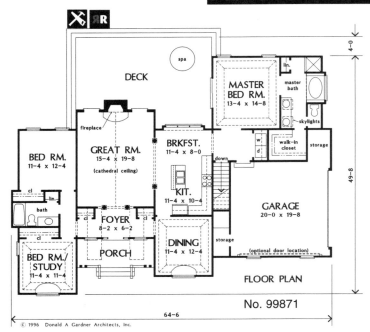

FLOOR PLAN
No. 99871

© 1996 Donald A Gardner Architects, Inc.

No. 92557
Elegant Brick Exterior

■ This plan features:
—Three bedrooms
—Two full baths

■ Detailing and accenting columns highlighting the covered front porch

■ Den is enhanced by a corner fireplace and adjoining with Dining Room

■ Efficient Kitchen well-appointed and with easy access to the utility/laundry room

■ Master Bedroom topped by a vaulted ceiling and pampered by a private bath and a walk-in closet

■ Two secondary bedrooms are located at the opposite end of home sharing a full bath located between the two rooms

■ An optional slab or crawl space foundation available — please specify when ordering

MAIN FLOOR — 1,390 SQ. FT.
GARAGE — 590 SQ. FT.

MAIN FLOOR
No. 92557

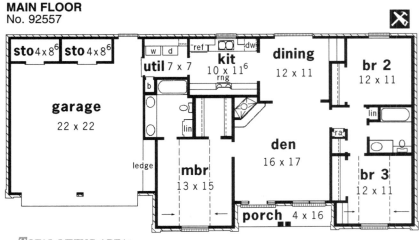

TOTAL LIVING AREA:
1,390 SQ. FT.

WIDTH 67'-4"
DEPTH 32'-10"

PRICE CODE B

No. 10394
Master Suite Crowns Plan

■ This plan features:
— Three bedrooms
— Two full baths

■ A Master Bedroom which occupies the entire second level

■ A passive solar design

■ A Living Room which rises two stories in the front

■ Skylights in the sloping ceilings of the Kitchen and Master Bath

FIRST FLOOR — 1,306 SQ. FT.
SECOND FLOOR — 472 SQ. FT.
GARAGE — 576 SQ. FT.

TOTAL LIVING AREA:
1,778 SQ. FT.

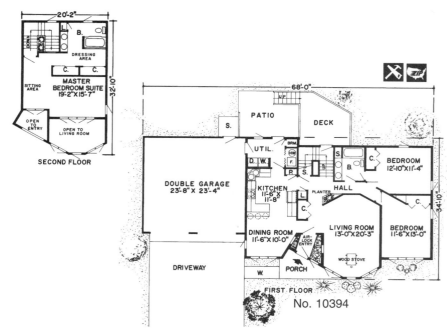

SECOND FLOOR
20'-2"
MASTER BEDROOM SUITE 19'-2"x15'-7"
DRESSING AREA
SITTING AREA
OPEN TO ENTRY
OPEN TO LIVING ROOM

FIRST FLOOR
No. 10394
68'-0"
DOUBLE GARAGE 23'-8" X 23'-4"
PATIO
DECK
UTIL.
KITCHEN 11'-6" X 11'-8"
HALL
BEDROOM 12'-10"X11'-4"
DINING ROOM 11'-6"X 10'-0"
LIVING ROOM 13'-0"X20'-3"
BEDROOM 11'-6"X13'-0"
PORCH
WOOD STOVE
DRIVEWAY

PRICE CODE B

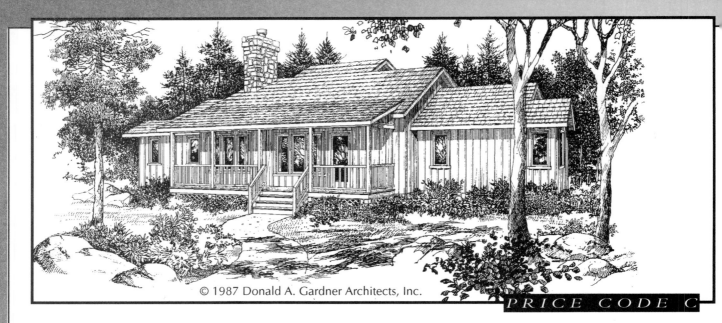

© 1987 Donald A. Gardner Architects, Inc.

No. 99864
Rustic Simplicity

- This plan features:
  — Three bedrooms
  — Two full and one half baths
- The central living area is large and boasts a cathedral ceiling, exposed wood beams and a clerestory
- A long screened porch has a bank of skylights
- The open Kitchen contains a convenient serving and eating counter
- The generous Master Suite opens to the screened Porch, and is enhanced by a walk-in closet and a whirlpool tub
- Two more bedrooms share a second full bath

MAIN FLOOR — 1,426 SQ. FT.

TOTAL LIVING AREA:
1,426 SQ. FT.

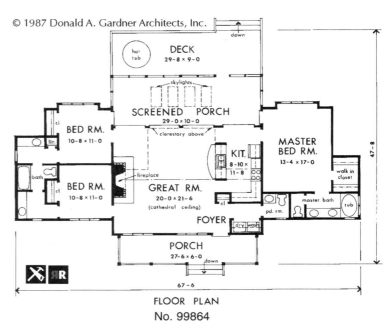

© 1987 Donald A. Gardner Architects, Inc.

FLOOR PLAN
No. 99864

No. 90671
Adapt this Colonial to Your Lifestyle

- This plan features:
  — Four bedrooms
  — Two full baths
- A Living Room with a beam ceiling and a fireplace
- An eat-in Kitchen efficiently serving the formal Dining Room
- A Master Bedroom with his and her closets
- Two upstairs bedrooms sharing a split bath

FIRST FLOOR — 1,056 SQ. FT.
SECOND FLOOR — 531 SQ. FT.

TOTAL LIVING AREA:
1,587 SQ. FT.

SECOND FLOOR

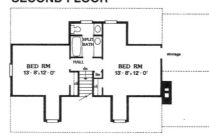

FIRST FLOOR
No. 90671

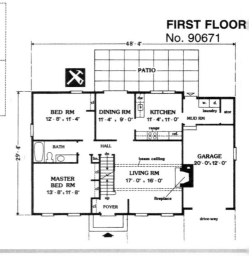

No. 98434

Expansive Living Room

■ This plan features:
—Three bedrooms
—Two full baths

■ Vaulted ceiling crowns spacious Living Room highlighted by a fireplace

■ Built-in pantry and direct access from the Garage adding to the conveniences of the Kitchen

■ Walk-in closet and a private five-piece bath topped by a vaulted ceiling in the Master Bedroom suite

■ Proximity to the full bath in the hall from the secondary bedrooms

■ An optional basement, slab or crawl space available — please specify when ordering

MAIN FLOOR — 1,346 SQ. FT.
GARAGE — 385 SQ. FT.
BASEMENT — 1,358 SQ. FT.

TOTAL LIVING AREA:
1,346 SQ. FT.

© Frank Betz Associates

MAIN FLOOR
No. 98434

No. 98456
High Ceilings Add Volume

■ This plan features:
— Three bedrooms
— Two full baths

■ A covered entry gives way to a 14-foot high ceiling in the Foyer

■ An arched opening greets you in the Great Room that also has a vaulted ceiling and a fireplace

■ The Dining Room is brightened by triple windows with transoms above

■ The Kitchen is a gourmet's delight and is open to the Breakfast nook

■ The Master Suite is sweet with a tray ceiling, vaulted Sitting Area and private bath

■ Two bedrooms on the opposite side of the home share a bath in the hall

■ An optional basement, slab or crawl space foundation available — please specify when ordering

MAIN FLOOR — 1,715 SQ. FT.
BASEMENT — 1,715 SQ. FT.
GARAGE — 450 SQ. FT.

TOTAL LIVING AREA: 1,715 SQ. FT.

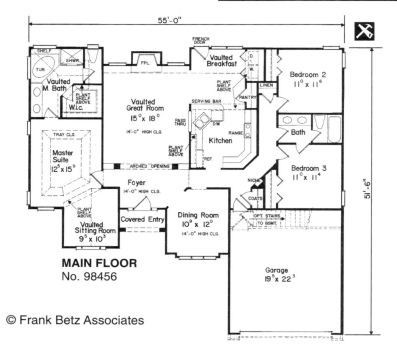

MAIN FLOOR
No. 98456

© Frank Betz Associates

No. 35001
Today's Family Living Made Easy

■ This plan features:
— Three bedrooms
— Two full and one half baths

■ A welcoming Country Porch sheltering the entrance

■ A large Living Room that flows into the Dining Room creating a great area for entertaining

■ An efficient U-shaped Kitchen that includes an informal Breakfast area and a Laundry Center

■ A private Master Suite with a full Bath and two closets

■ A Den/Office with ample closet space, enabling it to double as a Guest Room

■ Two additional bedrooms on the second floor that share a full hall bath

FIRST FLOOR — 1,081 SQ. FT.
SECOND FLOOR — 528 SQ. FT.
GARAGE — 528 SQ. FT.

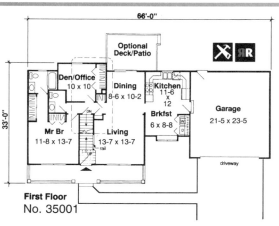

First Floor
No. 35001

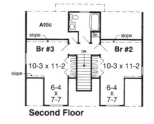

Second Floor

Crawl Space / Slab Option

TOTAL LIVING AREA: 1,609 SQ. FT.

No. 92647

Plenty of Room to Grow

■ This plan features:
— Three or Four bedrooms
— Two full and one half baths

■ Fieldstone and wood siding accent Porch entrance into open Foyer with lovely landing staircase

■ Sunken Great Room with large fireplace, built-in entertainment center and access to rear yard

■ Hub Kitchen with built-in Pantry, serving counter, bright Breakfast area and adjoining Dining Room, Laundry and Garage entry

■ Corner Master bedroom with walk-in closet, pampering bath with double vanity and whirlpool tub topped by sloped ceiling

■ Two or three additional bedrooms share a full bath and a study/computer area

■ No materials list is available for this plan

FIRST FLOOR — 1,065 SQ. FT.
SECOND FLOOR — 833 SQ. FT.
BONUS ROOM — 254 SQ. FT.
GARAGE — 652 SQ. FT.
BASEMENT — 995 SQ. FT.

TOTAL LIVING AREA:
1,898 SQ. FT.

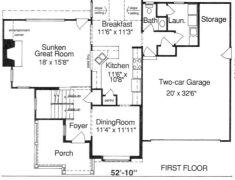

No. 92647

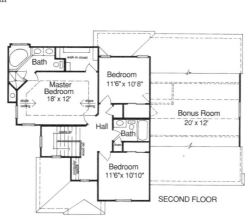

No. 99844
Clever Use of Interior Space

- This plan features:
— Three bedrooms
— Two full baths
- Efficient interior with cathedral and tray ceilings create feeling of space
- Great Room boosts cathedral ceiling above cozy fireplace, built-in shelves and columns
- Octagon Dining Room and Breakfast alcove bathed in light and easily access Porch
- Open Kitchen features island counter sink and Pantry
- Master Bedroom suite enhance by tray ceiling and plush bath

MAIN FLOOR — 1,737 SQ. FT.
GARAGE & STORAGE — 517 SQ. FT.

TOTAL LIVING AREA:
1,737 SQ. FT.

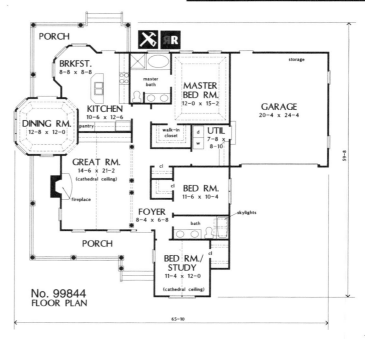

No. 99844
FLOOR PLAN

No. 96487
Perfect Home for Narrow Lot

- This plan features:
— Three bedrooms
— Two full and one half baths
- Wraparound Porch and two-car Garage features unusual for narrow lot floor plan
- Alcove of windows and columns add distinction to Dining Room
- Cathedral ceiling above inviting fireplace accent spacious Great Room
- Efficient Kitchen with peninsula counter accesses side Porch and Deck
- Master Suite on first floor and two additional bedrooms and Bonus Room on second floor

FIRST FLOOR — 1,219 SQ. FT.
SECOND FLOOR — 450 SQ. FT.
BONUS ROOM — 406 SQ. FT.
GARAGE — 473 SQ. FT.

TOTAL LIVING AREA:
1,669 SQ. FT.

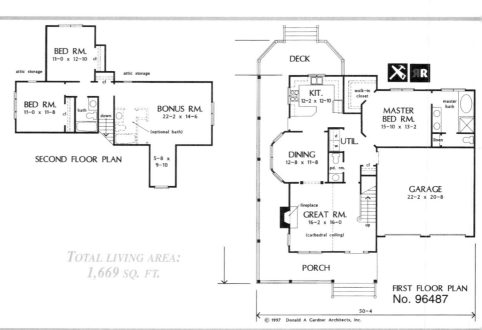

SECOND FLOOR PLAN

FIRST FLOOR PLAN
No. 96487

© 1997 Donald A. Gardner Architects, Inc.

No. 90680
Affordable Energy-Saver

■ This plan features:
— Three bedrooms
— Two full baths

■ A covered Porch leading into an open Foyer and Living/Dining Room with skylights and front to back exposure

■ An efficient Kitchen with a bay window Dinette area, a walk-in Pantry and adjacent to the Mud Room, Garage area

■ A private Master Bedroom with a luxurious Master Bath leading to a private Deck complete with a Hot Tub

■ Two additional bedrooms with access to a full hall bath

MAIN FLOOR — 1,393 SQ. FT.
BASEMENT — 1,393 SQ. FT.

TOTAL LIVING AREA:
1,393 SQ. FT.

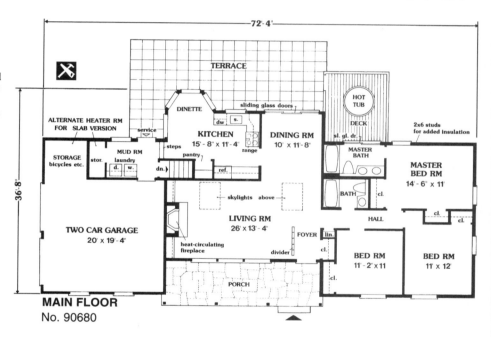

MAIN FLOOR
No. 90680

© 1997 Donald A. Gardner Architects, Inc.

PRICE CODE C

No. 98454
Family-Sized Accommodations

■ This plan features:
— Four bedrooms
— Two full and one half baths
■ This home has been designed for today's hectic lifestyle
■ The spacious feeling provided by a vaulted ceiling in Foyer carries into Family Room
■ A fireplace is nestled by an alcove of windows in Family Room which invites cozy gatherings
■ An angled Kitchen with a work island and a pantry easily serves the Breakfast area and the Dining Room
■ The Master Bedroom is accented by a tray ceiling, a lavish bath and a walk-in closet
■ On second floor find three additional bedrooms that share a double vanity bath and an optional Bonus Room
■ An optional basement or crawl space foundation available — please specify when ordering

FIRST FLOOR — 1,320 SQ. FT.
SECOND FLOOR — 554 SQ. FT.
BONUS ROOM — 155 SQ. FT.
GARAGE — 406 SQ. FT.
BASEMENT — 1,320 SQ. FT.

TOTAL LIVING AREA: 1,874 SQ. FT.

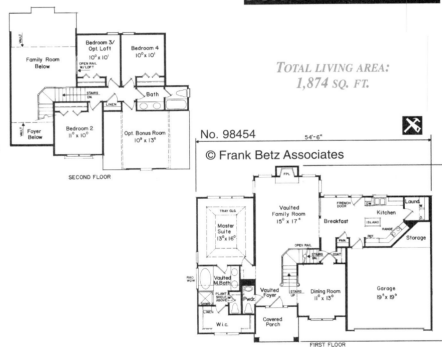

No. 98454
© Frank Betz Associates

No. 96458
Country Charm and Convenience

■ This plan features:
— Three bedrooms
— Two full baths
■ The open design pulls the Great Room, Kitchen and Breakfast Bay into one common area
■ Cathedral ceilings in the Great Room, Master Bedroom and a secondary bedroom
■ The rear deck expands the living and entertaining space
■ The Dining Room provides a quiet place for relaxed family dinners
■ Two additional bedrooms share a full bath

MAIN FLOOR — 1,512 SQ. FT.
GARAGE & STORAGE — 455 SQ. FT.

TOTAL LIVING AREA: 1,512 SQ. FT.

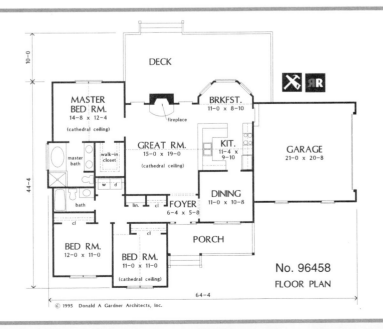

No. 96458
FLOOR PLAN

© 1995 Donald A Gardner Architects, Inc.

242

No. 98414

Three Bedroom Ranch

- This plan features:
  – Three bedrooms
  – Two full baths
- Formal Dining Room enhanced by a plant shelf and a side window
- Wetbar located between the Kitchen and the Dining Room
- Built-in pantry, a double sink and a snack bar highlight the Kitchen
- Breakfast Room containing a radius window and a French door to the rear yard
- Large cozy fireplace framed by windows in the Great Room
- Master Suite with a vaulted ceiling over the sitting area, a master bath and a walk-in closet
- Two additional bedrooms sharing the full bath in the hall
- An optional basement or crawl space foundation available — please specify when ordering

MAIN FLOOR — 1,575 SQ. FT.
GARAGE — 459 SQ. FT.
BASEMENT — 1,658 SQ. FT.

© Frank Betz Associates

OPT. BASEMENT STAIR LOCATION

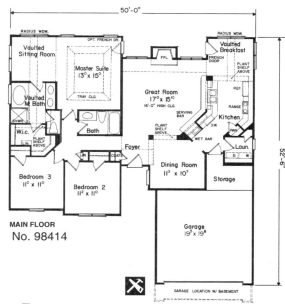

MAIN FLOOR
No. 98414

TOTAL LIVING AREA:
1,575 SQ. FT.

©1995 Donald A. Gardner Architects, Inc.

No. 10521
Elegant Design Offers Special Living

■ This plan features:
— Four bedrooms
— Two and one half baths
■ A balcony overlooking the two-story foyer
■ A Master Suite including a five-piece bath, an oversized walk-in closet, and a separate linen closet
■ A Kitchen including a Breakfast Nook, Pantry and Desk
■ A formal Living Room with access to a rear deck

FIRST FLOOR — 1,191 SQ. FT.
SECOND FLOOR — 699 SQ. FT.
BASEMENT — 1,191 SQ. FT.
GARAGE — 454 SQ. FT.

TOTAL LIVING AREA:
1,890 SQ. FT.

No. 10521

An
EXCLUSIVE DESIGN
By Karl Kreeger

No. 98357
First Floor Master Suite

■ This plan features:
— Three bedrooms
— Two full and one half baths
■ The front Porch and dormer add to the country appeal of this home
■ An elegant Dining Room is topped by a decorative ceiling and has direct Kitchen access
■ The Kitchen/Breakfast Room includes a cook top island, a double corner sink, a walk-in Pantry, a built-in desk and a vaulted ceiling
■ The Great Room is accented by a vaulted ceiling and a fireplace
■ A double door entrance, a box bay window, a vaulted ceiling and a plush five-piece bath are all features of the Master suite
■ Two additional bedrooms share use of the full bath in the hall

MAIN FLOOR — 1,490 SQ. FT.
UPPER FLOOR — 436 SQ. FT.
BASEMENT — 1,490 SQ. FT.
GARAGE — 400 SQ. FT.

UPPER FLOOR

TOTAL LIVING AREA:
1,926 SQ. FT.

No. 98357
MAIN FLOOR

No. 96462

Farmhouse Charm

■ This plan features:
— Three bedrooms
— Two full and one half baths

■ Nine foot ceilings and vaulted ceilings in Great Room and Master Bedroom add spaciousness

■ Dining Room accented by columns and accesses Deck for outdoor living

■ Efficient Kitchen features peninsula counter with serving bar for Breakfast area

■ Master Bedroom suite includes luxurious bath with walk-in closet, garden tub, shower and double vanity

■ Two upstairs bedrooms. one with walk-in closet, share full bath with skylight

FIRST FLOOR — 1,380 SQ. FT.
SECOND FLOOR — 466 SQ. FT.
BONUS ROOM — 326 SQ. FT.
GARAGE — 523 SQ. FT.

TOTAL LIVING AREA:
1,846 SQ. FT.

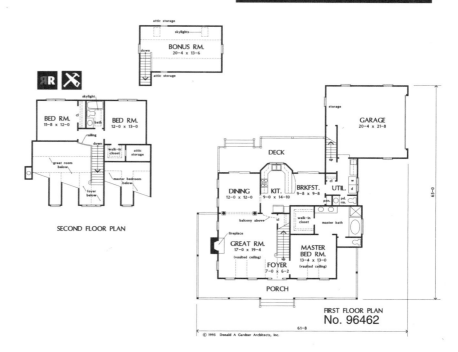

SECOND FLOOR PLAN

FIRST FLOOR PLAN
No. 96462

Everything You Need...
...to Make Your Dream Come True!

You pay only a fraction of the original cost for home designs by respected professionals.

You've Picked Your Dream Home!

You can already see it standing on your lot... you can see yourselves in your new home... enjoying family, entertaining guests, celebrating holidays. All that remains ahead are the details. That's where we can help. Whether you plan to build-it-yourself, be your own contractor, or hand your plans over to an outside contractor, your Garlinghouse blueprints provide the perfect beginning for putting yourself in your dream home right away.

We even make it simple for you to make professional design modifications. We can also provide a materials list for greater economy.

My grandfather, L.F. Garlinghouse, started a tradition of quality when he founded this company in 1907. For over 90 years, homeowners and builders have relied on us for accurate, complete, professional blueprints. Our plans help you get results fast... and save money, too! These pages will give you all the information you need to order. So get started now... I know you'll love your new Garlinghouse home!

Sincerely,

EXTERIOR ELEVATIONS

Elevations are scaled drawings of the front, rear, left and right sides of a home. All of the necessary information pertaining to the exterior finish materials, roof pitches and exterior height dimensions of your home are defined.

CABINET PLANS

These plans, or in some cases elevations, will detail the layout of the kitchen and bathroom cabinets at a larger scale. This gives you an accurate layout for your cabinets or an ideal starting point for a modified custom cabinet design. Available for most plans in our collection. You may also show the floor plan without a cabinet layout. This will allow you to start from scratch and design your own dream kitchen.

TYPICAL WALL SECTION

This section is provided to help your builder understand the structural components and materials used to construct the exterior walls of your home. This section will address insulation, roof components, and interior and exterior wall finishes. Your plans will be designed with either 2x4 or 2x6 exterior walls, but most professional contractors can easily adapt the plans to the wall thickness you require. Available for most plans in our collection.

FIREPLACE DETAILS

If the home you have chosen includes a fireplace, the fireplace detail will show typical methods to construct the firebox, hearth and flue chase for masonry units, or a wood frame chase for a zero-clearance unit. Available for most plans in our collection.

FOUNDATION PLAN

These plans will accurately dimension the footprint of your home including load bearing points and beam placement if applicable. The foundation style will vary from plan to plan. Your local climatic conditions will dictate whether a basement, slab or crawlspace is best suited for your area. In most cases, if your plan comes with one foundation style, a professional contractor can easily adapt the foundation plan to an alternate style.

ROOF PLAN

The information necessary to construct the roof will be included with your home plans. Some plans will reference roof trusses, while many others contain schematic framing plans. These framing plans will indicate the lumber sizes necessary for the rafters and ridgeboards based on the designated roof loads.

TYPICAL CROSS SECTION

A cut-away cross-section through the entire home shows your building contractor the exact correlation of construction components at all levels of the house. It will help to clarify the load bearing points from the roof all the way down to the basement.

DETAILED FLOOR PLANS

The floor plans of your home accurately dimension the positioning of all walls, doors, windows, stairs and permanent fixtures. They will show you the relationship and dimensions of rooms, closets and traffic patterns. The schematic of the electrical layout may be included in the plan. This layout is clearly represented and does not hinder the clarity of other pertinent information shown. All these details will help your builder properly construct your new home.

STAIR DETAILS

If stairs are an element of the design you have chosen, the plans will show the necessary information to build these, either through a stair cross section, or on the floor plans. Either way, the information provides your builders the essential reference points that they need to build the stairs.

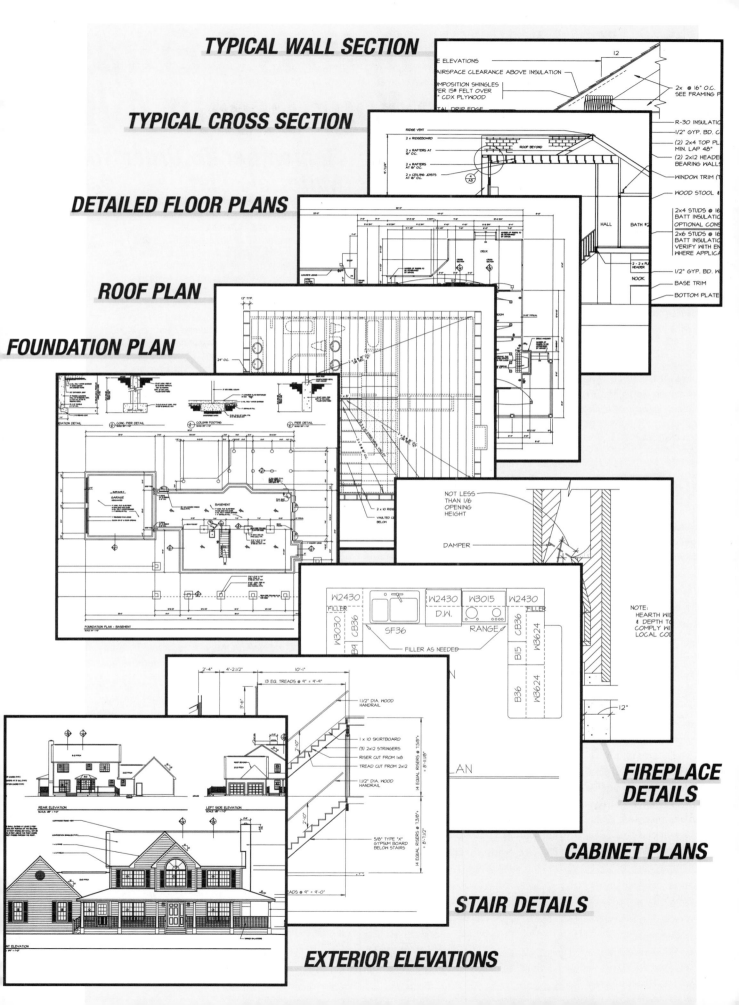

TYPICAL WALL SECTION

TYPICAL CROSS SECTION

DETAILED FLOOR PLANS

ROOF PLAN

FOUNDATION PLAN

FIREPLACE DETAILS

CABINET PLANS

STAIR DETAILS

EXTERIOR ELEVATIONS

Garlinghouse Options & Extras ...Make Your Dream A Home

Reversed Plans Can Make Your Dream Home Just Right!

"That's our dream home...if only the garage were on the other side!"

You could have exactly the home you want by flipping it end-for-end. Check it out by holding your dream home page of this book up to a mirror. Then simply order your plans "reversed." We'll send you one full set of mirror-image plans (with the writing backwards) as a master guide for you and your builder.

The remaining sets of your order will come as shown in this book so the dimensions and specifications are easily read on the job site...but most plans in our collection come stamped "REVERSED" so there is no construction confusion.

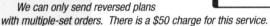

As Shown   Reversed

We can only send reversed plans with multiple-set orders. There is a $50 charge for this service.

Some plans in our collection are available in Right Reading Reverse. Right Reading Reverse plans will show your home in reverse, with the writing on the plan being readable. This easy-to-read format will save you valuable time and money. Please contact our Customer Service Department at (860) 343-5977 to check for Right Reading Reverse availability. (There is a $125 charge for this service.)

Specifications & Contract Form

We send this form to you free of charge with your home plan order. The form is designed to be filled in by you or your contractor with the exact materials to use in the construction of your new home. Once signed by you and your contractor it will provide you with peace of mind throughout the construction process.

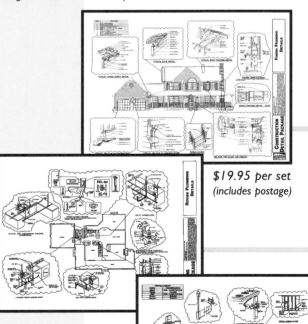

$19.95 per set
(includes postage)

Remember To Order Your Materials List

It'll help you save money. Available at a modest additional charge, the Materials List gives the quantity, dimensions, and specifications for the major materials needed to build your home. You will get faster, more accurate bids from your contractors and building suppliers — and avoid paying for unused materials and waste. Materials Lists are available for all home plans except as otherwise indicated, but can only be ordered with a set of home plans. Due to differences in regional requirements and homeowner or builder preferences... electrical, plumbing and heating/air conditioning equipment specifications are not designed specifically for each plan. However, non-plan specific detailed typical prints of residential electrical, plumbing and construction guidelines can be provided. Please see below for additional information. If you need a detailed materials cost you might need to purchase a Zip Quote. (Details follow)

Detail Plans Provide Valuable Information About Construction Techniques

Because local codes and requirements vary greatly, we recommend that you obtain drawings and bids from licensed contractors to do your mechanical plans. However, if you want to know more about techniques — and deal more confidently with subcontractors — we offer these remarkably useful detail sheets. These detail sheets will aid in your understanding of these technical subjects. **The detail sheets are not specific to any one home plan and should be used only as a general reference guide.**

RESIDENTIAL CONSTRUCTION DETAILS

Ten sheets that cover the essentials of stick-built residential home construction. Details foundation options — poured concrete basement, concrete block, or monolithic concrete slab. Shows all aspects of floor, wall and roof framing. Provides details for roof dormers, overhangs, chimneys and skylights. Conforms to requirements of Uniform Building code or BOCA code. Includes a quick index and a glossary of terms.

RESIDENTIAL PLUMBING DETAILS

Eight sheets packed with information detailing pipe installation methods, fittings, and sized. Details plumbing hook-ups for toilets, sinks, washers, sump pumps, and septic system construction. Conforms to requirements of National Plumbing code. Color coded with a glossary of terms and quick index.

RESIDENTIAL ELECTRICAL DETAILS

Eight sheets that cover all aspects of residential wiring, from simple switch wiring to service entrance connections. Details distribution panel layout with outlet and switch schematics, circuit breaker and wiring installation methods, and ground fault interrupter specifications. Conforms to requirements of National Electrical Code. Color coded with a glossary of terms.

Modifying Your Favorite Design, Made *EASY*!

OPTION #1

Modifying Your Garlinghouse Home Plan

Simple modifications to your dream home, including minor non-structural changes and material substitutions, can be made between you and your builder by marking the changes directly on your blueprints. However, if you are considering making significant changes to your chosen design, we recommend that you use the services of The Garlinghouse Co. Design Staff. We will help take your ideas and turn them into a reality, just the way you want. Here's our procedure!

When you place your Vellum order, you may also request a free Garlinghouse Modification Kit. In this kit, you will receive a red marking pencil, furniture cut-out sheet, ruler, a self addressed mailing label and a form for specifying any additional notes or drawings that will help us understand your design ideas. Mark your desired changes directly on the Vellum drawings. NOTE: Please use only a **red pencil** to mark your desired changes on the Vellum. Then, return the redlined Vellum set in the original box to The Garlinghouse Company at, 282 Main Street Extension, Middletown, CT 06457. **IMPORTANT**: Please **roll** the Vellums for shipping, **do not fold** the Vellums for shipping.

We also offer modification estimates. We will provide you with an estimate to draft your changes based on your specific modifications before you purchase the vellums, for a $50 fee. After you receive your estimate, if you decide to have The Garlinghouse Company Design Staff do the changes, the $50 estimate fee will be deducted from the cost of your modifications. If, however, you choose to use a different service, the $50 estimate fee is non-refundable.

Within 5 days of receipt of your plans, you will be contacted by a member of The Garlinghouse Co. Design Staff with an estimate for the design services to draw those changes. A 50% deposit is required before we begin making the actual modifications to your plans.

Once the preliminary design changes have been made to the floor plans and elevations, copies will be sent to you to make sure we have made the exact changes you want. We will wait for your approval before continuing with any structural revisions. The Garlinghouse Co. Design Staff will call again to inform you that your modified Vellum plan is complete and will be shipped as soon as the final payment has been made. For additional information call us at 1-860-343-5977. Please refer to the Modification Pricing Guide for estimated modification costs. Please call for Vellum modification availability for plan numbers 85,000 and above.

OPTION #2

Reproducible Vellums for Local Modification Ease

If you decide not to use the Garlinghouse Co. Design Staff for your modifications, we recommend that you follow our same procedure of purchasing our Vellums. You then have the option of using the services of the original designer of the plan, a local professional designer, or architect to make the modifications to your plan.

With a Vellum copy of our plans, a design professional can alter the drawings just the way you want, then you can print as many copies of the modified plans as you need to build your house. And, since you have already started with our complete detailed plans, the cost of those expensive professional services will be significantly less than starting from scratch. Refer to the price schedule for Vellum costs. Again, please call for Vellum availability for plan numbers 85,000 and above.

IMPORTANT RETURN POLICY: Upon receipt of your Vellums, if for some reason you decide you do not want modified plan, then simply return the Kit and the unopened Vellums. Reproducible Vellum copies of our home plans are copyright protected and only sold under the terms of a license agreement that you will receive with your order. Should you not agree to the terms, then the Vellums may be returned, **unopened,** for a full refund less the shipping and handling charges, plus a 15% restocking fee. For any additional information, please call us at 1-860-343-5977.

MODIFICATION PRICING GUIDE

CATEGORIES	ESTIMATED COST
KITCHEN LAYOUT — PLAN AND ELEVATION	$175.00
BATHROOM LAYOUT — PLAN AND ELEVATION	$175.00
FIREPLACE PLAN AND DETAILS	$200.00
INTERIOR ELEVATION	$125.00
EXTERIOR ELEVATION — MATERIAL CHANGE	$140.00
EXTERIOR ELEVATION — ADD BRICK OR STONE	$400.00
EXTERIOR ELEVATION — STYLE CHANGE	$450.00
NON BEARING WALLS (INTERIOR)	$200.00
BEARING AND/OR EXTERIOR WALLS	$325.00
WALL FRAMING CHANGE — 2X4 TO 2X6 OR 2X6 TO 2X4	$240.00
ADD/REDUCE LIVING SPACE — SQUARE FOOTAGE	QUOTE REQUIRED
NEW MATERIALS LIST	$.20 SQUARE FOOT
CHANGE TRUSSES TO RAFTERS OR CHANGE ROOF PITCH	$300.00
FRAMING PLAN CHANGES	$325.00
GARAGE CHANGES	$325.00
ADD A FOUNDATION OPTION	$300.00
FOUNDATION CHANGES	$250.00
RIGHT READING PLAN REVERSE	$575.00
ARCHITECTS SEAL (Available for most states)	$300.00
ENERGY CERTIFICATE	$150.00
LIGHT AND VENTILATION SCHEDULE	$150.00

Questions?

Call our customer service department at **1-860-343-5977**

"How to obtain a construction cost calculation based on labor rates and building material costs in <u>your</u> Zip Code area!"

ZIP-QUOTE!
HOME COST CALCULATOR

ZIP QUOTE
HOME COST CALCULATOR

WHY?

Do you wish you could quickly find out the building cost for your new home without waiting for a contractor to compile hundreds of bids? Would you like to have a benchmark to compare your contractor(s) bids against? **Well, Now You Can!!,** with **Zip-Quote** Home Cost Calculator. Zip-Quote is only available for zip code areas within the United States.

HOW?

Our new **Zip-Quote** Home Cost Calculator will enable you to obtain the calculated building cost to construct your new home, based on labor rates and building material costs within your zip code area, without the normal delays or hassles usually associated with the bidding process. Zip-Quote can be purchased in two separate formats, an itemized or a bottom line format.

"How does **Zip-Quote** actually work?" When you call to order, you must choose from the options available, for your specific home, in in order for us to process your order. Once we receive your **Zip-Quote** order, we process your specific home plan building materials list through our Home Cost Calculator which contains up-to-date rates for all residential labor trades and building material costs in your zip code area. "The result?" A calculated cost to build your dream home in your zip code area. This calculation will help you (as a consumer or a builder) evaluate your building budget. This is a valuable tool for anyone considering building a new home.

All database information for our calculations is furnished by Marshall & Swift, L.P. For over 60 years, Marshall & Swift L.P. has been a leading provider of cost data to professionals in all aspects of the construction and remodeling industries.

OPTION 1

The **Itemized Zip-Quote** is a detailed building material list. Each building material list line item will separately state the labor cost, material cost and equipment cost (if applicable) for the use of that building material in the construction process. Each category within the building material list will be subtotaled and the entire Itemized cost calculation totaled at the end. This building materials list will be summarized by the individual building categories and will have additional columns where you can enter data from your contractor's estimates for a cost comparison between the different suppliers and contractors who will actually quote you their products and services.

OPTION 2

The **Bottom Line Zip-Quote** is a one line summarized total cost for the home plan of your choice. This cost calculation is also based on the labor cost, material cost and equipment cost (if applicable) within your local zip code area.

COST

The price of your **Itemized Zip-Quote** is based upon the pricing schedule of the plan you have selected, in addition to the price of the materials list. Please refer to the pricing schedule on our order form. The price of your initial **Bottom Line Zip-Quote** is $29.95. Each additional **Bottom Line Zip-Quote** ordered in conjunction with the initial order is only $14.95. **Bottom Line Zip-Quote** may be purchased separately and does NOT have to be purchased in conjunction with a home plan order.

FYI

An **Itemized Zip-Quote** Home Cost Calculation can ONLY be purchased in conjunction with a Home Plan order. The **Itemized Zip-Quote** can not be purchased separately. The **Bottom Line Zip-Quote** can be purchased separately and doesn't have to be purchased in conjunction with a home plan order. Please consult with a sales representative for current availability. If you find within 60 days of your order date that you will be unable to build this home, then you may exchange the plans and the materials list towards the price of a new set of plans (see order info pages for plan exchange policy). The **Itemized Zip-Quote** and the **Bottom Line Zip-Quote** are NOT returnable. The price of the initial **Bottom Line Zip-Quote** order can be credited towards the purchase of an **Itemized Zip-Quote** order only. Additional **Bottom Line Zip-Quote** orders, within the same order can not be credited. Please call our Customer Service Department for more information.

Zip-Quote is available for plans where you see this symbol. ☐
Please call for current availability.

SOME MORE INFORMATION

The Itemized and Bottom Line Zip-Quotes give you approximate costs for constructing the particular house in your area. These costs are not exact and are only intended to be used as a preliminary estimate to help determine the affordability of a new home and/or a guide to evaluate the general competitiveness of actual price quotes obtained through local suppliers and contractors. However, Zip-Quote cost figures should never be relied upon as the only source of information in either case. The Garlinghouse Company and Marshall & Swift L.P. can not guarantee any level of data accuracy or correctness in a Zip-Quote and disclaim all liability for loss with respect to the same, in excess of the original purchase price of the Zip-Quote product. All Zip-Quote calculations are based upon the actual blueprint materials list with options as selected by customer and do not reflect any differences that may be shown on the published house renderings, floor plans, or photographs.

Ignoring Copyright Laws Can Be
A $1,000,000 Mistake

Recent changes in the US copyright laws allow for statutory penalties of up to **$100,000** per incident for copyright infringement involving any of the copyrighted plans found in this publication. The law can be confusing. So, for your own protection, take the time to understand what you can and cannot do when it comes to home plans.

···WHAT YOU CANNOT DO···

You Cannot Duplicate Home Plans

Purchasing a set of blueprints and making additional sets by reproducing the original is **illegal**. If you need multiple sets of a particular home plan, then you must purchase them.

You Cannot Copy Any Part of a Home Plan to Create Another

Creating your own plan by copying even part of a home design found in this publication is called "creating a derivative work" and is **illegal** unless you have permission to do so.

You Cannot Build a Home Without a License

You must have specific permission or license to build a home from a copyrighted design, even if the finished home has been changed from the original plan. It is **illegal** to build one of the homes found in this publication without a license.

What Garlinghouse Offers

Home Plan Blueprint Package

By purchasing a multiple set package of blueprints or a vellum from Garlinghouse, you not only receive the physical blueprint documents necessary for construction, but you are also granted a license to build one, and only one, home. You can also make simple modifications, including minor non-structural changes and material substitutions, to our design, as long as these changes are made directly on the blueprints purchased from Garlinghouse and no additional copies are made.

Home Plan Vellums

By purchasing vellums for one of our home plans, you receive the same construction drawings found in the blueprints, but printed on vellum paper. Vellums can be erased and are perfect for making design changes. They are also semi-transparent making them easy to duplicate. But most importantly, the purchase of home plan vellums comes with a broader license that allows you to make changes to the design (ie, create a hand drawn or CAD derivative work), to make copies of the plan, and to build one home from the plan.

License To Build Additional Homes

With the purchase of a blueprint package or vellums you automatically receive a license to build one home and only one home, respectively. If you want to build more homes than you are licensed to build through your purchase of a plan, then additional licenses may be purchased at reasonable costs from Garlinghouse. Inquire for more information.

Order Code No. H98A4

Order Form

Plan prices guaranteed until 10/26/99 — After this date call for updated pricing

_____ set(s) of blueprints for plan #_____ $_____

_____ Vellum & Modification kit for plan #_____ $_____

_____ Additional set(s) @ $35 each for plan #_____ $_____

_____ Mirror Image Reverse @ $50 each $_____

_____ Right Reading Reverse @ $125 each $_____

_____ Materials list for plan #_____ $_____

_____ Detail Plans @ $19.95 each

      ❏ Construction ❏ Plumbing ❏ Electrical $_____

_____ Bottom line ZIP Quote@$29.95 for plan #_____ $_____

_____ Additional Bottom Line Zip Quote

    @ $14.95 for plan(s) #_____

_____ $_____

_____ Itemized ZIP Quote for plan(s) #_____ $_____

  Shipping (see charts on opposite page) $_____

  Subtotal $_____

  Sales Tax(CT residents add 6% sales tax, KS residents add
     6.15% sales tax) (Not required for other states) $_____

TOTAL AMOUNT ENCLOSED $_____

Send your check, money order or credit card information to:
(No C.O.D.'s Please)

Please submit all <u>United States</u> & <u>Other Nations</u> orders to:

Garlinghouse Company
P.O. Box 1717
Middletown, CT. 06457

Please Submit all <u>Canadian</u> plan orders to:

Garlinghouse Company
60 Baffin Place, Unit #5
Waterloo, Ontario N2V 1Z7

ADDRESS INFORMATION:

NAME:_____

STREET:_____

CITY:_____

STATE:_____ **ZIP:**_____

DAYTIME PHONE:_____

Credit Card Information	
Charge To: ❏ Visa	❏ Mastercard
Card # ⎵⎵⎵⎵⎵⎵⎵⎵⎵⎵⎵⎵⎵⎵⎵	
Signature _____ Exp. ___/___	

IMPORTANT INFORMATION TO READ BEFORE YOU PLACE YOUR ORDER

How Many Sets Of Plans Will You Need?

The Standard 8-Set Construction Package

Our experience shows that you'll speed every step of construction and avoid costly building errors by ordering enough sets to go around. Each tradesperson wants a set — the general contractor and all subcontractors; foundation, electrical, plumbing, heating/air conditioning and framers. Don't forget your lending institution, building department and, of course, a set for yourself. * Recommended For Construction *

The Minimum 4-Set Construction Package

If you're comfortable with arduous follow-up, this package can save you few dollars by giving you the option of passing down plan sets as work progresses. You might have enough copies to go around if work goes exactly as scheduled and no plans are lost or damaged by subcontractors. But for only $50 more, the 8-set package eliminates these worries. * Recommended For Bidding *

The Single Study Set

We offer this set so you can study the blueprints to plan your dream home in detail. They are stamped "study set only-not for construction", and you can-not build a home from them. In pursuant to copyright laws, it is <u>illegal</u> to repro-duce any blueprint.

Our Reorder and Exchange Policies:

If you find after your initial purchase that you require additional sets of plans you may purchase them from us at special reorder prices (please call for pricing details) provided that you reorder within 6 months of your original order date. There is a $28 reorder processing fee that is charged on all reorders. For more information on reordering plans please contact our Customer Service Department at (860) 343-5977.

We want you to find your dream home from our wide selection of home plans However, if for some reason you find that the plan you have purchased from us does not meet your needs, then you may exchange that plan for any other plan in our col-lection. We allow you sixty days from your original invoice date to make an exchange At the time of the exchange you will be charged a processing fee of 15% of the total amount of your original order plus the difference in price between the plans (if applicable) plus the cost to ship the new plans to you. Call our Customer Service Department at (860) 343-5977 for more information. Please Note: Reproducible vel-lums can only be exchanged if they are unopened.

Important Shipping Information

Please refer to the shipping charts on the order form for service availability for your specific plan number. Our delivery service must have a street address or Rural Route Box number — never a post office box. (PLEASE NOTE: Supplying a P.O. Box number <u>only</u> will delay the shipping of your order.) Use a work address if no one is home during the day.

Orders being shipped to APO or FPO must go via First Class Mail. Please include the proper postage.

For our International Customers, only Certified bank checks and money orders are accepted and must be payable in U.S. currency. For speed, we ship internation-al orders Air Parcel Post. Please refer to the chart for the correct shipping cost.

Important Canadian Shipping Information

To our friends in Canada, we have a plan design affiliate in Kitchener, Ontario. This relationship will help you avoid the delays and charges associated with ship-ments from the United States. Moreover, our affiliate is familiar with the building requirements in your community and country. We prefer payments in U.S. Curren-cy. If you, however, are sending Canadian funds please add 40% to the prices of the plans and shipping fees.

An Important Note About Building Code Requirements:

All plans are drawn to conform to one or more of the industry's major national building standards. However, due to the variety of local building regulations, your plan may need to be modified to comply with local requirements — snow loads, energy loads, seismic zones, etc. Do check them fully and consult your local building officials.

A few states require that all building plans used be drawn by an architect registered in that state. While having your plans reviewed and stamped by such an architect may be prudent, laws requiring non-conforming plans like ours to be completely redrawn forces you to unnecessarily pay very large fees. If your state has such a law, we strongly recommend you contact your state representative to protest.

The rendering, floor plans, and technical information contained within this publication are not guaranteed to be totally accurate. Consequently, no information from this publication should be used either as a guide to constructing a home or for estimating the cost of building a home. Complete blueprints must be purchased for such purposes.

Garlinghouse 1998 Blueprint Price Code Schedule

Additional sets with original order $35

PRICE CODE	A	B	C	D	E	F	G	H
8 SETS OF SAME PLAN	$385	$425	$470	$510	$550	$595	$635	$675
4 SETS OF SAME PLAN	$335	$375	$420	$460	$500	$545	$585	$625
1 SINGLE SET OF PLANS	$285	$325	$370	$410	$450	$495	$535	$575
VELLUMS	$495	$540	$590	$635	$680	$730	$775	$820
MATERIALS LIST	$50	$50	$55	$55	$60	$60	$65	$65
ITEMIZED ZIP QUOTE	$75	$80	$85	$85	$90	$90	$95	$95

Shipping — (Plans 1-84999)

	1-3 Sets	4-6 Sets	7+ & Vellums
Standard Delivery (UPS 2-Day)	$25.00	$30.00	$35.00
Overnight Delivery	$35.00	$40.00	$45.00

Shipping — (Plans 85000-99999)

	1-3 Sets	4-6 Sets	7+ & Vellums
Ground Delivery (7-10 Days)	$15.00	$20.00	$25.00
Express Delivery (3-5 Days)	$20.00	$25.00	$30.00

International Shipping & Handling

	1-3 Sets	4-6 Sets	7+ & Vellums
Regular Delivery Canada (7-10 Days)	$25.00	$30.00	$35.00
Express Delivery Canada (5-6 Days)	$40.00	$45.00	$50.00
Overseas Delivery Airmail (2-3 Weeks)	$50.00	$60.00	$65.00

Option Key

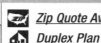

- Zip Quote Available
- Right Reading Reverse
- Duplex Plan
- Materials List Available

Index

Plan	Pg.	Price	Plan	Pg.	Price	Plan	Pg.	Price	Plan	Pg.	Price	Plan	Pg.	Price
9964	228	C	34600	24	A	91413	115	B	93432	52	C	98460	113	B
10394	235	B	34601	190	A	91418	64	B	93909	53	B	98463	204	B
10515	76	C	34602	200	B	91514	104	B	94105	131	B	98473	164	C
10521	244	C	34603	210	B	91731	71	B	94116	96	C	98474	215	B
10652	70	D	34901	226	B	91807	107	A	94203	229	B	98747	47	A
10674	59	B	35001	238	B	91901	38	D	94248	221	C	98912	111	A
10690	132	D	35007	194	A	92220	105	C	94307	116	A	99045	138	B
10785	82	C	90048	212	A	92238	139	B	94801	89	B	99115	231	C
10839	18	B	90288	33	A	92283	153	B	94902	230	C	99208	35	C
19422	143	B	90353	101	A	92400	159	A	94904	128	C	99238	163	A
20062	85	C	90356	129	B	92502	39	B	94907	155	B	99255	162	A
20069	217	C	90358	205	B	92503	127	B	94911	191	C	99285	185	B
20070	230	B	90378	78	A	92523	79	B	94917	208	B	99327	119	A
20083	66	B	90406	54	B	92525	196	B	94923	152	B	99365	108	A
20100	222	B	90409	95	B	92527	112	C	94944	193	C	99404	87	B
20156	36	A	90412	122	A	92531	176	C	94956	202	D	99420	51	B
20160	8	C	90423	75	B	92539	214	D	94986	48	B	99450	63	E
20161	158	A	90433	103	A	92557	234	B	96404	110	D	99639	121	A
20164	65	A	90436	124	C	92560	211	C	96408	189	D	99641	69	B
20198	23	B	90440	97	B	92609	12	B	96417	22	C	99757	123	C
20205	134	B	90441	180	C	92610	17	C	96442	31	D	99800	169	C
20220	150	B	90444	68	D	92622	201	D	96452	77	B	99801	30	D
20368	6	D	90450	91	D	92625	100	B	96456	203	C	99802	177	C
20501	148	C	90458	72	D	92629	102	C	96458	242	B	99804	25	C
24245	149	C	90476	90	B	92630	117	B	96462	245	C	99805	28	C
24302	126	A	90601	133	B	92631	142	C	96476	172	C	99806	58	C
24309	37	A	90606	183	C	92640	73	D	96479	165	C	99808	32	C
24319	173	B	90671	236	B	92642	15	C	96480	232	C	99809	98	B
24326	136	B	90680	241	A	92643	86	D	96487	240	C	99810	27	C
24400	147	C	90682	154	A	92644	16	D	96491	67	C	99811	135	B
24402	157	B	90689	168	A	92646	61	D	96493	144	C	99812	151	B
24404	181	D	90844	62	B	92647	239	C	96506	197	B	99826	167	B
24610	187	B	90847	145	A	92649	21	B	96509	170	A	99829	81	C
24654	27	B	90905	141	B	92655	216	B	96513	192	B	99830	220	B
24700	29	A	90930	182	B	92692	13	D	96522	209	B	99831	45	C
24701	20	B	90934	195	A	92705	224	C	97108	184	B	99835	174	C
24706	199	A	90966	94	D	93015	84	A	98357	244	C	99836	55	C
24708	30	B	90983	223	A	93017	92	A	98406	188	B	99844	240	C
24718	83	A	90986	207	B	93021	60	A	98407	161	C	99851	125	C
26112	10	A	90990	227	A	93048	120	A	98410	175	D	99852	14	C
26740	4	B	91002	140	B	93133	179	B	98411	137	A	99858	146	B
32084	1	C	91021	40	A	93161	218	B	98414	243	B	99859	233	C
32109	171	C	91026	93	A	93191	198	B	98415	42	A	99860	213	B
34003	166	A	91031	232	A	93212	57	C	98416	156	B	99864	236	C
34011	160	B	91033	109	A	93213	2	C	98423	106	B	99871	234	C
34029	178	B	91053	49	C	93219	206	B	98425	80	C	99873	99	C
34043	56	B	91055	46	B	93222	130	A	98431	118	B			
34049	43	C	91081	186	B	93261	225	B	98432	228	B			
34054	19	A	91340	74	A	93269	44	B	98454	237	A			
34077	114	B	91342	88	A	93279	34	A	98456	238	B			
34150	50	A	91343	41	C	93413	219	C						

GARAGE PLANS

Save money by Doing-It-Yourself using our Easy-To-Follow plans. Whether you intend to build your own garage or contract it out to a building professional, the Garlinghouse garage plans provide you with everything you need to price out your project and get started. Put our 90+ years of experience to work for you. *Order now!!*

No. 06016C   **$86.00**

Apartment Garage With One Bedroom

- 24' x 28' Overall Dimensions
- 544 Square Foot Apartment
- 12/12 Gable Roof with Dormers
- Slab or Stem Wall Foundation Options

No. 06015C   **$86.00**

Apartment Garage With Two Bedrooms

- 26' x 28' Overall Dimensions
- 728 Square Foot Apartment
- 4/12 Pitch Gable Roof
- Slab or Stem Wall Foundation Options

No. 06012C   **$54.00**

30' Deep Gable &/or Eave Jumbo Garages

- 4/12 Pitch Gable Roof
- Available Options for Extra Tall Walls, Garage & Personnel Doors, Foundation, Window, & Sidings
- Package contains 4 Different Sizes
  - 30' x 28'   • 30' x 32'   • 30' x 36'   • 30' x 40'

No. 06013C   **$68.00**

Two-Car Garage With Mudroom/Breezeway

- Attaches to Any House
- 24' x 24' Eave Entry
- Available Options for Utility Room with Bath, Mudroom, Screened-In Breezeway, Roof, Foundation, Garage & Personnel Doors, Window, & Sidings

No. 06001C $48.00

12', 14' & 16' Wide-Gable 1-Car Garages

- Available Options for Roof, Foundation, Window, Door, & Sidings
- Package contains 8 Different Sizes
- 12' x 20' Mini-Garage   • 14' x 22'   • 16' x 20'   • 16' x 24'
- 14' x 20'   • 14' x 24'   • 16' x 22'   • 16' x 26'

No. 06003C $48.00

24' Wide-Gable 2-Car Garages

- Available Options for Side Shed, Roof, Foundation, Garage & Personnel Doors, Window, & Sidings
- Package contains 5 Different Sizes
- 24' x 22'   • 24' x 24'   • 24' x 26'
- 24' x 28'   • 24' x 32'

No. 06007C $60.00

Gable 2-Car Gambrel Roof Garages

- Interior Rear Stairs to Loft Workshop
- Front Loft Cargo Door With Pulley Lift
- Available Options for Foundation, Garage & Personnel Doors, Window, & Sidings
- Package contains 5 Different Sizes
- 22' x 26'   • 22' x 28'   • 24' x 28'   • 24' x 30'   • 24' x 32'

No. 06006C $48.00

22' & 24' Deep Eave 2 & 3-Car Garages

- Can Be Built Stand-Alone or Attached to House
- Available Options for Roof, Foundation, Garage & Personnel Doors, Window, & Sidings
- Package contains 6 Different Sizes
- 22' x 28'   • 22' x 32'   • 24' x 32'
- 22' x 30'   • 24' x 30'   • 24' x 36'

No. 06002C $48.00

20' & 22' Wide-Gable 2-Car Garages

- Available Options for Roof, Foundation, Garage & Personnel Doors, Window, & Sidings
- Package contains 7 Different Sizes
- 20' x 20'   • 20' x 24'   • 22' x 22'   • 22' x 28'
- 20' x 22'   • 20' x 28'   • 22' x 24'

No. 06008C $60.00

Eave 2 & 3-Car Clerestory Roof Garages

- Interior Side Stairs to Loft Workshop
- Available Options for Engine Lift, Foundation, Garage & Personnel Doors, Window, & Sidings
- Package contains 4 Different Sizes
- 24' x 26'   • 24' x 28'   • 24' x 32'   • 24' x 36'

How to Order Garage Plans

Garage Order Form

Order Code No.	G98A4

Please send me 3 complete sets of the following GARAGE PLANS:

Item no. & description   Price

Additional Sets $ _____

      (@ $10.00 each)

Shipping Charges: UPS-$3.75, First Class- $4.50 $ _____

Subtotal: $ _____

Resident sales tax: KS-6.15%, CT-6% $ _____
(NOT REQUIRED FOR OTHER STATES)

                         $ _____

Total Enclosed: $ _____

My Billing Address is:

Name _____

Address _____

City _____

State _____ Zip _____

Daytime Phone No. (_____) _____

My Shipping Address is:

Name _____

Address _____
          (UPS will not ship to P.O. Boxes)

City _____

State _____ Zip _____

For Faster Service...Charge It!
U.S. & Canada Call
1(800)235-5700

All foreign residents call 1(860)343-5977

❏ Mastercard ❏ Visa

Card # | | | | | | | | | | | | | | | | | |

Signature _____ Exp. ___ / ___

If paying by credit card, to avoid delays:
billing address must be as it appears on credit card statement
or FAX us at (860) 343-5984

256

Here's What You Get

◆ Three complete sets of drawings for each plan ordered

◆ Detailed step-by-step instructions with easy-to-follow diagrams on how to build your garage (not available with apartment garages)

◆ For each garage style, a variety of size and garage door configuration options

◆ Variety of roof styles and/or pitch options for most garages

◆ Complete materials list

◆ Choice between three foundation options: Monolithic Slab, Concrete Stem Wall or Concrete Block Stem Wall

◆ Full framing plans, elevations and cross-sectionals for each garage size and configuration

Build-It-Yourself PROJECT PLAN

Order Information For Garage Plans:
All garage plan orders contain three complete sets of drawings with instructions and are priced as listed next to the illustration. Additional sets of plans may be obtained for $10.00 each with your original order. UPS shipping is used unless otherwise requested. Please include the proper amount for shipping.

GARLINGHOUSE

Send your order to:
(With check or money order payable in U.S. funds only)

The Garlinghouse Company

P.O. Box 1717
Middletown, CT 06457

No C.O.D. orders accepted; U.S. funds only. UPS will not ship to Post Office boxes, FPO boxes, APO boxes, Alaska or Hawaii. Canadian orders must be shipped First Class.

Prices subject to change without notice.